T0296633

Living with Robots

Living with Robots
Emerging Issues on the Psychological and Social Implications of Robotics

Edited by

Richard Pak
Department of Psychology
Clemson University
Clemson, SC, United States

Ewart J. de Visser
Warfighter Effectiveness Research Center (WERC)
U.S. Air Force Academy
Colorado Springs, CO, United States

Ericka Rovira
Department of Behavioral Sciences and Leadership
U.S. Military Academy
West Point, NY, United States

ELSEVIER

ACADEMIC PRESS
An imprint of Elsevier

Academic Press is an imprint of Elsevier
125 London Wall, London EC2Y 5AS, United Kingdom
525 B Street, Suite 1650, San Diego, CA 92101, United States
50 Hampshire Street, 5th Floor, Cambridge, MA 02139, United States
The Boulevard, Langford Lane, Kidlington, Oxford OX5 1GB, United Kingdom

Notices
Knowledge and best practice in this field are constantly changing. As new research and experience broaden our understanding, changes in research methods, professional practices, or medical treatment may become necessary.

Practitioners and researchers must always rely on their own experience and knowledge in evaluating and using any information, methods, compounds, or experiments described herein. In using such information or methods they should be mindful of their own safety and the safety of others, including parties for whom they have a professional responsibility.

To the fullest extent of the law, neither the Publisher nor the authors, contributors, or editors, assume any liability for any injury and/or damage to persons or property as a matter of products liability, negligence or otherwise, or from any use or operation of any methods, products, instructions, or ideas contained in the material herein.

Library of Congress Cataloging-in-Publication Data
A catalog record for this book is available from the Library of Congress

British Library Cataloguing-in-Publication Data
A catalogue record for this book is available from the British Library

ISBN: 978-0-12-815367-3

For information on all Academic Press publications visit our website at
https://www.elsevier.com/books-and-journals

Publisher: Nikki Levy
Acquisition Editor: Anita Koch
Editorial Project Manager: Lindsay Lawrence
Production Project Manager: Paul Prasad Chandramohan
Cover Designer: Matthew Limbert

Working together
to grow libraries in
developing countries

www.elsevier.com • www.bookaid.org

Typeset by TNQ Technologies

Contents

3.   Robotics to support aging in place

George Mois and Jenay M. Beer

4.   Kill switch: The evolution of road rage in an increasingly AI car culture

Julie Carpenter

5.   Development and current state of robotic surgery

Rana Pullatt and Benjamin L. White

6.   Regulating safety-critical autonomous systems: past, present, and future perspectives

M.L. Cummings and David Britton

7.   The role of consumer robots in our everyday lives

Heather C. Lum

8.   Principles of evacuation robots

Alan R. Wagner

9. **Humans interacting with intelligent machines: at the crossroads of symbiotic teamwork**
Michael D. McNeese and Nathaniel J. McNeese

Contributors

Jenay M. Beer, Institute of Gerontology, University of Georgia, Athens, GA, United States

David Britton, Department of Mechanical Engineering and Materials Science and the Law School, Duke University, Durham, NC, USA

Julie Carpenter, Ethics + Emerging Sciences Group, California Polytechnic State University, San Luis Obispo, CA, United States

Jessie Y.C. Chen, U.S. Army Research Laboratory, Human Research and Engineering Directorate, Aberdeen Proving Ground, MD, United States

M.L. Cummings, Department of Electrical and Computer Engineering, Duke University, Durham, NC, USA

Shan G. Lakhmani, U.S. Army Research Laboratory, Human Research and Engineering Directorate, Orlando, FL, United States

Heather C. Lum, Embry-riddle Aeronautical University, Daytona Beach, FL, United States

Michael D. McNeese, College of Information Sciences and Technology, Pennsylvania State University, University Park, PA, United States

Nathaniel J. McNeese, Clemson University, Clemson, SC, United States

George Mois, School of Social Work, University of Georgia, Athens, GA, United States

Rana Pullatt, Department of Surgery, Medical University of South Carolina, Charleston, SC, USA

Steven J. Stroessner, Barnard College, Columbia University, New York, NY, United States

Alan R. Wagner, Department of Aerospace Engineering and Rock Ethics Institute, Pennsylvania State University, University Park, PA, United States

Benjamin L. White, General Surgery, Medical University of South Carolina, Charleston, SC, USA

Julia L. Wright, U.S. Army Research Laboratory, Human Research and Engineering Directorate, Orlando, FL, United States

Foreword

Maggie Jackson

A decade ago, I held hands with a robot. Developed at MIT Media Lab as a prototype domestic servant, Domo was legless and fused to a table but could speak, track faces, and gently grasp objects such as cups and plates (Jackson, 2018). On the day that I visited the Lab, I tried to touch Domo to see how it would react, and it promptly reached out its steely fingers and grasped my hand. I was enchanted.

Now our robots are no longer rare creatures caged in laboratories. In 2018, global sales of service robots rose nearly 60 percent to 16.6 million robots worth $12.9 billion from the previous year (International Federation of Robotics, 2019). Bolstered by advances in AI and programmed to respond to us with "emotion," they are increasingly becoming our teammates, tutors, and companions. And yet for all their rising complexity, it still takes very little on their part to win us over. If a robot cheats while playing a game with a human, it need only put a finger to its lips—offering a conspiratorial shhh!—to persuade the human *not* to report its transgression (Scassellati, 2018). Savvy technologists "coo like children at the petting zoo" when playing with social robots at electronics shows (Calo et al., 2011, p. 22). Soldiers mourn when their bomb-detection robot, which resembles little more than a souped-up toy truck, is destroyed (Hall, 2017).

It almost does not matter what a robot looks like, we are willing to hug and touch them, talk to them, and befriend them. We quickly forget that it is, in the words of researcher Gill Pratt, "like a hollow doll," with smarts that cannot match ours and no capacity to return our love or care (Metz, 2018, p. B3). Humanity has been longing since Biblical times to create autonomous creatures in its own image. Now the Grand Experiment has begun. Who will profit, who will benefit, and who may get hurt?

Such questions carry a real urgency, as some of the most vulnerable members of human society are at the front lines of efforts to make robots a part of everyday life. As William Gibson noted, "the future is already here. It's just not very evenly distributed" (Gibson, 2018). Robots now comfort sick children in hospitals; tutor children with autism in social skills; and serve as companions, assistants, and therapy pets to older people (Jeong et al., 2015; Scassellati et al., 2018, Pedersen, Reid & Aspevig, 2018). The rapid aging of the world's population, in fact, is a main driver of the rise of the service robot industry (Pedersen et al., 2018). (I can imagine a time not far off when self-driving cars and drones are marketed as Grandma's friendly helpers.) Yet delegating some of the most intricate and challenging forms of human care to autonomous devices may wind up threatening the dignity and freedom of the very people that society is trying to help.

Consider the case of Paro, the robot baby seal used in eldercare facilities since 2003, often with those who have cognitive impairments such as dementia (Turner, Personal Communication, Nov. 14, 2018). Although more robust research remains to be done, studies show that the furry creatures can lower stress, offer tactile stimulation, and stimulate patient's involvement with their environment (Mordoch et al., 2013). In one study in an Australian facility for the aged, residents with dementia reacted most strongly to Paro, "their eyes sparkle," one recreational therapist reported (Birks et al., 2016, p. 3). But is it a fair yardstick of a robot's value to society if its success is measured by the reactions of those least able to choose how and when to use them? It may be both a victory and a defeat for humanity if a robot wins over those most easily deceived by the fiction of its "care." Paro is marketed as a nonpharmacological intervention for depression, anxiety, and symptoms of dementia, yet classified by the USDA as a medical device, a point of confusion that further underscores how its effects and our intentions are as yet far from clear (Turner, Personal Communication, Nov. 14, 2018).

Before we can understand who might benefit from robots, we must clarify what we want from these mechanical creatures, now and in future. Only recently have older people begun to be consulted in the design of robots designed for their use, a lapse that echoes the insufficient attention historically paid to technology users. And early findings reveal numerous disconnects between what many older people want, and what robots are designed to offer. Senior citizens are well aware that robotic companions are mostly built for those who are mentally frail, physically weak, and lonely, stereotypes of aging that many elderly belie and reject. In one recent US focus group study, most participants said they were willing to open their homes to a robot, but wanted one that might help augment their social lives, not position itself as their intimate friend (Lazar et al., 2016).

Consumers and some roboticists further wonder if making robots with humanlike charm may make it easier for people to evade responsibility for one another. A majority of Americans say that they would *not* use a robot caregiver for themselves or a family member, and nearly 65% expect such devices to *increase* feelings of isolation in the elderly (Smith & Anderson, 2017, p. 4). When an older person who is sad or in pain smiles at a robot or eagerly anticipates its visit, it might be easier for a relative or friend to evade the difficult act of consoling them. "I won't be visiting mum … on Thursday, could you please take [the robot] up to her?," a resident's daughter told a therapist at a facility using robotic companions (Birks et al., 2016, p. 4).

The task of aiding the vulnerable in any society is deeply complex, but we must take care that in deputizing robots as our partners in this work, we do not wind up diminishing ourselves as humans. Designing devices that promote human flourishing, rather than simply remedying our assumed deficiencies, should be our aim. That might mean, for instance, creating robots that quiet when humans are interacting with one another, thereby ceding their charms to the emotional nourishing that we need most.

To understand something fully "we need not only proximity but also distance," the philosopher Walter Ong once wrote (Ong, 1982, 2002, p. 81). He was referring to the impact of writing on culture, yet his words can inspire us as we prepare to interact with robots each day. It is alluring to draw close to these creatures, yet we must guard our distance in order to gain perspective on them.

We can do so firstly by remembering that technology's effects on life are a mix of augmentation and subtraction, of tensions and trade-offs, and unintended consequences. That is why it is crucial to keep looking beyond moments of easy enchantment to the wider issues raised by our relations with these machines: the unspoken values embedded in their design; their long-term effects on our notions of good care; the digital divides that may surface over time (forty-two percent of Americans think robot caregivers will only be used by those who cannot afford human help) (Smith & Anderson, 2017, p. 4). Going forward, we can heed a lesson long taught by technology: turning a device "on" marks only the beginning of its reach.

Second, we can wisely integrate robots into society only by clearly recognizing the lines that still divide our species from our devices. In this realm, transparency is key, as some leading roboticists now argue (Scheutz, 2011). The routine practice in the field of calling a robot with a low battery "in pain" or referring to an inventor as a robot's "caregiver" (Lim, 2017) furthers the fallacy that such devices are human, a deception that can only muddy our efforts to discover the true limits and powers of both technology and humanity itself. "On the Internet, nobody knows you're a dog," we once joked, celebrating the masquerade ball-flavor of the virtual. Yet as we have learned online, knowing who or what we are dealing with is crucial for fostering human autonomy in relationships and in thought.

In future, we may be enchanted each and everyday by a robot, as I was once long ago. But let us endeavor *not* to get carried away. This book, with its deep and varied perspectives on living with some of humanity's most astonishing inventions, can help us answer one of the most crucial dilemmas confronting us today: when to let a robot take us by the hand, and when to let it go.

References

Birks, M., et al. (2016). Robotic seals as therapeutic tools in an aged care facility: A qualitative study. *Journal of Aging Research, 2016*. https://doi.org/10.1155/2016/8569602. Article ID 8569602, 7 pages.

Calo, C., et al. (2011). Ethical implications of using the Paro robot with a focus on dementia patient care. In *Proceedings of the 12th AAAI conference on human-robot interaction in elder care* (p. 22).

Gibson, W. (2018). The Future is Already Here — it's just not Very Evenly Distributed: Fluctuating Proximities and Clusters.

Hall, L. (2017). How we feel about robots that feel. *MIT Technology Review, 120*(6), 75—78.

International Federation of Robotics. (2019). *World Robotics 2019 Service Robots Report.*

Jackson, M. (2018). *Distracted: Reclaiming our focus in a world of lost attention* (2nd ed.). Amherst, NY: Prometheus Books, 185—188, 212—213.

Joeng, S., et al. (March 2—5, 2015). A social robot to mitigate stress, anxiety, and pain in hospital pediatric care. In *Proceedings of the tenth annual ACM/IEEE international conference on human-robot interaction extended abstracts* (pp. 103—104). https://doi.org/10.1145/2701973.2702028.

Lazar, A., et al. (June 4—8, 2016). Rethinking the design of robotic pets for older adults. In *Proceedings of the 2016 ACM conference on designing interactive systems* (pp. 1034—1046). https://doi.org/10.1145/2901790.2901811.

Lim, A. (2017). Can you teach a Robot to Love? UC Berkeley's Greater Good Magazine. https://ggsc.berkeley.edu/?_ga=2.36671584.1716233812.1574449319-298686721.1571768229.

Metz, C. (October 1, 2018). Robots are improving quickly, but they can still be dumb. *The New York Times*, B3.

Mordoch, E., et al. (2013). Use of social commitment robots in the care of elderly people with dementia: A literature review. *Maturitas, 74*(1), 14—20. https://doi.org/10.1016/j.maturitas.2012.10.015.

Ong, W. (1982, 2002). Writing restructures consciousness. In *Orality and literacy* (p. 81). New York: Routledge.

Pedersen, I., Reid, & Aspevig. (2018). Developing social robots for aging populations: A literature review of recent academic sources. *Sociology Compass, 12*, e12585. https://doi.org/10.1111/soc412585, 1—10.

Scassellati, B. (November 13, 2018) Personal communication.

Scassellati, B., et al. (2018). Improving social skills in children with ASD using a long-term, in-home social robot. *Science Robotics, 3*(21), eaat7544. https://doi.org/10.1126/scirobotics.aat7544.

Scheutz, M. (2011). The inherent dangers of unidirectional emotional bonds between humans and social robots,. In P. Lin, G. Bekey, & K. Abney (Eds.), *Robot ethics: The ethical and social implications of robotics* (pp. 205—222). Cambridge, MA: MIT Press.

Smith, A., & Anderson, M. (October 4, 2017). *Automation in everyday life*. New York: Pew Research Center.

Turner, T. General Manager, PARO Robots US. Personal Communication, Nov. 14, 2018. Note: There are currently 300 Paro robots in use in the United States and about 5000 in the world.

Further reading

Gladstone, B. (Host). (October 22, 2018). The science in science fiction [radio program]. In Carline Watson (Executive Producer), *Talk of the nation*. Washington, D.C.: NPR.

Chapter 1

Transparent interaction and human—robot collaboration for military operations

Shan G. Lakhmani[1], Julia L. Wright[1], Jessie Y.C. Chen[2]

[1]*U.S. Army Research Laboratory, Human Research and Engineering Directorate, Orlando, FL, United States;* [2]*U.S. Army Research Laboratory, Human Research and Engineering Directorate, Aberdeen Proving Ground, MD, United States*

Chapter outline

Introduction

The military's idea of what a robot is will change over the next decade. We are in a point of transition, where the future of military robotics lies in pursuit of autonomous teammates, rather than teleoperated tools. This shift in vision, however, changes the way soldiers and robots will interact. Rather than a human soldier having to complete many tasks—some in person, some via robot—to attain a goal, instead, the soldier and robot can share the taskload and fulfill the goal together. This more collaborationist approach, however,

Living with Robots. https://doi.org/10.1016/B978-0-12-815367-3.00001-3

1

introduces the robot as an independent entity, which can act autonomously. Autonomy introduces a level of uncertainty that would not occur with a teleoperated robot. So, as we transition from teleoperated robots to autonomous, intelligent robots, we have to figure out the informational needs that must be established for this future human–robot relationship.

The relationship between humans and robots is relatively unique, given that robots can be independent actors, but only in the ways they have been designed to act independently. While robots are not exactly human, human teamwork is an appropriate metaphor for human–robot interaction (HRI) (Morrow & Fiore, 2012). To accomplish a goal, members of a human team engage in two tracks of behavior. The first track is taskwork, which is the specific, work-related activities needed to accomplish the team's goals (Salas, Shuffler, Thayer, Bedwell, & Lazzara, 2015). The second track is teamwork, which includes coordination, sharing knowledge, and all the other actions needed for interdependent operation (Burke, Salas, Wilson-Donnelly, & Priest, 2004). Robots are already being designed to do taskwork. However, with the expected trend toward greater autonomous capabilities, robots must provide an analog to the teamwork behaviors that human team members perform. Team behaviors, such as communication and coordination, can be simulated by robots to support important facets of HRI, such as mutual predictability and shared knowledge (Demir et al., 2015; Sycara & Sukthankar, 2006).

Transparent HRI can support mutual predictability and shared knowledge. Transparency has been described as an emergent property of the HRI process whereby the human operator has a clear and accurate understanding of how the robot gathers information, processes that information, and makes decisions (Ososky, Sanders, Jentsch, Hancock, & Chen, 2014; Phillips, Ososky, Grove, & Jentsch, 2011). Robot designers can facilitate transparent interactions by implementing elements in the interface that support understanding of the robot's decision-making process (Boyce, Chen, Selkowitz, & Lakhmani, 2015; Chen et al., 2014; Stowers et al., 2016).

In this chapter, we will be exploring the trends of military robotics from teleoperation to autonomy and how that change influences both the human–robot relationship and the informational needs of a human–robot team. Furthermore, we will talk about the flow of information between humans and robots, the patterns between them, and the communication styles it can take. By grappling with these questions now, we prepare ourselves for a future where autonomous robots are more ubiquitous.

Humans and robots in the military

Why robots?

Robots in the military serve many of the same purposes as they do in the private sector: they go where soldiers cannot, do things that soldiers cannot, and increase the soldiers' scope of influence. First and foremost, military robots keep both soldiers and civilians safe. Military robots replace soldiers in a variety of situations: clearing buildings, search and rescue in disaster areas and battlefields, detonation and disposal of explosives, reconnaissance and surveillance, etc. (Chen & Barnes, 2014; Murphy & Burke, 2010). They also augment soldier capabilities, such as gathering data to support soldiers' situation awareness, transporting soldier equipment, distributing supplies to soldiers in the most forward resupply positions, facilitating commanders' decision-making (collecting, organizing, and prioritizing data), and otherwise keeping soldier's safe by providing greater stand-off distance from the enemy for maneuvers and convoys (US Army, 2017). The development and advancement of autonomous robots is a key factor in the Department of Defense's Third Offset Strategy, which seeks to achieve and maintain a technological advantage over the United States' top adversaries (Eaglen, 2016). Currently, most robots fielded by the military are teleoperated.

Teleoperation

Teleoperation is when a human (i.e., teleoperator) can mechanically manipulate items or sense objects at a different location than where they are currently located, using a mechanical or robotic apparatus (Sheridan, 1995). It is important for even semiautonomous and fully autonomous robots to have a teleoperation mode, for those instances where its programming is insufficient to meet the environmental or task challenges at hand, and a human operator is needed for mission success. However, teleoperation presents unique challenges in supporting the human operators' situation awareness (Chen, Haas, & Barnes, 2007). Operators experience issues related to cognitive tunneling, decreased field of vision, degraded sense of spatial orientation, attention switching, and motion sickness. Many of these issues can be addressed by supporting the operator's sense of presence. The sense of presence can be increased through a variety of methods, such as multiple or operator-controlled views and multimodal feedback (Chen et al., 2007).

Supervisory control

Soon, it is expected that military applications of robots and unmanned systems will increase, and as such, humans will find themselves supervising increasingly large numbers of robotic assets. When an operator manages multiple robots by interacting with them individually, multiple performance decrements occur. As the number of robots being supervised increases, the operators' workload increases, their situation awareness decreases, their response times increase, the number of tasks that can be successfully completed within a designated time interval decreases, and the number of system failures and accidents increase (Adams, 2009; Chen & Barnes, 2012; Chen, Durlach,

Sloan, & Bowens, 2008; Squire & Parasuraman, 2010; Wang, Jamieson, & Hollands, 2009; Wang, Lewis, Velagapudi, Scerri, & Sycara, 2009). As a result, the current state of the art is a many-to-one supervision model, i.e., multiple humans are required to oversee a single robotic asset. As the complexity of the operating environment and/or robots' task increase, so does the number of human supervisors required for operation (Murphy & Burke, 2010). However, this growth in human team size also creates issues for those supervisors—e.g., physical exposure to dangerous environments, distractions, and back seat driving—so the move from a many-to-one model to a one-to-many model is desired. Development of systems, such as the mixed-initiative system that can assist human operators to oversee teams of robots is the first step toward achieving this goal.

Mixed-initiative systems

Mixed-initiative systems incorporate elements of both adaptive automation—where the level of automation is changeable by the system (Parasuraman, Sheridan, & Wickens, 2000)—and adjustable automation—where the level of automation is changeable by an external operator or system (Bradshaw et al., 2003). Systems with these capabilities allow for mixed-initiative interactions between humans and robots, allowing them to work in concert, each with authority to make decisions (Allen, Guinn, & Horvtz, 1999; Goodrich, 2010). Although both have the ability to make changes, the human operator is the ultimate authority in mixed-initiative systems. Mixed-initiative systems are effective in keeping the human supervisor in the loop, reducing operator workload, and thus increasing the number of subordinate robots that the operator can direct (Barnes et al., 2014; Chen & Barnes, 2010, 2014). While mixed-initiative systems have been lauded as the most flexible system for supervisory control (Calhoun, Ruff, Draper, & Wright, 2011), these systems are also particularly susceptible to mode confusion (Goodrich, 2010; Sarter, 2008). Mode confusion is when the operator believes the automation is in a different mode than it currently is, and as a result, their responses to the automation are inappropriate (Joshi, Miller, & Heimdahl, 2003).

Autonomous systems

Autonomy, with respect to robots, refers to a system that can use its understanding of the world, itself, and its situation to independently compose and select among different courses of action to accomplish its goals (David & Nielsen, 2016). Autonomy, rather than being a feature that might or might not be present, is an anticipated interaction between the robot, the robot's work, and the situation (Bradshaw, Hoffman, Woods, & Johnson, 2013). A robot might have autonomous capabilities in some contexts, but lack those capabilities in others, and thus require human intervention (David & Nielsen, 2016; Fong et al., 2005).

Numerous industries have leveraged the unique abilities of computerized systems to solve difficult problems quickly. Autonomous systems have been used to identify fraudulent financial transactions, provide recommendations based on medical content, and authenticate users' logins, all of which would require experts to exert a not-insignificant amount of time (David & Nielsen, 2016). Adjustable autonomy attempts to facilitate better performance by having the robot manipulate itself, what it can and must do, and the situation it is in so that it can use its capabilities to pursue its goals (Bradshaw et al., 2003). This combination of independence and flexibility is particularly desirable in complex, dynamic environments, the kind in which the US military anticipates operating (US Army, 2017). The US military has explored the potential of autonomy in robotic platforms—such as unmanned ground vehicles used as mules or explorers—or in software—such as decision aides or mission planners (Chen et al., 2008; Cooke, Demir, & McNeese, 2016; Selkowitz, Lakhmani, & Chen, 2017; Stowers et al., 2016).

Autonomous robots and human–robot teamwork

To gain the advantages of incorporating robots with autonomous capabilities into military teams, we must understand the way that autonomy changes the nature of the human–robot interaction and how that interaction can be modulated to support effective performance.

The importance of human–autonomy interaction

A hammer is a relatively simple tool. It is designed to pursue a specific goal, it cannot fulfill that goal without you, and it is unlikely to surprise you. Robots are not hammers. They can be designed to pursue multiple goals, often without you, and have a greater opportunity to surprise you. Robots with autonomous capabilities can do more but have their own set of shortcomings. One shortcoming, for instance, is the possibility that humans working with a robot can fall "out of the loop," completely delegating a task to the robot and losing awareness of that task and the robot (Chen & Barnes, 2014; Schuster, 2013). This problem is exacerbated when the robot is designed to be "strong and silent" (Kilgore & Voshell, 2014). Even if a robot is entirely reliable, its failure to communicate relevant information about itself and its actions—its lack of transparency—would inhibit a human's ability to work interdependently with it (Bradshaw et al., 2013). If a robot is not entirely reliable, then any humans working with it may trust it inappropriately. One human working with the robot might trust it too much, overrelying on the robot and missing errors (Lee & See, 2004). Another human may see the robot make a mistake and completely distrust the robot after, not using it and losing all the benefits that the robot might have provided (Dzindolet, Peterson, Pomranky, Pierce, & Beck, 2003). Effective teamwork between humans and robots, like effective teamwork between people, depends on a mutual understanding of what all the team members are capable of doing, what they are responsible for doing, and what they are currently doing (Bradshaw et al., 2009; Sycara & Sukthankar, 2006).

Human—autonomy interaction and allocation of responsibilities

One aspect of that interaction that must be considered is function allocation. In 1951, Paul Fitts and associates essentially begat function allocation research with the publication of a list delineating tasks where either humans or machines excelled (de Winter & Dodou, 2014). This list suggests that there are some tasks which humans are better suited to doing than machines, and conversely, there are some tasks which machines are better suited to than people. While this delineation may be clear in some cases, there is a swathe of situations where both the human and the robot are capable of doing a task suitably. The human and robot's capabilities can also change over time, or if contextual factors change (Bradshaw et al., 2003). Finally, situations may arise where neither human nor robot can do the task by themselves but can do so jointly as a team (Bradshaw, Dignum, Jonker, & Sierhuis, 2012a). In order to effectively act in all of these situations, the human has to work with a robot that supports mixed-initiative interaction, keeping the human apprised of the overall situation, soliciting additional information as needed, completing predefined tasks without human intervention, and even dynamically negotiating for initiative when appropriate (Allen et al., 1999). Supporting mixed-initiative HRI for both individual and joint action is a subject for future study far beyond the next decade.

Working with a robot

In the military, HRI is often focused around teleoperation. This approach styles the interaction between humans and robots as one between operator and tool. In this approach, the robot is a piece of equipment, and the operator needs to know about its operating procedures, functions, and limitations (Cannon-Bowers, Salas, & Converse, 1993; Ososky, Schuster, Phillips, & Jentsch, 2013). This approach increases operators' capabilities, allowing them to execute tasks more safely, accurately, and reliably than they would alone (Parasuraman et al., 2000). Fully manually controlled robots are extensions of the operators' will (Sheridan, 1995). While this form of interaction keeps the operator in the loop, the task is engrossing, and the operator can only control a single robot at a time (Adams, 2005). A supervisory control approach allows the operator to allocate tasks to one or more robots, monitor their performance, and intervene when necessary (Inagaki, 2012; Johnson et al., 2014; Sheridan, 1995). Increasing the autonomous capabilities of a robot reduces the amount of work an operator has to do to direct a single robot, leaving them free to supervise more robots or to engage in other, separate tasks (Lyons, 2013).

Task delegation frees the operator to do more, but having both robots and humans doing tasks near one another is hardly an efficient use of resources. Collaboration between the two groups, the interdependent pursuit of shared objectives, allows humans and robots to complete tasks together that they could not do separately (Bradshaw, Feltovich, & Johnson, 2012b; Fan & Yen, 2004). For humans and robots to successfully engage in a joint activity, however, they must share a common ground—a shared set of knowledge, beliefs, and assumptions (Johnson et al., 2014; Stubbs, Wettergreen, & Hinds, 2007). To establish and maintain this common ground, humans and robots must be able to communicate in some way (Chen & Barnes, 2014). With this understanding in place, both parties can predict one another's future actions and use that knowledge to coordinate on a shared task (Bradshaw et al., 2012b; Sycara & Sukthankar, 2006). This need for mutual understanding differentiates autonomous robots from their more teleoperated brethren (Chen et al., 2018). Robots with autonomous capabilities have their own "understanding" of a situation and use that to make decisions independently from their human counterparts (David & Nielsen, 2016). Given the agency of these robots, humans may need to treat robots more like their human teammates (Morrow & Fiore, 2012).

Human–robot teamwork

Humans, especially when undertaking a task, maintain an awareness of what's going on (Endsley, 1995). This awareness is continually updating, depending on the feedback that people get from the environment and the understanding they have of that environment (Endsley, 2015). Robots can be used to extend that awareness of the environment, using sensors and other capabilities (Schuster, 2013; US Army, 2017). Robots with autonomous capabilities not only broaden human knowledge of the environment, but also become part of the environment of which humans must be aware (Grote, Weyer, & Stanton, 2014). Consequently, human–robot interfaces have to be designed so that human operators remain "in the loop," maintaining an adequate understanding of the robot and its invisible processes (Chen & Barnes, 2014). The US Army's long-term plans, however, are to create and use robots with greater autonomous capabilities, able to deal with complex, dynamic environments (David & Nielsen, 2016). One of the factors in these complex, dynamic environments is the intent of the human operator, whose goals the robot pursues (Sukthankar, Shumaker, & Lewis, 2012).

In a human–human team, each person has their awareness and their understandings of the situation, so working alongside one another and working on tasks together requires some communication to maintain common ground

(Cooke, Salas, Kiekel, & Bell, 2004; Salmon et al., 2008). In a human—robot team, the human can gain information about the situation by observing the environment (including the robot) and getting information from the robot that it is designed to provide; similarly, a robot can gain information about its situation by observing its environment (including the human) to update its model of the world and getting information from the human that it is designed to interpret (Kaupp, Makarenko, & Durrant-Whyte, 2010; Sycara & Suk-thankar, 2006). A mutual exchange of information between humans and robots can mitigate the potential adverse effects of humans depending on robots—e.g., loss of situation awareness, complacency, automation surprises—and provide robots with the usually hidden human intention that the robot would otherwise have to infer (Chen et al., 2018; Matignon, Karami, & Mouaddib, 2010). By exchanging information, humans and robots would be able to establish common ground and subsequently coordinate on shared tasks (Bradshaw et al., 2012a). Determining what specific information needs to be exchanged, however, requires an examination of transparency in HRI.

Transparency

Definition/history

According to the *Merriam-Webster Dictionary*, there are multiple definitions for the word "transparent"; "a: free from pretense or deceit; b: easily detected or seen through; c: readily understood; d: characterized by visibility or accessibility of information" (Merriam-Webster, 2013). Interestingly, when discussing automation and robotics, each of these definitions has been used. The idea of what transparency is, and how this idea should be applied to automation in general, has evolved. Prior to the advent of computers, the discussion of transparency centered on teleoperation.

In teleoperations, the preferred definition of transparent is "easily detected or seen through." A transparent interface is one that supports telepresence, or the sensation or illusion of being elsewhere (Sheridan, 1995). Workers performing tasks in dangerous or inaccessible environments need interfaces that, while not necessarily enhancing their skills, allow them to perform tasks without adding to their workload by being difficult to use or interfering with the work. These interfaces augment the sense of presence in various ways: with sensors, audio and/or haptic feedback, and visually with remote camera feeds. Studies have demonstrated that creating telepresence in teleoperations improves performance (Kaber, Riley, Zhou, & Draper, 2000; Pacchierotti, Tirmizi, Bianchini, & Prattichizzo, 2013).

When computers came into use, the predominant definition of transparency also changed. Where transparency once meant something that could be seen through or was invisible, now it was "characterized by visibility or accessibility of information." Maass (1983) began this transition with her definition of system transparency, which emphasized that the system must support the users' mental model of its functions, be intuitive, and not interfere with the users' thought processes. The computer (or system) was still a tool, but now it was a tool that enhanced user performance rather than merely being the conduit through which the user performed a task.

As more advanced automation was developed, the meaning of transparency evolved again. Where once computers simply allowed people to conduct tasks quicker and more efficiently, programs that assisted humans by making decisions were beginning to appear. Now to "be transparent" meant to be "readily understood," as the human operators needed to understand not only what decisions or actions the automation was initializing but what were the underlying reasons for doing so.

Today, when describing transparency in automation and technology, any of the three dictionary definitions may be meant, as automation level spans the spectrum from teleoperations to full autonomy. The complexity of the tasks performed by automation has also increased: once these were simple machines performing difficult, dirty, or repetitive tasks, today automation conducts tasks as complex as driving along city streets. Thus, what it means to be transparent, or "understood," also becomes more complex.

As the level of automation increases, so does the level of difficulty the operator experiences maintaining awareness of the automation's actions. Often this is due to an overwork situation, where the operator is performing multiple tasks, leaving them to allow the automation to continue with less (or no) supervision.

The loop—what it is and why we want to be in it

The interactions between a human operator and automation while conducting one or more tasks are often referred to as "the loop of control" (Endsley & Kiris, 1995). The idea is that control over the task passes between the two, as task demands, workload, and individual abilities dictate. The human is considered "in-the-loop" so long as they are aware of what the automation is doing, how the task is progressing, and can reasonably estimate what the next step or outcome will be. Often the operator is conducting multiple tasks or has other demands upon their attention. When this is the case one typical response to their increasing workload or demands is to increase the level of automated assistance on the shared task, thus switching the burden of task performance from the operator to the automation. However, the unintended consequence of this increase in the level of automation is that the operator steadily becomes more removed from the inner loop of control as their role changes from actor to supervisor. As the human loses awareness of the shared task, they are said to be "out of the loop" (Chen & Barnes, 2014; Endsley & Kiris, 1995; Kilgore & Voshell, 2014; Parasuraman, Molloy, & Singh, 1993).

Human out-of-the-loop conditions result in adverse outcomes, for example, reduced performance, reduced situation awareness, increased automation bias.

When humans are not the ones making decisions, they tend to ignore or overlook changes, both environmental and system state (Endsley & Kiris, 1995; Sarter & Woods, 1995). Losing sight of the state of the system can result in mode errors due to confusion; it takes the human time to regain their situation awareness of the system (Kaber, Omal, & Endsley, 1999). This loss of situation awareness is particularly likely when the automation is reliable and highly autonomous; so long as the automation is handling the task, the human tends to become complacent and overtrust, laying the groundwork for potentially devastating errors to occur (Kasdaglis, Newton, & Lakhmani, 2014; Stubbs, Hinds, & Wettergreen, 2007; Wright, Chen, & Barnes, 2018).

Additionally, the automation may not communicate its intentions well, creating the out-of-the-loop condition inadvertently. When the human has difficulty understanding the automation's state and/or status, they will question its accuracy, effectiveness, and rationale behind its actions (Linegang et al., 2006; Stanton, Young, & Walker, 2007). Thus it is critical for the humans to understand the behaviors, reasoning, and expected outcomes of the autonomous agents (de Visser, Cohen, Freedy, & Parasuraman, 2014; Lee & See, 2004). To address these issues in human—agent teaming, Chen and colleagues developed the Situation awareness—based Agent Transparency (SAT) model (Chen et al., 2014, 2018). According to the SAT model, an agent has to answer three questions in order to maintain a transparent interaction with its human operator: what is the agent trying to achieve; why is the agent doing what it is doing; What should the operator expect to happen in the future (Chen et al., 2014).

Communication between humans and robots

Robots with increasing autonomous capabilities are being pursued in the US military. This increased independence can make it difficult for people working with these robots to stay informed about the robot's actions and the decision-making processes that lead to those actions. Designing human—robot interfaces to facilitate transparent interactions help alleviate some of the negative outcomes that can result from humans and autonomous robots working together (Chen et al., 2014; Stubbs et al., 2007). However, given the breadth of information transfer strategies available—using human—computer interaction and human—human interaction as guides—a variety of different factors have to be examined to get information from the robot to the human operator (Morrow & Fiore, 2012; Sycara & Sukthankar, 2006). Furthermore, the US Army's long-term goals for robots include facilitating shared mental models and mutual predictability, which has implications for patterns of communication between human operator and robot (Chen et al., 2018; David & Nielsen, 2016).

Communication modality

Robots are not humans, and consequently, they are neither bound by human limitations nor proficient at human capabilities (Barnes, Chen, & Hill, 2017). Robots using some form of a visual interface can convey information using text and graphics (Moreno & Mayer, 2007). If using an avatar, or if the robot is physically instantiated, robots can use animal-like or human-like gestures (Krämer, 2010; Ososky et al., 2013). While the visual modality is the most commonly used, robots can convey information using auditory cues—including synthetic and human voices, tones, and alarms—and haptic feedback—including vibrations and controller torque (Johns et al., 2016; Sims, ChinLumUpham-Ellis, Ballion, & Lagattuta, 2009; Teo, Wohleber, Lin, & Reinerman-Jones, 2017; Vitense, Jacko, & Emery, 2003). Robots can use any one of these feedback methods, or a combination of them, to communicate with humans, depending on the capabilities of the robot and the needs of the mission. Conversely, robots can receive information from humans, depending on their abilities as well.

Robots with autonomous capabilities use sensors to detect what's going on in their environment and use that information to make decisions (Wooldridge & Jennings, 1995). Consequently, robots can gain information from humans by observing them (Gori, Aggarwal, Matthies, & Ryoo, 2016). Robots can even make suppositions of human intent, based on their actions, and use that information in their decision-making (Hayes & Scassellati, 2013). More direct means of communication include translational input devices—keyboard, mouse, and touch screen—as well as more multimodal inputs, such as gesture detectors and natural language processing (Teo et al., 2017). These methods of communication, both human-to-robot and robot-to-human open up different patterns and styles of communication.

Communication patterns

Human–robot teams can be made up of one or multiple humans, one or multiple robots, and can be colocated or distributed. Each of these actors can either send or receive information, unidirectionally, or do both, allowing for a bidirectional flow of information between the team members (Kaupp et al., 2010). This bidirectional flow can be used to build a common ground built on sharing individual knowledge (Barnlund, 1970; Chen et al., 2018). In addition to sending each other information, human–robot teams can interact by having a human team member send directives, a robot team member soliciting feedback, or a human and robot can negotiate initiative, depending on the robot's built-in capabilities (Johnson et al., 2014; Kaupp et al., 2010). These communication patterns, which can be used when humans are teamed with autonomous robots, facilitate a mutual flow of information that more closely resembles communication in human teams (Salas et al., 2015). A reciprocal flow of information facilitates the fulfillment of the requirements for effective human–robot collaboration (Bradshaw et al., 2012b).

Human–robot communication in the future

Human teamwork is limited by the capabilities of the human team members and the technology used to facilitate teamwork. Robots *are* technology, and hence, their capacities set what the team is capable of doing (Fiore & Wiltshire, 2016). The future of military robotics encompasses robots with differing capabilities, each used in discrete circumstances. This necessitates developing unique methods of interaction and, consequently, ways of presenting different information. With teleoperation, for example, the robot needs to feel like an extension of the operator. By submitting information nonconspicuously, the robot would be able to facilitate the human's sense of being physically present at a remote location, e.g., transported to where the robot is (IJsselsteijn, de Ridder, Freeman, & Avons, 2000; McMahan, 2003). Communicating relevant information can be even more difficult, given that current teleoperated robots require one or more human operators to operate it (Chen et al., 2008). The approach to communication needed for a teleoperated robot is different than the approach needed when the human is working with a more autonomous robot that requires supervisory control.

Robots that require supervisory control are expected to be used in the future. With increasingly autonomous robots, human operators can delegate tasks, which transform the human's role to that of a supervisor. Because the nature of the task has changed, the information needed to do the task, and how the information needs to be presented, needs to change. Furthermore, with increased autonomous capabilities, human operators are expected to be able to supervise multiple robots, given the proper support. One research paradigm that explores this approach is RoboLeader, a mixed-initiative supervisory control robot test bed (Wright, Chen, Barnes, & Hancock, 2017). RoboLeader acts as a mediator between a human operator and multiple robots, allowing humans to direct multiple robots without having to micromanage them. By providing some information about the decisions that were being made and the underlying rationale behind them, participants were able to improve their performance and decrease complacent behavior. However, providing ambiguous information about the underlying reasoning of decisions hurt participants' performance (Wright et al., 2017). Furthermore, people who rated themselves as more vulnerable to complacent behavior experienced with this effect more than their less vulnerable counterparts. These findings suggest that future soldiers may be operating groups of robots who give customized feedback, depending on their operators' needs (Chen et al., 2018).

Another anticipated approach to the future of military robotics is the mixed-initiative systems. The Intelligent Multi-UxV planner with adaptive collaborative/control technologies (IMPACT) system is a decision recommendation agent that helps operators set up patterns of behavior for unmanned vehicles, i.e., plays (Stowers et al., 2017). This agent provides the operator with a number of factors that could influence the unmanned vehicles' performance and a choice between the top two plays. Participants were shown different variants of the agent, which provided basic plan information, the previous information and decision rationale information, the previous information and added projected outcomes, or the previous information and how uncertain that information was. Providing information that facilitates transparent interactions benefited participants' performance on the decision-making task (Chen et al., 2018). These findings suggest that when soldiers in the future are engaging in decision-making tasks, they will have the help of agentic decision aids and that these aids will provide supplementary information about not only the decision but about how it will have reached that decision.

Unlike a decision aid or a robotic supervisee, a more autonomous robot can interact with a human similarly to a human teammate. In the future, a robot that acts like a synthetic teammate can work with humans to make decisions and accomplish shared goals where both robot and human skills are needed. The way that this kind of robot would interact with a human is still being explored, though both human team communication and HRI guide the interaction model. Currently, different approaches to bidirectional human—robot communication are being investigated, focusing on robots asking questions and providing visual information to support transparent interaction. These questions range from simple confirmation to a more complex negotiation of response. This approach, however, is only one of many that can be used. The future of communication with synthetic teammates may range in modality and content, but we know that it must be able to be used to build a shared understanding between teammates, both synthetic and human. While much work needs to be done concerning HRI, existing models of human teamwork, transparency, human—computer interaction, and automation can be used to guide that work.

Conclusion

In the following decade and beyond, the US Army is pursuing a strategy whereby human soldiers will be teamed with autonomous agents (US Army, 2017). A tool, be it a hammer or teleoperated robot, is a thing that an operator needs to know how to use. However, autonomy changes the nature of a relationship. Robots with autonomous capabilities operate independently and with a set of knowledge that may not be directly provided by the operator (Fan & Yen, 2004). That independent knowledge transforms the relationship from operator—tool to human teammate—synthetic teammate (Phillips et al., 2011). Synthetic teammates can do more than automated systems, but also have higher informational requirements (Bradshaw et al., 2012a). As researchers, we are exploring these informational requirements, so that our human—robot teams can jointly make decisions and perform effectively on the dynamic, complex battlefields of the future (David & Nielsen, 2016).

References

Adams, J. A. (September 2005). Human-robot interaction design: Understanding user needs and requirements. *Proceedings of the Human Factors and Ergonomics Society Annual Meeting* (Vol. 49,(3), 447–451. Sage, CA, Los Angeles, CA: SAGE Publications.

Adams, J. A. (2009). Multiple robot/single human interaction: Effects on perceived workload. *Behaviour & Information Technology, 28*(2), 183–198.

Allen, J. E., Guinn, C. I., & Horvtz, E. (1999). Mixed-initiative interaction. *IEEE Intelligent Systems and Their Applications, 14*(5), 14–23.

Barnes, M. J., Chen, J. Y., & Hill, S. (2017). *Humans and autonomy: Implications of shared decision Making for military operations (No. ARL-TR-7919).* MD, United States: US Army Research Laboratory Aberdeen Proving Ground.

Barnes, M. J., Chen, J. Y., Jentsch, F., Oron-Gilad, T., Redden, E., Elliott, L., et al. (2014). *Designing for humans in autonomous systems: Military applications (No. ARL-TR-6782).* Army Research Lab Aberdeen Proving Ground, MD, Human Research and Engineering Directorate.

Barnlund, D. C. (1970). A transactional model of communication. In J. Akin, A. Goldberg, G. Myers, & J. Stewart (Eds.), *Language behavior: A book of readings in communication* (pp. 43–61). The Hague, NL: Mouton & Co. N.V.

Boyce, M. W., Chen, J. Y., Selkowitz, A. R., & Lakhmani, S. G. (2015). *Agent transparency for an autonomous squad member (No. ARL TR 7298).* Army Research Lab Aberdeen Proving Ground, MD, Human Research And Engineering Directorate.

Bradshaw, J. M., Dignum, V., Jonker, C., & Sierhuis, M. (2012a). Human-agent-robot teamwork. *IEEE Intelligent Systems, 27*(2), 8–13.

Bradshaw, J. M., Feltovich, P. J., & Johnson, M. (2012b). Human-agent interaction. In G. A. Boy (Ed.), *The handbook of human-machine interaction: A human-centered design approach.* Boca Raton, FL: CRC Press.

Bradshaw, J. M., Feltovich, P., Johnson, M., Breedy, M., Bunch, L., Eskridge, T., et al. (July 2009). From tools to teammates: Joint activity in human-agent-robot teams. In *International conference on human centered design* (pp. 935–944). Berlin, Heidelberg: Springer.

Bradshaw, J. M., Feltovich, P. J., Jung, H., Kulkarni, S., Taysom, W., & Uszok, A. (July 2003). Dimensions of adjustable autonomy and mixed-initiative interaction. In *International workshop on computational autonomy* (pp. 17–39). Berlin, Heidelberg: Springer.

Bradshaw, J. M., Hoffman, R. R., Woods, D. D., & Johnson, M. (2013). The seven deadly myths of "autonomous systems". *IEEE Intelligent Systems, 28*(3), 54–61.

Burke, C., Salas, E., Wilson-Donnelly, K., & Priest, H. (2004). How to turn a team of experts into an expert medical team: Guidance from the aviation and military communities. *BMJ Quality and Safety, 13*(Suppl. 1), i96–i104.

Calhoun, G. L., Ruff, H. A., Draper, M. H., & Wright, E. J. (2011). Automation-level transference effects in simulated multiple unmanned aerial vehicle control. *Journal of Cognitive Engineering and Decision Making, 5*(1), 55–82.

Cannon-Bowers, J. A., Salas, E., & Converse, S. (1993). Shared mental models in expert team decision making. In *Individual and group decision making: Current issues* (pp. 221–246). Hillsdale, NJ: Erlbaum.

Chen, J. Y., & Barnes, M. J. (September 2010). Supervisory control of robots using RoboLeader. *Proceedings of the Human Factors and Ergonomics Society Annual Meeting* (Vol. 54,(19), 1483—1487. Sage, CA, Los Angeles, CA: SAGE Publications.

Chen, J. Y. C., & Barnes, M. J. (2012). Supervisory control of multiple robots effects of imperfect automation and individual differences. *Human Factors: The Journal of the Human Factors and Ergonomics Society, 54*(2), 157—174.

Chen, J. Y. C., & Barnes, M. J. (2014). Human—agent teaming for multirobot control: A review of human factors issues. *IEEE Transactions on Human-Machine Systems, 44*(1), 13—29.

Chen, J. Y., Durlach, P. J., Sloan, J. A., & Bowens, L. D. (2008). Human-robot interaction in the context of simulated route reconnaissance missions. *Military Psychology, 20*(3), 135—149.

Chen, J. Y., Haas, E. C., & Barnes, M. J. (2007). Human performance issues and user interface design for teleoperated robots. *IEEE Transactions on Systems, Man, and Cybernetics, Part C (Applications and Reviews), 37*(6), 1231—1245.

Chen, J. Y., Lakhmani, S. G., Stowers, K., Selkowitz, A. R., Wright, J. L., & Barnes, M. (2018). Situation awareness-based agent transparency and human-autonomy teaming effectiveness. *Theoretical Issues in Ergonomics Science, 19*(3), 259—282.

Chen, J. Y., Procci, K., Boyce, M., Wright, J. L., Garcia, A., & Barnes, M. J. (2014). *Situation awareness-based agent transparency (ARL-TR-6905)*. Army Research Lab Aberdeen Proving Ground, MD, Human Research and Engineering Directorate.

Cooke, N. J., Demir, M., & McNeese, N. (2016). *Synthetic teammates as team players: Coordination of human and synthetic teammates (No. RE2016844 01)*. Mesa, United States: Cognitive Engineering Research Institute.

Cooke, N. J., Salas, E., Kiekel, P. A., & Bell, B. (2004). Advances in measuring team cognition. In *Team cognition: Understanding the factors that drive process and performance* (pp. 83—106).

David, R. A., & Nielsen, P. (2016). *Defense science board summer study on autonomy*. Washington, United States: Defense Science Board.

Demir, M., McNeese, N. J., Cooke, N. J., Ball, J. T., Myers, C., & Frieman, M. (September 2015). Synthetic teammate communication and coordination with humans. *Proceedings of the Human Factors and Ergonomics Society Annual Meeting* (Vol. 59,(1), 951—955. Sage, CA, Los Angeles, CA: SAGE Publications.

Dzindolet, M. T., Peterson, S. A., Pomranky, R. A., Pierce, L. G., & Beck, H. P. (2003). The role of trust in automation reliance. *International Journal of Human-Computer Studies, 58*(6), 697—718.

Eaglen, M. (2016). What is the third offset strategy? *RealClearDefense*. http://www. realcleardefense.com/articles/2016/02/16/what_is_the_third_offset_strategy_109034.html.

Endsley, M. R. (1995). Toward a theory of situation awareness in dynamic systems. *Human Factors, 37*, 85—104.

Endsley, M. R. (2015). Situation awareness misconceptions and misunderstandings. *Journal of Cognitive Engineering and Decision Making, 9*(1), 4—32.

Endsley, M. R., & Kiris, E. O. (1995). The out-of-the-loop performance problem and level of control in automation. *Human Factors, 37*(2), 381—394.

Fan, X., & Yen, J. (2004). Modeling and simulating human teamwork behaviors using intelligent agents. *Physics of Life Reviews, 1*(3), 173—201.

Fiore, S. M., & Wiltshire, T. J. (2016). Technology as teammate: Examining the role of external cognition in support of team cognitive processes. *Frontiers in Psychology, 7*, 1531.

Fong, T. W., Nourbakhsh, I., Kunz, C., Fluckiger, L., Schreiner, J., Ambrose, R., et al. (2005). The peer-to-peer human-robot interaction project. In *Space 2005* (pp. 1—11). Long Beach, CA.

Goodrich, M. (2010). On maximizing fan-out: Towards controlling multiple unmanned vehicles. In *Human-robot interactions in future military operations* (pp. 375–395).

Gori, I., Aggarwal, J., Matthies, L., & Ryoo, M. S. (2016). Multitype activity recognition in robot-centric scenarios. *IEEE Robotics and Automation Letters, 1*(1), 593–600.

Grote, G., Weyer, J., & Stanton, N. A. (2014). *Beyond human-centred automation—concepts for human—machine interaction in multi-layered networks.* Milton Park, Abingdon, UK: Taylor & Francis.

Hayes, B., & Scassellati, B. (2013). Challenges in shared-environment human-robot collaboration. In *Collaborative manipulation workshop at the 8th ACM/IEEE international conference on human-robot interaction* (Vol. 8).

IJsselsteijn, W. A., de Ridder, H., Freeman, J., & Avons, S. E. (2000). June). Presence: Concept, determinants, and measurement. In *Human vision and electronic imaging V* (Vol. 3959, pp. 520–530). International Society for Optics and Photonics.

Inagaki, T. (2012). *Special issue on human—automation coagency.* Switzerland: Springer.

Johns, M., Mok, B., Sirkin, D. M., Gowda, N. M., Smith, C. A., Talamonti, W. J., Jr., et al. (March 2016). Exploring shared control in automated driving. In *The eleventh ACM/IEEE international conference on human robot interaction* (pp. 91–98). IEEE Press.

Johnson, M., Bradshaw, J. M., Feltovich, P. J., Jonker, C. M., Van Riemsdijk, M. B., & Sierhuis, M. (2014). Coactive design: Designing support for interdependence in joint activity. *Journal of Human-Robot Interaction, 3*(1), 43–69.

Joshi, A., Miller, S. P., & Heimdahl, M. P. (October 2003). Mode confusion analysis of a flight guidance system using formal methods. In *Digital avionics systems conference, 2003. DASC'03. The 22nd* (Vol. 1, pp. 2.D.11–2.D.112). IEEE.

Kaber, D. B., Omal, E., & Endsley, M. (1999). Level of automation effects on telerobot performance and human operator situation awareness and subjective workload. *Automation Technology and Human Performance: Current Research and Trends,* 165–170.

Kaber, D. B., Riley, J. M., Zhou, R., & Draper, J. (July 2000). Effects of visual interface design, and control mode and latency on performance, telepresence and workload in a teleoperation task. *Proceedings of the Human Factors and Ergonomics Society Annual Meeting* (Vol. 44,(5), 503–506. Sage, CA, Los Angeles, CA: SAGE Publications.

Kasdaglis, N., Newton, O., & Lakhmani, S. (September 2014). System state awareness: A human centered design approach to awareness in a complex world. *Proceedings of the Human Factors and Ergonomics Society Annual Meeting* (Vol. 58,(1), 305–309. Sage, CA, Los Angeles, CA: SAGE Publications.

Kaupp, T., Makarenko, A., & Durrant-Whyte, H. (2010). Human—robot communication for collaborative decision making—a probabilistic approach. *Robotics and Autonomous Systems, 58*(5), 444–456.

Kilgore, R., & Voshell, M. (June 2014). Increasing the transparency of unmanned systems: Applications of ecological interface design. In *International conference on virtual, augmented and mixed reality* (pp. 378–389). Cham, Switzerland: Springer.

Krämer, N. C. (2010). Psychological research on embodied conversational agents: The case of pedagogical agents. *Journal of Media Psychology, 22*(2), 47–51.

Lee, J. D., & See, K. A. (2004). Trust in automation: Designing for appropriate reliance. *Human Factors: The Journal of the Human Factors and Ergonomics Society, 46*(1), 50–80.

Linegang, M. P., Stoner, H. A., Patterson, M. J., Seppelt, B. D., Hoffman, J. D., Crittendon, Z. B., et al. (October 2006). Human-automation collaboration in dynamic mission planning: A challenge requiring an ecological approach. *Proceedings of the Human Factors and*

Ergonomics Society Annual Meeting (Vol. 50,(23), 2482—2486. Sage, CA, Los Angeles, CA: SAGE Publications.

Lyons, J. B. (2013). Being transparent about transparency: A model for human-robot interaction. In *AAAI spring symposium. Palo Alto, CA.*

Maass, S. (1983). Why systems transparency? In T. R. G. Green, S. J. Payne, & G. C. van der Veer (Eds.), *The psychology of computer use* (pp. 19—28). Orlando, FL: Academic Press, Inc.

Matignon, L., Karami, A. B., & Mouaddib, A. I. (November 2010). A model for verbal and non-verbal human-robot collaboration. In *AAAI fall symposium: Dialog with robots* (Vol. 10, pp. 62—67).

McMahan, A. (2003). Immersion, engagement, and presence: A method for analysing 3-D video games. In M. J. P Wolf, & B. Perron (Eds.), *The video game theory reader* (pp. 67—86). New York, NY: Routledge.

Merriam-Webster, S. (2013). *Dictionary.* Merriam-Webster Inc.

Moreno, R., & Mayer, R. (2007). Interactive multimodal learning environments. *Educational Psychology Review, 19*(3), 309—326.

Morrow, P. B., & Fiore, S. M. (September 2012). Supporting human-robot teams in social dynamicism: An overview of the metaphoric inference framework. *Proceedings of the Human Factors and Ergonomics Society Annual Meeting* (Vol. 56,(1), 1718—1722. Sage, CA, Los Angeles, CA: SAGE Publications.

Murphy, R. R., & Burke, J. L. (2010). The safe human-robot ratio. In M. Barnes, & F. Jentsch (Eds.), *Human-robot interactions in future military operations, human factors in defense.* Burlington, VT: Ashgate Publishing.

Ososky, S., Sanders, T., Jentsch, F., Hancock, P., & Chen, J. Y. (June 2014). Determinants of system transparency and its influence on trust in and reliance on unmanned robotic systems. In *Unmanned systems technology XVI* (Vol. 9084)International Society for Optics and Photonics, 90840E-90840E.

Ososky, S., Schuster, D., Phillips, E., & Jentsch, F. G. (March 2013). Building appropriate trust in human-robot teams. In *AAAI spring symposium: Trust and autonomous systems.*

Pacchierotti, C., Tirmizi, A., Bianchini, G., & Prattichizzo, D. (November 2013). Improving transparency in passive teleoperation by combining cutaneous and kinesthetic force feedback. In *Intelligent robots and systems (IROS), 2013 IEEE/RSJ international conference on* (pp. 4958—4963). IEEE.

Parasuraman, R., Molloy, R., & Singh, I. L. (1993). Performance consequences of automation-induced 'complacency'. *The International Journal of Aviation Psychology, 3*(1), 1—23.

Parasuraman, R., Sheridan, T. B., & Wickens, C. D. (2000). A model for types and levels of human interaction with automation. *IEEE Transactions on Systems, Man, and Cybernetics-Part A: Systems and Humans, 30*(3), 286—297.

Phillips, E., Ososky, S., Grove, J., & Jentsch, F. (September 2011). From tools to teammates: Toward the development of appropriate mental models for intelligent robots. *Proceedings of the Human Factors and Ergonomics Society Annual Meeting* (Vol. 55,(1), 1491—1495. Sage, CA, Los Angeles, CA: SAGE Publications.

Salas, E., Shuffler, M. L., Thayer, A. L., Bedwell, W. L., & Lazzara, E. H. (2015). Understanding and improving teamwork in organizations: A scientifically based practical guide. *Human Resource Management, 54*(4), 599—622.

Salmon, P. M., Stanton, N. A., Walker, G. H., Baber, C., Jenkins, D. P., McMaster, R., et al. (2008). What really is going on? Review of situation awareness models for individuals and teams. *Theoretical Issues in Ergonomics Science, 9*(4), 297—323.

Sarter, N. (2008). Investigating mode errors on automated flight decks: Illustrating the problem-driven, cumulative, and interdisciplinary nature of human factors research. *Human Factors, 50*(3), 506–510.

Sarter, N. B., & Woods, D. D. (1995). How in the world did we ever get into that mode? Mode error and awareness in supervisory control. *Human Factors, 37*(1), 5–19.

Schuster, D. (2013). *The effects of diagnostic aiding on situation awareness under robot unreliability.* Orlando, FL: University of Central Florida.

Selkowitz, A. R., Lakhmani, S. G., & Chen, J. Y. (2017). Using agent transparency to support situation awareness of the Autonomous Squad Member. *Cognitive Systems Research, 46,* 13–25.

Sheridan, T. B. (1995). Teleoperation, telerobotics and telepresence: A progress report. *Control Engineering Practice, 3*(2), 205–214.

Sims, V. K., Chin, M. G., Lum, H. C., Upham-Ellis, L., Ballion, T., & Lagattuta, N. C. (2009). Robots' auditory cues are subject to anthropomorphism. *Proceedings of the Human Factors and Ergonomics Society Annual Meeting* (Vol. 53,(18), 1418–1421. Sage, CA, Los Angeles, CA: SAGE Publications.

Squire, P., & Parasuraman, R. (2010). Effects of automation and task load on task switching during human supervision of multiple semi-autonomous robots in a dynamic environment. *Ergonomics, 53*(8), 951–961.

Stanton, N. A., Young, M. S., & Walker, G. H. (2007). The psychology of driving automation: A discussion with professor Don Norman. *International Journal of Vehicle Design, 45*(3), 289–306.

Stowers, K., Kasdaglis, N., Newton, O., Lakhmani, S., Wohleber, R., & Chen, J. (September 2016). Intelligent agent transparency: The design and evaluation of an interface to facilitate human and intelligent agent collaboration. *Proceedings of the Human Factors and Ergonomics Society Annual Meeting* (Vol. 60,(1), 1706–1710. Sage, CA, Los Angeles, CA: SAGE Publications.

Stowers, K., Kasdaglis, N., Rupp, M., Chen, J. Y. C., Barber, D., & Barnes, M. (2017). Insights into human-agent teaming: Intelligent agent transparency and uncertainty. In *Advances in human factors in robots and unmanned systems* (pp. 149–160). Orlando, FL: Springer International Publishing.

Stubbs, K., Hinds, P. J., & Wettergreen, D. (2007). Autonomy and common ground in human-robot interaction: A field study. *IEEE Intelligent Systems, 22*(2).

Sukthankar, G., Shumaker, R., & Lewis, M. (2012). Intelligent agents as teammates. In *Theories of team cognition: Cross-disciplinary perspectives* (pp. 313–343).

Sycara, K., & Sukthankar, G. (2006). *Literature review of teamwork models* (p. 31). Robotics Institute, Carnegie Mellon University.

Teo, G., Wohleber, R., Lin, J., & Reinerman-Jones, L. (2017). The relevance of theory to human-robot teaming research and development. In *Advances in human factors in robots and unmanned systems* (pp. 175–185). Cham, Switzerland: Springer.

U.S. Army. (2017). *The U.S. Army robotic and autonomous systems strategy.* Fort Eustis, VA: TRADOC.

de Visser, E. J., Cohen, M., Freedy, A., & Parasuraman, R. (June 2014). A design methodology for trust cue calibration in cognitive agents. In *International conference on virtual, augmented and mixed reality* (pp. 251–262). Cham, Switzerland: Springer.

Vitense, H. S., Jacko, J. A., & Emery, V. K. (2003). Multimodal feedback: An assessment of performance and mental workload. *Ergonomics, 46*(1–3), 68–87.

Wang, L., Jamieson, G. A., & Hollands, J. G. (2009). Trust and reliance on an automated combat identification system. *Human Factors, 51*(3), 281—291.

Wang, H., Lewis, M., Velagapudi, P., Scerri, P., & Sycara, K. (March 2009). How search and its subtasks scale in N robots. In *Proceedings of the 4th ACM/IEEE international conference on human robot interaction* (pp. 141—148). ACM.

de Winter, J. C., & Dodou, D. (2014). Why the Fitts list has persisted throughout the history of function allocation. *Cognition, Technology & Work, 16*(1), 1—11.

Wooldridge, M., & Jennings, N. R. (1995). Intelligent agents: Theory and practice. *The Knowledge Engineering Review, 10*(2), 115—152.

Wright, J. L., Chen, J. Y., & Barnes, M. J. (2018). Human—automation interaction for multiple robot control: The effect of varying automation assistance and individual differences on operator performance. *Ergonomics*, 1—13.

Wright, J. L., Chen, J. Y., Barnes, M. J., & Hancock, P. A. (2017). *Agent reasoning transparency: The influence of information level on automation induced complacency (No. ARL-TR-8044).* United States: US Army Research Laboratory Aberdeen Proving Ground.

Chapter 2

On the social perception of robots: measurement, moderation, and implications

Steven J. Stroessner
Barnard College, Columbia University, New York, NY, United States

Chapter outline

Readers of this book are undoubtedly aware of the growing importance of robots in everyday life. Robots—mobile machines that can perform tasks autonomously by sensing and manipulating their environments—have existed since the late 1960s (Simon, 2018). However, early robots were primarily novelties offering proofs of concept rather than full-fledged machines capable of completing complex tasks and interacting with humans. That has changed dramatically in recent years, and robots are now involved in many aspects of people's lives. For example, robots are now used to teach children songs, protect homes, vacuum living rooms, distribute medicine in hospitals, and serve as companions. Human-facing robots will become increasingly common, relevant, and important over the next decades.

Living with Robots. https://doi.org/10.1016/B978-0-12-815367-3.00002-5

Given the anticipated increase in the centrality of robots in our lives, it becomes critical to understand social aspects of human–robot interaction (HRI). For robots to effectively interact with humans, they must generate social impressions consistent with their roles. A teaching robot that scares children or a security robot that elicits laughter will likely be ineffective in completing their intended responsibilities. Conversely, a companion robot that produces feelings of warmth and connection or a concierge robot that is judged to be trustworthy will be more successful in their tasks. It is therefore critical to understand how people think about and react to robots based on their appearance, movement, and behavior. Being able to measure the inferences that human interactants might draw about a robot should also prove useful in robotic design. The ability to anticipate how a robot will likely be perceived will help avoid design errors, saving both time and money while increasing a robot's effectiveness.

This chapter focuses on the social perception of human-facing robots. It begins with a discussion of existing measures of social aspects of HRI, culminating in the description of a newly developed psychometrically valid scale, the Robot Social Attributes Scale (RoSAS), that is proving useful in assessing fundamental trait inferences about robots. The chapter then examines how social perceptions of robots captured by the RoSAS vary based on robots' features. This section highlights how robots' perceived association with social categories affects how they are judged and whether (or not) this aligns what is known about human social perception. Finally, we end by discussing future avenues of research to improve the measurement of social factors in HRI.

Previous research measuring social reactions to robots

Over the last two decades, numerous measures of social responses to robots have been developed and used in research. Many of these scales measure specific judgments that are central to assess the effectiveness of interactions in HRI. For example, existing scales measure trust (Jian, Bisantz, & Drury, 2000; Yagoda & Gillan, 2012), perceived safety (Kamide et al., 2012), and negative reactions (Nomura, Kanda, Suzuki, & Kato, 2004; Nomura, Suzuki, Kanda, & Kato, 2006) in HRI. These scales and others are invaluable in assessing social reactions to robots in specific roles that especially require confidence and comfort, such as socially assistive robots (Heerink, Kröse, Evers, & Wielinga, 2010).

Other scales have attempted to look at a broader array of reactions to robots, assessing multiple aspects of social judgment. These reactions include various kinds of trait inferences and emotional responses, going beyond specific inferences (e.g., trust) or emotions (e.g., fear). Such multifaceted scales are useful in detecting whether a given robot is conveying an intended social impression (e.g., friendly) while avoiding an unintended impression (e.g., strange, awkward). The most commonly used general scale in HRI to date has been the Godspeed Questionnaire (Bartneck, Kulić, Croft, & Zoghbi, 2009), so named "because it is intended to help creators of robots on their development journey" (p. 78). This scale brought together a series of items from the existing literature to measure five concepts that are typically of interest in HRI: (1) anthropomorphism (the attribution of human features and behaviors to a robots); (2) animacy (that attribution of life to the robot); (3) likeability (the attribution of friendliness to the robot); (4) perceived intelligence (the attribution of intellectual competence to the robot); and (5) perceived safety (how anxious the perceiver feels in response to the robot). The Godspeed measures these constructs using semantic differentials, where respondents indicate their responses to items on scales anchored by two opposing words (e.g., artificial-lifelike).

In bringing together these five subscales, the authors presented Cronbach's αs from previous research reflecting the internal consistency of each. These reliability data generally exceeded 0.70 which has been commonly considered to be a minimum acceptable value (Nunnally, 1978). Specifically, the reported range of Cronbach's αs from studies that used these subscales or variants thereof were anthropomorphism (0.86–0.93), animacy (0.70–0.76), likeability (0.84–0.92), perceived intelligence (0.75–0.92), and perceived safety (0.91). Therefore, it was suggested that these subscales produced sufficiently consistent responding for them to be useful as a reliable standardized measurement tool in HRI.

Since it was initially proposed, the Godspeed Questionnaire (either in its entirety or its subscales) has been used in dozens of studies to investigate a variety of topics in HRI (see Weiss & Bartneck, 2015, for a metaanalytic review). The breadth of issues examined with the Godspeed include persuasion by robots (Ham, Bokhorst, Cuijpers, Pol, & Cabibihan, 2011), the influence of robotic attention on interactions (Schillaci, Bodiroza, & Hafner, 2013), the uncanny valley (Złotowski et al., 2015), evaluations of specific robots (Foster et al., 2012), and evaluations of robotic behavior (Torta, van Heumen, Cuijpers, & Juola, 2012).

Although the Godspeed Questionnaire has been widely used in HRI, questions have been raised about various properties of the measure. First, concerns have been voiced about whether the Godspeed focuses on the actual constructs that people focus on when thinking about or interacting with robots. It would be optimal first to identify the kinds of judgments, inferences, and reactions that occur in HRI before creating a scale to measure such responses. Second, the use of semantic differential scales is complicated by the fact that whereas some items use antonyms as endpoints (e.g., unfriendly–friendly), other items appear not so well aligned (e.g., awful–nice). This raises the possibility that any single item might capture more than one dimension of judgment. Third, as was acknowledged by the developers of the Godspeed when it was first proposed (Bartneck et al., 2009), there is conceptual overlap between the constructs being measured. Items designed to identify anthropomorphism and animacy, for example, are very similar, and one item (the dead—lifelike item) even appears on each subscale. Because the original study did not involve the collection of responses to all subscales from a single set of participants, it was impossible to establish the independence of the Godspeed subscales empirically.

In sum, although there are several scales for measuring specific judgments of robots, there has not until recently existed a general measure that captures the fundamental aspects of robot social perception. The Godspeed Questionnaire was designed as such a measure, but questions have been raised about various psychometric aspects of the measure. As such, further research seemed warranted. In initiating such work, my colleagues and I accepted the solicitation that accompanied the introduction of Godspeed that "interested readers, in particular experimental psychologists, are invited to continue to develop these questionnaires, and to validate them further" (Bartneck et al., 2009).

Goals in measuring social reactions to robots

Psychometrics is a field of study focused on the theories and techniques involved in measuring psychological constructs. Psychometrics provides researchers with a set of standards by which to judge the effectiveness and likely success of measuring psychological phenomena. As we argued earlier in this chapter, social reactions to robots are central in accounting for various important aspects of HRI. As such, we can look to psychometrics to assess measures used in HRI and to guide further development and refinement.

Several goals are important in developing a psychometrically sound testing instrument. First, an instrument should be capturing what it purports to be measuring. As applied to HRI, a general measure of social responses to robots should identify and capture what people spontaneously focus on when they think about, look at, or interact with a robot. Second, measures should successfully capture the intended and not unintended constructs. And third, measures should be responded to consistently, both within items designed to measure a specific construct and over time in response to a consistent stimulus. Of course, as most readers are undoubtedly aware, these characteristics correspond to *construct validity*, *discriminant validity*, and *reliability* in measurement, respectively.

Although psychometrics is likely well understood by many readers, a brief discussion of several key issues highlights important issues in HRI. Generally, a measure is psychometrically sound to the degree that it is both reliable and valid. Although reliability generally refers to consistency in responding to a measure, there are several distinct aspects of reliability. One aspect of reliability pertains to consistency over time; Are identical stimuli judged consistently with different research participants in different testing contexts? Another critical aspect of reliability involves internal consistency (commonly reflected in the statistic, Cronbach's α), indicating whether individuals respond consistently to items that supposedly measure the same underlying construct.

Validity is the degree that a score derived from a measure can be interpreted as a measure of a specific psychological construct. Validity is high when a measure successfully captures the construct or constructs that it is intended to assess. Instruments should have high *discriminant validity* if they presume to evaluate more than one aspect of judgment. This type of validity is high if responses to a scale or subscale are distinct from responses to scales assessing theoretically different concepts. When different concepts are being measured within a single scale, the scale's *dimensionality*, or factor structure, is used to identify the number and nature of distinct constructs being assessed. Unidimensional scales contain a set of coherent items measuring a single psychological construct, whereas multidimensional scales contain sets of items capturing different psychological constructs. In sum, measures should elicit consistent responses in assessing any given construct and different responses to different constructs.

There are several distinct benefits to using psychometrically valid measures in HRI. First, the use of a standardized measure that is both reliable and valid allows comparison of results on a single metric, both over time and across different contexts. Use of a valid instrument becomes particularly crucial when trying to compare reactions to different robots or similar robots by different sets of respondents. Second, such a scale can be used to study a variety of related but distinct phenomena within a given area of research. If constructs are similar but distinct, measurement instruments should reflect those relations. Third, using a valid measure provides a solid foundation for examining other judgments or behaviors concerning a robot. Fourth, such a scale allows researchers and practitioners to avoid using intuition or speculation as the basis of research. In sum, reliance on psychometric data to develop and assess a measure ensures that crucial constructs are being studied while avoiding measurement of constructs that are indistinct or unimportant in accounting for reactions to robots. Given these myriad benefits, it should not be surprising that several scales assessing responses to robots have emerged in HRI research.

What are the psychometric properties of the Godspeed Questionnaire? As we reported earlier, the various subscales produce moderate to high consistency in responding, indicating an acceptable level of reliability. However, empirical work raised questions about the discriminant validity for the Godspeed subscales. In a study on the uncanny valley, Ho and MacDorman (2010) had participants rate computer animated characters and robots displayed via video clips using the Godspeed Questionnaire. Various statistical tests were performed to assess the psychometric properties of the Godspeed. Subscale reliabilities were similar to those reported in Bartneck et al. (2009) except for perceived safety (Cronbach's $\alpha = 0.60$). However, responses to the subscales were highly correlated, reaching as high as 0.89. In fact, the average correlation in responses to the first four subscales was 0.74, suggesting that similar and highly overlapping concepts were being measured. Only perceived safety appeared to be a distinct construct (all correlations with other subscales <0.20). This conclusion was confirmed by a factor analysis, a statistical method for generating a small, meaningful set of conceptual variables (factors) from analyzing variability among scale responses (see Furr, 2011 for an overview). Factor analysis is ideal for identifying whether different subscales are capturing distinct constructs, and Ho and MacDorman's analysis suggested the Godspeed subscales did not. Instead, the factor analysis did not support the existence of the five hypothesized factors. Moreover, responses to many of the items that were intended to measure specific concepts were only weakly related to that factor. For example, Surprised—Quiescent judgments were loosely related to the perceived safety factor that it supposedly measured. This work has been criticized for using video clips rather than actual robots (Weiss & Bartneck, 2015). In spite of that caveat, the research did raise questions about the utility of the Godspeed as a general measure of robot social perceptions.

The Robot Social Attributes Scale

In light of these concerns, my colleagues (Colleen Carpinella, Alisa Wyman, Michael Perez, and Jonathan Benitez) and I set about developing a new generalized scale, the RoSAS, to capture fundamental social reactions to robots. Specifically, the RoSAS measures trait judgments of robots. Trait inferences are subjective judgments about the characteristic regularities in the thoughts and actions of other people (friendly? smart? helpful?), and they play a critical role in the social perception of humans. Inferences about people's traits of people often serve as the foundation for other important reactions such as evaluations (deciding whether you like or dislike a person; e.g., Schneid, Crawford, Skowronski, Irwin, & Carlston, 2015) and desire for contact (deciding whether you want to approach or avoid the person; e.g. Snyder, Tanke, & Berscheid, 1977). Moreover, large literature show that even from a young age, trait inferences are affected by the humans' features (Cogsdill, Todorov, Spelke, & Banaji, 2014) and social category memberships (Diesendruck & Eldror, 2011). Given that people regularly anthropomorphize nonsocial entities such as robots (Waytz, Epley, & Cacioppo, 2010), we sought to explore whether similar effects would also characterize judgments in HRI.

The RoSAS explicitly built upon the Godspeed, recognizing that this widely used measure of robot social perception provided a good foundation for additional scale development. In both the general approach and in the choice of specific items we utilized in developing the RoSAS, we were indebted to the developers of the Godspeed. Nonetheless, we felt that additional work could be done to create a more psychometrically valid scale of robot social perception, thereby overcoming the concerns raised about the prior scale. Moreover, we fully expect that others will build upon the work we discuss here.

Scale development and reliability

We began this work by conducting several studies to identify constructs that are of central concern when people think about robots and to identify items to measure those constructs (Carpinella, Wyman, Perez, & Stroessner, 2017, Studies 1−3). This was done through the use of exploratory factor analysis, a technique similar to the one that initially raised questions about the discriminant validity of the Godspeed subscales (Ho & MacDorman, 2010). We first explored judgments of robots on the items contained in the Godspeed. We told experimental participants that we were interested in how people perceive groups in our society and that when we encounter the name of a group, certain words might come to mind. We then presented them with the category label "robots" and asked them to indicate, "Using the scale provided, what is your impression of the category robots?" All semantic differential pairs from the Godspeed Questionnaire were then presented. We intentionally did not include any images, definitions, or descriptions of robots to avoid tethering the responses to any specific exemplar or type of robot. In doing so, we hoped to identify what factors underlie people's thinking about the general category of robots.

These judgments were then factor analyzed. Three factors emerged rather than the five factors specified by the Godspeed. Based on the items that loaded highly on these factors (i.e., items for which responses were strongly correlated with the factor), we termed those factors: *anthropomorphism* (captured by judgments on the items machinelike−humanlike, mechanical−organic, artificial−lifelike, and moving rigidly−moving elegantly); *intelligence* (incompetent−competent, ignorant−knowledgeable, foolish−sensible, unintelligent−intelligent, inert−interactive, and irresponsible−responsible); and *likeability* (awful−nice, dislike−like, unpleasant−pleasant, and unkind−kind.) In sum, these factors bore little resemblance to the constructs supposedly measured by the Godspeed subscales.

A second study was then performed that included both items from the Godspeed Questionnaire and also a much broader set of items pulled from the empirical literature on the social perception of humans. Specifically, we included traits items that have been shown to be central in stereotyping, broadly, and gender stereotyping, specifically (Fiske, Cuddy, & Glick, 2007; Bem, 1974, respectively). To standardize items, we separated out the endpoints from the semantic differential Godspeed items and presented them in Likert-format scales ($1 = definitely\ not\ associated$ to $9 = definitely\ associated$) along with the traits from the social perception literature. After eliminating duplicates, items included a total set of 83 characteristics.

After collecting data following the same procedure as in the first study, we factor analyzed responses to this larger set of items. Three statistically significant factors again emerged. Coincidentally, six items loaded highly on each factor and no items loaded on more than one factor (all factor loadings can be seen in Table 2.1). Based on the items that loaded on these factors, we labeled them as signifying *warmth*, *competence*, and *discomfort*. We then calculated Cronbach's αs for each set of traits to determine reliability if they were used as subscales. These indices were good to excellent for warmth (happy, feeling, sociable, organic, compassionate, emotional; Cronbach's α = 0.91), competence (capable, responsive, interactive, reliable, competent, knowledgeable; Cronbach's α = 0.84), and discomfort (scary, strange, awkward, dangerous, awful, aggressive; Cronbach's α = 0.82). Eliminating any of the items from these calculations reduced the reliability of each subscale, indicating that all

TABLE 2.1 Factor loadings for Robotic Social Attributes Scale trait items.

Trait	Warmth	Competence	Discomfort
Happy	**0.83**	−0.01	−0.01
Feeling	**0.81**	−0.15	0.04
Sociable	**0.79**	0.13	−0.18
Organic	**0.78**	−0.15	−0.02
Compassionate	**0.78**	−0.04	0.03
Emotional	**0.78**	−0.20	0.05
Capable	−0.21	**0.71**	−0.05
Responsive	−0.14	**0.68**	0.04
Interactive	−0.23	**0.65**	−0.01
Reliable	−0.06	**0.65**	−0.03
Competent	−0.11	**0.65**	−0.04
Knowledgeable	−0.01	**0.62**	−0.02
Scary	0.05	−0.01	**0.69**
Strange	−0.05	0.15	**0.60**
Awkward	0.05	0.04	**0.60**
Dangerous	−0.04	0.02	**0.60**
Awful	0.36	−0.25	**0.56**
Aggressive	0.27	0.01	**0.55**
Eigenvalue	22.03	9.34	5.05
Percent variance explained	26.5%	11.3%	6.1%

From Carpinella, C. M., Wyman, A. B., Perez, M. A., & Stroessner, S. J. (2017). The robotic social attributes scale (RoSAS): Development and validation. In: Proceedings of the 2017 ACM/IEEE international conference on human-robot interaction, Vienna, Austria (pp. 254–262) (Study 2).

traits should be measured to maximize consistency. Moreover, correlations between factors were low (rs ranging from 0.18 to 0.34), providing additional evidence that these factors reflected independent constructs.

It is intriguing that two of the three factors that emerged in judgments of robots bear a close resemblance to fundamental factors underlying social cognition. Research in social psychology has established two universal dimensions of judgments of human individuals and groups: warmth and competence (Fiske, 2018; Fiske et al., 2007; Kervyn, Yzerbyt, & Judd, 2010; Rosenberg, Nelson, & Vivekananthan, 1968). These two dimensions are thought to reflect questions concerning basic survival—whether a person or group intends us help or harm us and whether they can be effective doing so. In general, when people or groups are evaluated as warm and competent, they are judged more favorably and interacted with more positively. Warmth judgments are particularly important in social cognition. They are commonly made more quickly than competence judgments and carry more weight in interpersonal interactions (Willis & Todorov, 2006). Warmth has been shown to be an underlying focal dimension of robot perception as well (Ho & MacDorman, 2010).

The notable discovery from this study was the emergence of a factor related to discomfort. Although the importance of these concerns was foreshadowed by the "perceived safety" subscale in the Godspeed Questionnaires (containing the items anxious—relaxed, agitated—calm, and quiescent—surprised), discomfort emerged as a coherent construct that, along with warmth and competence, appears to play a fundamental role in the social perception of robots. Although our initial attempt in developing the RoSAS was to focus on trait judgments, it is also clear that discomfort, as a construct, is somewhat distinct from the traits that comprise warmth and competence. Discomfort can be better characterized as a *reaction* or an *evaluative response* that arises uniquely in HRI.

We initially wondered how unique this was to HRI, speculating that discomfort might emerge in judgments of robots simply because of their unfamiliarity. In other words, we wondered whether discomfort might be a concern in imagining any unknown entity. To test this idea, we conducted a study (Carpinella et al., 2017, Study 3) in which participants were asked to respond to familiar and unfamiliar social groups (Australians and Nauruans, respectively) and animals (giraffe and okapi, respectively) using the RoSAS. These ratings were then factor analyzed. In each case, only two significant factors emerged, and neither of these factors reflected discomfort. Therefore, the factor focusing on discomfort in thinking about robots does not appear to merely reflect low familiarity. Instead, it seems that people spontaneously consider discomfort when judging robots but do not do so when thinking about other unfamiliar entities.

The RoSAS has now been used in numerous studies performed by independent labs using a variety of methods and purposes, and psychometric data suggest that measures of warmth, competence, and discomfort are reliable. A review of all papers offering detailed data for all dimensions of the RoSAS (see Table 2.2) indicates that the subscales demonstrate good to excellent reliabilities (Nunnally, 1978). The only exception was one study (Bonani et al., 2018) that reported low reliabilities for discomfort in one condition and competence in a second condition (both Cronbach's αs < 0.80). It is important to note that this study used a small sample size (N = 12), and, as would be expected, reliabilities were lower than those that emerged from studies with larger samples. In sum, existing data show that responses to the RoSAS subscales are highly consistent, matching, and usually exceeding the reliability of scales that are commonly used in HRI.

TABLE 2.2 Robotic Social Attributes Scale subscale reliabilities (Cronbach's α).

			Dimension		
Study	Stimuli	N	W	C	D
Benitez et al. (2017, Study 1)	Synthetic robot faces	124	0.93	0.94	0.90
Benitez et al. (2017, Study 2)	Imagined robot roles	121	0.87	0.88	0.81
Benitez et al. (2017, Study 4)	Synthetic robot faces in imagined robot roles	381	0.90	0.93	0.90
Bonani et al. (2018, Condition 1)	Robot verbal instructions	12	0.86	0.84	0.74
Bonani et al. (2018, Condition 2)	Robot interaction	12	0.84	0.53	0.86
Carpinella et al. (2017, Study 2)	Imagined robots	210	0.91	0.84	0.82
Carpinella et al. (2017, Study 4)	Synthetic robot faces	252	0.92	0.95	0.90
Hoffman et al. (2018, Study 3)	Observed human–robot interaction	297	0.83	0.87	0.84
Pan et al. (2018)	Robot arm handoffs	22	0.94	0.90	0.81
Stroessner and Benitez (2019, Study 1)	Real humanoid robots	250	0.90	0.93	0.85
Stroessner and Benitez (2019, Study 2)	Real humanoid and nonhumanoid robots	196	0.91	0.89	0.87

Notes: C, competence; D, discomfort; N, sample size; W, warmth.

Scale validation

Evidence supporting the validity of the RoSAS has been provided by various types of evidence from several studies. The first indication of the validity of the RoSAS as a measure of robot social perception emerged from Carpinella et al. (2017), who examined RoSAS scores generated in response to synthetic robotic faces. Although the primary focus of this study was to investigate social categorization processes in HRI (which will be discussed in greater detail later in this chapter), the data also serve as a test of whether the RoSAS measures the constructs it is supposed to measure. In this study, participants were shown 12 different synthetic robot faces that are shown in Fig. 2.1. After developing an androgynous, humanlike base face (the face furthest left in the middle row of Fig. 2.1), commercial software was used to manipulate the gender-typicality of this face making it appear particularly feminine or masculine (displayed above and below the base face, respectively). Each of these humanlike images was then edited to look like a human−machine blend or strongly machinelike by altering the texture and color of the skin (shown in the second and third columns of Fig. 2.1).

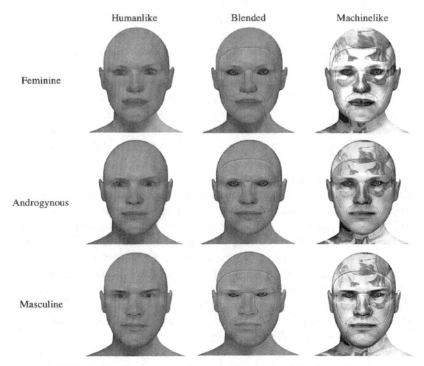

FIGURE 2.1 Synthetic robot faces varying in gender-typicality and machineness.

If the RoSAS is a valid measure of robot social perception, we would expect that several effects would emerge from ratings of these different robot faces based on their gender-typicality and machineness. First, based on prevailing gender stereotypes (Prentice & Carranza, 2002; Rudman & Glick, 2008), we would expect that feminine faces would be judged as warmer than masculine faces (Eyssel & Hegel, 2012; Haines, Deaux, & Lofaro, 2016) and that masculine faces would create higher feelings of discomfort than feminine faces (Johnson, Iida, & Tassinary, 2012). Both predictions were supported: more feminine faces were judged as warmer, and more masculine faces were judged with higher levels of discomfort. Interestingly, this pattern was true at every level of machineness. In other words, feminine faces were judged as warmer and masculine faces as creating high discomfort regardless of how machinelike the face appeared.

Effects based on the faces' machineness were also expected and obtained. We hypothesized that more machinelike faces would be seen as less warm and would produce higher levels of discomfort. Both of these effects also emerged, and these patterns were consistent across the different levels of sex-typicality. As a result of these effects for both gender-typicality and machineness, the female humanlike robot face was judged highest in warmth and lowest in discomfort, whereas the masculine machinelike face was judged lowest in warmth and highest in discomfort.

What about judgments of competence? We expected that humanlike robots would be seen as more competent than machinelike robots, and that hypothesis was confirmed. It might be assumed based on social stereotypes that men would be judged as more competent than women (Basow, 1986), but this effect did not emerge and has not been obtained consistently in subsequent studies. In fact, as will be discussed in further detail later in this chapter, the opposite has often been obtained. It is important to note, however, that the RoSAS competence factor (emphasizing reliability and responsiveness) is quite distinct from measures of human competence (emphasizing independence and self-confidence).

More broadly, we also sought to determine whether these synthetic faces might produce gender stereotyping in a manner that is characteristic of human competence. To that end, we (Benitez, Wyman, Carpinella, & Stroessner, 2017) asked a separate set of participants to judge the masculine humanlike and feminine humanlike robot faces using an established scale of warmth and competence from the social perception literature. Consistent with research on human gender stereotyping, the masculine robot was judged to be more competent than the feminine robot. In retrospect, it might have been wise to name the RoSAS factor relating to reliability as "reliability" or "capability," rather than "competence," given that this construct is different in flavor than the gender stereotype applied to humans.

Although these initial results were encouraging, one might reasonably question whether they tell us more about the stimuli than about the RoSAS

FIGURE 2.2 Images of real robot heads differing in gender-typicality and machines. *From Stroessner, S. J., & Benitez, J. (2019). The social perception of humanoid and non-humanoid robots: Effects of gendered and machinelike features. International Journal of Social Robotics (in press) (Study 1).*

itself. Is it possible that these results are limited to the particular synthetic robot faces that were used in this study? To answer this question, it would be beneficial to show similar effects with different stimuli, optimally with real robots. In fact, this has been done in two studies (Stroessner & Benitez, 2019). In the first study, a large set of images of real robot heads were collected and pretested for inclusion based on ratings of their gender-typicality and machineness. Participants then judged eight of these robots (see Fig. 2.2) that were most (and equally) extreme on these dimensions using the RoSAS. Regarding warmth, female and humanlike robots were judged higher than male and machinelike robots, confirming the prior findings for judgments of synthetic robot heads. On competence, humanlike robots were judged as more competent than machinelike robots, again replicating previous research. In this study, feminine robots were judged as more competent than masculine robots. On discomfort, masculine robots were judged higher than female robots, and machinelike robots tended to be judged higher than human robots.

In the second study, humanoid and nonhumanoid robots (depicted in Fig. 2.3) were judged on RoSAS dimensions and also for both gender-typicality and machineness. The goal was to examine how natural variations in these variables would correlate with trait ratings measured by the RoSAS. As was expected, judgments of machineness correlated significantly and negatively with perceived warmth and competence and positively with perceived discomfort. In other words, the more machinelike a robot, the less warm and competent it was judged to be and the more discomfort it produced. Gender-typicality judgments also correlated significantly with RoSAS judgments. The more feminine appearing a robot, the more likely it would be judged as high in warmth and low in competence and discomfort. These results

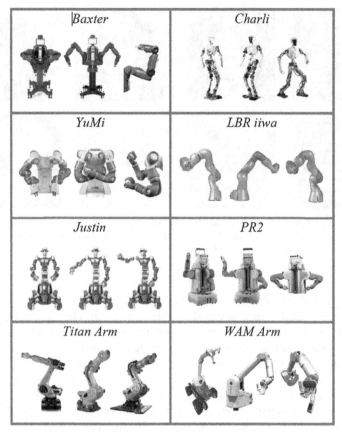

FIGURE 2.3 Images of humanoid and nonhumanoid real robots (Stroessner & Benitez, 2019, Study 2).

generally replicated the previous validation studies, this time using real robots and a different method.

Since these initial studies were conducted, several additional studies using diverse methods to study a range of issues provide further support to the validity of the RoSAS. Pan, Croft, and Niemeyer (2018), for example, examined social responses throughout a series of human–robot handovers from a robotic arm. The handovers varied over trials in their initial position, grasp method, and retraction speed. Over and above these variations, it was found that warmth increased and perceived discomfort decreased as the trials progressed. This would be expected to the degree that participants became familiar and comfortable with the robot with increased experience. Bonani et al. (2018) had participants with impaired sight assemble a puzzle with a robot who either provided voice instructions or interacted physically to assist in the puzzle assembly. The robot was perceived as warmer and more competent when the collaboration involved physical contact. Discomfort did not differ between conditions, consistent with participants self-reports. Finally, Sebo, Traeger, Jung, and Scassellati (2018) had human participants collaborate with a social robot that made statements indicating either vulnerability or neutrality. The vulnerable robot was judged more warmly, and engagement in the task was also heightened in this condition. All these findings indicate that the RoSAS effectively measures the intended constructs.

In this first part of this chapter, the focus has been on the development of the RoSAS. This scale was developed to provide the HRI research community a standardized, psychometrically robust, generalized scale of social reactions to robots. Preliminary tests of this instrument have been encouraging, although future refinement is both inevitable and welcomed. Of course, the RoSAS was not developed solely as an end in itself but as a tool that would prove useful in addressing substantive questions in HRI. The chapter now turns to a discussion of some of those questions, examining downstream consequences of trait inferences captured by the RoSAS and variation in responding based on robots' features.

Predictors and consequences of trait judgments of robots

In our laboratory, we have been examining numerous consequential responses to robots that vary in their features. Preliminary results regarding trait inferences in response to robots varying in gender- and machine-related features were described earlier in this chapter, but some additional justification for the importance of these dimensions is now merited. We chose to modify physical features because they are ubiquitous and integral aspects of HRI. All robots must be designed, and their design elements are readily observable. Moreover, appearance factors are highly relevant to cognition about both social and nonsocial entities, although the specific physical features involved in these two domains might differ. To ensure inclusion of variables relevant to both domains, we chose to manipulate the degree that a robot resembled a human or a machine (i.e., machineness) because of the importance of such variations for anthropomorphism. We also manipulated the second appearance factor— gender-typicality—because of its critical role in social cognition. There were good theoretical reasons to suspect that both factors would affect trait inferences and other consequential social judgments.

Machineness and robot perception

Numerous HRI researchers and theorists have emphasized how humanlike physical attributes of robots, even features that play no functional role, are central in fostering human engagement (Duffy, 2003; Eddy, Gallup, & Povinelli, 1993; Fink, 2012). Humanlike physical features are believed to enhance familiarity, affinity, and feelings of warmth (Branscomb, 1979;

Caporael, 1986; Mori, 1970/2012). These responses are presumed to arise from anthropomorphism, the attribution of human cognitions and emotions to human-looking inanimate objects. Theoretical accounts of the psychology of anthropomorphism highlight the importance of physical features in promoting the humanization of nonsocial entities:

> The perceived similarity of targets to humans should likewise influence the extent to which people anthropomorphize nonhuman agents...Readily observable humanlike features should therefore influence the accessibility of egocentric or anthropomorphic knowledge structures, thereby increasing the likelihood that such knowledge is applied to a nonhuman target of judgment.
>
> Epley, Waytz, & Cacioppo, 2007

Within robotics, it has been argued that the humanlike outer appearance of a robot can lead people to respond automatically to social cues emitted by a robot, applying human—human social schemas and norms in such interactions (Lee, Lau, Kiesler, & Chiu, 2005; Schmitz, 2011). Conversely, visible physical indicators that robots are in fact machines should reduce engagement and affinity by decreasing the degree they are seen as humanlike.

Gender-typicality and social perception

Much research in social cognition shows that people are ubiquitously and effortlessly categorized not merely as "human" but also as members of age, race, and gender categories (Brewer, 1988; Devine, 1989; Fiske & Neuberg, 1990). Gender categorization is particularly crucial given its evolutionary and social significance; it is typically the first category to be perceived in others (Quinn, Yahr, Kuhn, Slater, & Pascalis, 2002) and oneself (Bem, 1981). Infants differentiate by sex categories at an early age and show an overall preference for female faces (Quinn et al., 2002; Ramsey, Langlois, & Marti, 2005). Evidence from neuroscience (Ito & Urland, 2003) shows that electroencephalogram (EEG) signals differ in response to male and female facial stimuli within 200 ms.

Gender is inferred through the use of visually available cues (facial features, body morphology, and bodily motion) that are associated with gender categories (Alt & Johnson, 2018). Several key features distinguish male and female faces. Males typically have higher facial width-to-height ratios (FWHRs) than females, and higher FWHRs are associated with more masculine facial ratings. Women usually have fuller lips, higher cheekbones, more rounded foreheads, smaller chins and noses, and rounder eyes compared with men (Farkas, 1987). Men are marked by larger jawbones, prominent cheekbones, thin cheeks and lips, and prominent brow ridges (Little, Jones, & DeBruine, 2011).

Once a person is categorized by gender, several processes are triggered with minimal effort or intention. Categorization leads to the activation of gender stereotypes—cognitive structures containing a person's knowledge, beliefs, and expectancies about a gender group (Hamilton & Trolier, 1986)—that serve as the basis of subsequent judgment. Human stereotypes can be quite varied and specific, but, as was previously mentioned, they can be characterized in terms of two fundamental dimensions: warmth and competence. Whereas men are seen as competent but not particularly warm, women are likely to be judged as warm but not particularly competent. Gender categorization also activates evaluative responses (i.e., attitudes) associated with these gender categories. There is a general tendency for women to be favored over men (Eagly & Mladinic, 1994), although positive attitudes toward women often mask underlying paternalistic beliefs (Glick & Fiske, 1996). Both stereotypes and attitudes can influence the desire for interpersonal contact. Positive beliefs and evaluations generally predict approach behavior, although a variety of motives (e.g., willingness to please, desire for access to power) also can play critical roles in determining whether a person desires to interact with another person.

Effects of gender-typicality and machineness on social judgments of robots

In light of these considerations, our lab has conducted a series of studies where the machineness and gender-typicality of synthetic and real robot faces were manipulated or measured to examine social reactions. As was described in the section on the development of the RoSAS, we began by focusing on trait judgments. In subsequent studies, we extended our analysis to include evaluative reactions and desire for contact, as well as the relation between these different judgments.

Implications for trait judgments

We earlier reported the results of Carpinella et al. (2017, Study 4) that offered evidence validating the RoSAS. That study showed that trait judgments of synthetic robot faces (shown in Fig. 2.1) mirrored human gender stereotyping and attested to the influence of machineness on social inference. Feminine and humanlike faces were judged as warmer and more competent than masculine and machinelike faces. Masculine and machinelike faces produced higher levels of discomfort than feminine and humanlike faces. Two additional studies using these faces produced highly similar results (Benitez et al., 2017, Studies 1 and 4) as did a study using real robot faces that varied in gender-typicality and machineness (Stroessner & Benitez, 2019).

Across these studies, two additional caveats became clear. One, although findings for warmth and discomfort were consistent across studies, effects for competence were more mixed. Three of the studies showed higher judgments of feminine over masculine faces on competence, whereas one study did not. Two, there were some interactions between machineness and gender-typicality variables, such that the effects of gender-typicality were sometimes weaker for machinelike faces. This would be expected to the degree that machinelike robots are less likely to be anthropomorphized, decreasing the likelihood that gender information is seen as applicable and given any weight.

In sum, these studies consistently show that feminine and humanlike robot faces are perceived as warm, competent, and nonthreatening. Masculine and machinelike faces are seen as lower in warmth and sometimes competence and usually provoke higher levels of discomfort.

Implications for evaluative responses

Evaluative responses were measured in two of the experiments with synthetic robot faces (Benitez et al., 2017, Studies 1 and 4) as well as the study with real robots (Stroessner & Benitez, 2019). Specifically, participants in these studies were asked to indicate "the degree to which you like the robot" for each face they were shown. In all three studies, the feminine robots were evaluated more favorably than the masculine robots, and the humanlike robots were judged more favorably than the machinelike robots. One study (Benitez et al., 2017, Study 4) produced an interaction between these variables, such that feminine and masculine faces were evaluated equivalently when they were machinelike, even though feminine robots were judged more favorably overall. In general, feminine looking and humanlike robots were judged more favorably than masculine and machinelike robots.

Implications for contact desirability

The desire for contact with the robot was also measured in these three studies using two items: "How willing would you be to interact with the robot?" and "How willing would you be to spend time with the robot?" Responses to these two items were highly similar in all studies, so they were combined into a single composite measure of contact desirability. In all three studies, robots with humanlike faces produced a higher desire for contact than robots with machinelike faces. Also, feminine faces generally produced a higher desire for contact than masculine faces, although one study (Benitez et al., 2017, Study 4) again showed that gender-typicality was irrelevant when responding to machinelike faces. In general, the same faces that were judged with favorable traits and were evaluated favorably were most likely to produce a desire for contact.

Relations between social judgments

Although results were consistent across trait, evaluative, and contact desirability measures, several additional questions can be addressed by examining relations between these responses. For example, which trait judgments captured by the RoSAS correlate most strongly with evaluative responses? Which traits predict contact desirability? And what is the strength of relation between evaluative responses and contact desirability?

These questions were examined using data from four experiments in which all three dependent measures were collected (Benitez et al., 2017, Studies 1 and 2; Stroessner & Benitez, 2019, Studies 1 and 2). Each study used different methods and robot stimuli. The first of these studies involved participants rating nine synthetic robot faces (Fig. 2.1), and correlations between RoSAS trait judgments, evaluative responses (liking of the robot), and contact desirability (want to interact/spend time with this robot) for each robot were calculated. Regarding correlations between RoSAS dimensions and liking, discomfort was the strongest (and negative) predictor of liking judgments. For seven of the nine robots, perceived discomfort was most strongly, and negatively, correlated with liking (ranging from −0.25 to −0.51 with an average correlation of −0.41). Perceived warmth (range 0.15−0.52; average 0.29) and competence (range 0.20−0.44, average 0.30) were less strongly correlated with liking judgments, although warmth judgments were most highly correlated with liking judgments for two of the robots (the human-masculine and machinelike-feminine robots). Regarding correlations between RoSAS judgments and contact desirability, discomfort was always the most potent predictor (range −0.38 to −0.57, average −0.47), and warmth was the weakest predictor for eight of the nine robots (range 0.15−0.38, average 0.25).

The second study asked participants to make judgments of robots in various roles (companion, entertainment, military, and no role specified) without being provided with images. Discomfort was most highly correlated with liking for three of the four robot roles (range −0.16 to −0.32, average −0.26), and warmth was the weakest predictor of liking for three of the four robot roles (range 0.00−0.25, average 0.13). Warmth was also weakly correlated with contact desirability (range −0.03 to 0.18, average 0.10) with discomfort (range −0.27 to −0.33, average −0.30) and competence (range 0.18−0.34, average 0.27), each correlating more highly.

The third study involved ratings of the real robot heads depicted in Fig. 2.2. For liking judgments of every category of robots, discomfort judgments were always most highly correlated (range −0.41 to −0.54, average −0.48) and warmth judgment most poorly correlated (range 0.29−0.36, average 0.33). The same pattern emerged for contact desirability, with discomfort most highly correlated (range −0.40 to −0.59, average −0.52) and warmth most weakly correlated (range 0.25−0.34, average 0.28) with these judgments.

The fourth study involved judgments of the real robot bodies depicted in Fig. 2.3. Because these robots varied naturally in the variables of interest, correlations between the different measures were assessed collapsing across all of the robots. Liking judgments were highly correlated with competence (0.43) and discomfort (−0.41) but weakly correlated with warmth (0.30). Contact desirability judgments were most highly correlated with perceived discomfort (−0.49) and most weakly correlated with warmth (0.22).

The pattern of correlational relations between judgments was remarkably consistent across these four studies. Judgments of discomfort from the RoSAS were almost always most highly (and negatively) correlated with liking and were especially strongly predictive of contact desirability. To the degree that a robot was expected to create feelings of strangeness or danger, liking was lower and the desire for contact was reduced. Warmth was generally a poor predictor of liking and contact desirability. Although perceived warmth was positively correlated with these other judgments, the relationship was generally weaker than for the other two dimensions captured by the RoSAS.

This relative weakness of warmth in accounting for liking and contact desirability was surprising given its importance in accounting for evaluations of humans (Cuddy, Fiske, & Glick, 2008; Kervyn et al., 2010) and the fact that it was the strongest construct to emerge from our original factor analysis (see Table 2.1). There are at least three possible reasons for the relative weakness of perceived warmth in accounting for evaluative judgments of robots. One possibility is that judgments of warmth, although important, simply might have less relevance for robots compared with people. Warmth in the social domain reflects the perceived goals or intentions of another person concerning the self (Fiske, Cuddy, Glick, & Xu, 2002). If a person appears to have positive intentions toward the self, warm feelings tend to arise. Ill intentions tend to result in perceptions of low warmth and feelings of dislike. Although robots are often anthropomorphized, perceivers still might not credit them with the same degree of intentionality as they do humans. As such, warmth in HRI might arise from superficial aspects of robot appearance indicating pleasantness and friendliness rather based on assumptions about underlying motives and goals.

A second possibility is that warmth is important in HRI but that competence (e.g., reliability and capability) and discomfort (e.g., scariness and danger) might be even *more* critical. Knowing that a robot will be dependable and unlikely to provoke fear might be paramount considerations in HRI, but these issues might not even be contemplated before interacting with other people. Consequently, warmth might be unimportant in HRI only because its importance pales in comparison to other factors that are particularly germane to interactions with robots. Unfortunately, we have no comparable data using human stimuli with which to test this possibility.

Third, it is also possible that different trait judgments play key roles at different times in HRI. Discomfort, for example, might be a primary determinant of whether interaction with a robot is ever initiated. Only if a person expects to feel comfortable and safe will contact with a robot be sought and, once contact is initiated, variance in discomfort might become relatively unimportant. Once an interaction begins, judgments of warmth might then determine the quality of the interaction. As such, judgments of discomfort might serve a gatekeeping function determining whether an interaction will be sought whereas warmth will determine whether contact is enjoyable. All of these possibilities and others are interesting questions to consider in future research.

Future research

Our research has focused on understanding basic social responses to robots, focusing on how variations in robots' physical features affect how they are judged and evaluated. We began by identifying a need to be able to identify and measure fundamental aspects of social perception in HRI. These efforts led to the development of the RoSAS for assessing social responses to robots. We then conducted a series of studies examining two distinct questions: (1) how do gendered and machinelike features affect trait judgments, and (2) how do trait judgments affect other important judgments in HRI.

Although the research presented here provides novel insights in HRI, this work is preliminary and should offer many opportunities for extension and clarification. For example, all of the research reported relies on participant self-reports using a standardized scale. While self-reports have value especially in predicting deliberative, intentional behavior (Armitage & Conner, 2001; Fishbein & Ajzen, 2010), more spontaneous behavior is often directed by intuitive or implicit processes. These processes reflect mental associations that are often inaccessible to conscious awareness (Gawronski & Bodenhausen, 2011; Gawronski & De Houwer, 2014), and they are typically measured indirect measures not requiring self-report (De Houwer & Moors, 2010). There are now several investigations using such indirect measures in HRI (e.g., MacDorman, Vasudevan, & Ho, 2009; Sanders, Schafer, Volante, Reardon, & Hancock, 2016; Strasser, Weiss, & Tscheligi, 2012). However, no indirect measure of general trait inferences about robots appears to exist at this time. Fortunately, the items from the RoSAS can easily be integrated into existing indirect methods to allow comparison of explicit and implicit responses and how they might predict unique aspects of behavior in HRI.

The RoSAS was initially developed and validated using images of synthetic and real robots. During the development phase, it was not used extensively to measure responses to robots with whom humans interacted, even though the RoSAS was developed for this very purpose. Fortunately, the RoSAS is now beginning to be used to measure social responses in live interaction contexts (Bonani et al., 2018; Pan et al., 2018; Sebo et al., 2018). It is encouraging that the RoSAS continues to show good to excellent reliability when adequate sample sizes are used (see Table 2.2).

It will also be valuable and necessary to integrate the RoSAS with other types of measures. The field of HRI is notably multidisciplinary, and each discipline brings its own goals, assumptions, methodologies, and techniques (Baxter, Kennedy, Senft, Lemaignan, & Belpaeme, 2016; Bethel & Murphy, 2010). There are four main methods of evaluating user experiences in HRI beyond self-assessment: behavioral observation, psychophysiological measures, interviews, and measures of task performance (Bethel & Murphy, 2010). There are two obvious benefits in collecting RoSAS judgments, along with these other measures are collected simultaneously. First, doing so will provide a better understanding of what trait inferences do and do not predict in HRI. We have shown that RoSAS judgments correlate with evaluative responses and desire for contact, but behavioral responses and psychophysiological measures ideally would also be assessed and compared with trait inferences to determine what aspects of HRI are affected by these judgments. Second, including the RoSAS in a set containing other kinds of measures would provide greater depth and complexity in accounting for responses to robots. Reviews of methods in HRI suggest the use of three or more measures to increase the reliability and accuracy of results and to enhance convergent validity (Bethel & Murphy, 2010).

It is also important to recognize that the RoSAS is a general measure of robot social perception. There are many contexts where such an instrument should be of value, but it is also important to recognize that more specific responses to robots are often of particular interest. A designer of a robot to provide elderly care might be mainly concerned with minimizing fear, discomfort, and anxiety. Or it might be desirable for a teaching robot to convey authority and intelligence. In such cases, the RoSAS could be augmented or even replaced with measures of the specific focal responses. In other words, the RoSAS was not designed or intended to replace all other measures of social responses to robots but instead was developed as a research tool for capturing broad and fundamental aspects of robot social perception.

Summary

As the frequency of contact between humans and robots increases, it will be important to measure human responses and reactions accurately. The manner in which humans perceive a robot in social terms is likely to play a critical role in determining the success or failure of interactions with that robot. The RoSAS was developed to provide a psychometrically valid instrument of general social perception that can be used in assessing responses to a wide variety of robots. Studies involved in developing the scale pointed to the importance of three fundamental aspects of robot social perception—warmth, competence, and discomfort. Evidence was provided of the reliability and validity of subscales measuring these constructs, and the RoSAS is now beginning to be used to study a broad variety of topics in HRI.

We also used RoSAS to study social psychological issues of importance in robotic design. As was recently stated, one open question in the field that requires multidisciplinary consideration pertains to "the role that robot behavior and morphology relate to one another with respect to human perceptions and reactions" (Baxter et al., 2016). We have shown in several studies that facial and body morphology do indeed affect human responses to robots, and these effects appear to be related to inferences about gender categories and anthropomorphism. As our research begins to incorporate aspects of robot behavior, we suspect that the importance of these social psychological factors will become even more readily apparent.

Acknowledgment

The author would like to thank Kerri L. Johnson and David L. Hamilton for providing helpful comments on an earlier draft of this chapter.

References

Alt, N. P., & Johnson, K. L. (2018). Categorization by sex. In T. K. Shackelford, & V. A. Weekes-Shackelford (Eds.), *Encyclopedia of evolutionary psychological science*. https://doi.org/10. 1007/978-3-319-16999-6_2428-1.

Armitage, C. J., & Conner, M. (2001). Efficacy of the theory of planned behaviour: A meta-analytic review. *British Journal of Social Psychology, 40*, 471–499.

Bartneck, C., Kulić, D., Croft, E., & Zoghbi, S. (2009). Measurement instruments for the anthropomorphism, animacy, likeability, perceived intelligence, and perceived safety of robots. *International Journal of Social Robotics, 1*, 71–81.

Basow, S. A. (1986). *Gender stereotypes: Traditions and alternatives*. Monterey, CA: Brooks/Cole.

Baxter, P., Kennedy, J., Senft, E., Lemaignan, S., & Belpaeme, T. (2016). From characterising three years of HRI to methodology and reporting recommendations. In *11th ACM/IEEE international conference on human-robot interaction, Christchurch, New Zealand* (pp. 391–398). https://doi.org/10.1109/HRI.2016.7451777.

Bem, S. L. (1974). The measurement of psychological androgyny. *Journal of Clinical and Consulting Psychology, 42*, 155–162.

Bem, S. L. (1981). Gender schema theory: A cognitive account of sex typing. *Psychological Review, 88*, 354–364.

Benitez, J., Wyman, A. B., Carpinella, C. M., & Stroessner, S. J. (2017). The authority of appearance: How robot features influence trait inferences and evaluative responses. In *26th IEEE international symposium on robot and human interactive communication (RO-MAN), Lisbon, Portugal* (pp. 397–404).

Bethel, C. L., & Murphy, R. R. (2010). Review of human studies methods in HRI and recommendations. *International Journal of Social Robotics, 2*, 347–359.

Bonani, M., Oliveira, R., Correia, F., Rodrigues, A., Guerreiro, T., & Paiva, A. (2018). What my eyes can't see, a robot can show me: Exploring the collaboration between blind people and robots. In *20th international ACM SIGACCESS conference on computers and accessibility, Galway, Ireland*.

Branscomb, L. M. (1979). The human side of the computer. In *International symposium on computer, man and society, Haifa, Israel* (pp. 1–18).

Brewer, M. B. (1988). A dual process model of impression formation. In T. K. Srull, & R. S. Wyer, Jr. (Eds.), *Advances in social cognition* (Vol. 1, pp. 1–36). Hillsdale, NJ: Erlbaum.

Caporael, L. R. (1986). Anthropomorphism and mechanomorphism: Two faces of the human machine. *Computers in Human Behavior, 2*, 215–234.

Carpinella, C. M., Wyman, A. B., Perez, M. A., & Stroessner, S. J. (2017). The robotic social attributes scale (RoSAS): Development and validation. In *Proceedings of the 2017 ACM/IEEE international conference on human-robot interaction, Vienna, Austria* (pp. 254–262).

Cogsdill, E. J., Todorov, A. T., Spelke, E. S., & Banaji, M. R. (2014). Inferring character from faces: A developmental study. *Psychological Science, 25*, 1132–1139.

Cuddy, A. J., Fiske, S. T., & Glick, P. (2008). Warmth and competence as universal dimensions of social perception: The stereotype content model and the BIAS map. *Advances in Experimental Social Psychology, 40*, 61–149.

De Houwer, J., & Moors, A. (2010). Implicit measures: Similarities and differences. In B. Gawronski, & B. K. Payne (Eds.), *Handbook of implicit social cognition: Measurement, theory, and applications* (pp. 176–193). New York: Guilford.

Devine, P. G. (1989). Stereotypes and prejudice: Their automatic and controlled components. *Journal of Personality and Social Psychology, 56*, 5–18.

Diesendruck, G., & Eldror, E. (2011). What children infer from social categories. *Cognitive Development, 26*, 118–126.

Duffy, B. R. (2003). Anthropomorphism and the social robot. *Robotics and Autonomous Systems, 42*, 177–190.

Eagly, A. H., & Mladinic, A. (1994). Are people prejudiced against women? Some answers from research on attitudes, gender stereotypes, and judgments of competence. *European Review of Social Psychology, 5*, 1–35. https://doi.org/10.1080/14792779543000002.

Eddy, T. J., Gallup, G. G., Jr., & Povinelli, D. J. (1993). Attribution of cognitive states to animals: Anthropomorphism in comparative perspective. *Journal of Social Issues, 49*, 87–101.

Epley, N., Waytz, A., & Cacioppo, J. T. (2007). On seeing human: A three-factor theory of anthropomorphism. *Psychological Review, 114*, 864–886.

Eyssel, F., & Hegel, F. (2012). (S)he's got the look: Gender-stereotyping of social robots. *Journal of Applied Social Psychology, 42*, 2213–2230. https://doi.org/10.1111/j.1559-1816.2012.00937.x.

Farkas, L. G. (1987). Age- and sex-related changes in facial proportions. In L. G. Farkas, & I. R. Munro (Eds.), *Anthropometric proportions in medicine* (pp. 29–56). Springfield, IL: Thomas.

Fink, J. (2012). Anthropomorphism and human likeness in the design of robots and human-robot interaction. In *ICSR'12 proceedings of the 4th international conference on social robotics, Chengdu, China* (pp. 199–208).

Fishbein, M., & Ajzen, I. (2010). *Predicting and changing behavior: The reasoned action approach.* New York: Taylor & Francis.

Fiske, S. T. (2018). Stereotype content: Warmth and competence endure. *Current Directions in Psychological Science, 27*, 67–73. https://doi.org/10.1177/0963721417738825.

Fiske, S. T., Cuddy, A. J. C., & Glick, P. (2007). Universal dimensions of social perception: Warmth and competence. *Trends in Cognitive Sciences, 11*, 77–83.

Fiske, S. T., Cuddy, A. J., Glick, P., & Xu, J. (2002). A model of (often mixed) stereotype content: Competence and warmth respectively follow from perceived status and competition. *Journal of Personality and Social Psychology, 82*, 878–902.

Fiske, S. T., & Neuberg, S. L. (1990). A continuum model of impression formation from category-based to individuation processes: Influences of information and motivation on attention and interpretation. In M. P. Zanna (Ed.), *Advances in experimental social psychology* (Vol. 23, pp. 1–74). New York: Academic Press.

Foster, M. E., Gaschler, A., Giuliani, M., Isard, A., Pateraki, M., & Petrick, R. P. A. (2012). Two people walk into a bar: Dynamic multi-party social interaction with a robot agent. In *Proceedings of the 14th ACM international conference on multimodal interaction (ICMI 2012), Santa Monica, CA* (pp. 3–10). https://doi.org/10.1145/2388676.2388680.

Furr, R. M. (2011). *Scale construction and psychometrics for social and personality psychology.* Los Angeles, CA: Sage.

Gawronski, B., & Bodenhausen, G. V. (2011). The associative-propositional evaluation model: Theory, evidence, and open questions. *Advances in Experimental Social Psychology, 44*, 59–127.

Gawronski, B., & De Houwer, J. (2014). Implicit measures in social and personality psychology. In H. T. Reis, & C. M. Judd (Eds.), *Handbook of research methods in social and personality psychology* (2nd ed., pp. 283−310). New York, NY: Cambridge University Press.

Glick, P., & Fiske, S. T. (1996). The ambivalent sexism inventory: Differentiating hostile and benevolent sexism. *Journal of Personality and Social Psychology, 70*(3), 491−512. https://doi. org/10.1037/0022-3514.70.3.491.

Haines, E. L., Deaux, K., & Lofaro, N. (2016). The times they are a-changing...or are they not? A comparison of gender stereotypes, 1983−2014. *Psychology of Women Quarterly, 40*, 353−363. https://doi.org/10.1177/0361684316634081.

Ham, J., Bokhorst, R., Cuijpers, R., Pol, D., & Cabibihan, J.-J. (2011). Making robots persuasive: The influence of combining persuasive strategies (gazing and gestures) by a storytelling robot on its persuasive power. In *Proceedings of the third international conference on social robotics, Amsterdam, The Netherlands* (pp. 71−73). https://doi.org/10.1007/978-3-642-25504-5_8.

Hamilton, D. L., & Trolier, T. K. (1986). Stereotypes and stereotyping: An overview of the cognitive approach. In S. L. Gaertner, & J. F. Dovidio (Eds.), *Prejudice, discrimination, and stereotyping* (pp. 127−157). New York: Academic Press.

Heerink, M., Kröse, B., Evers, V., & Wielinga, B. (2010). Assessing acceptance of assistive social agent technology by older adults: The Almere model. *International Journal of Social Robotics, 2*, 361−375. https://doi.org/10.1007/s12369-010-0068-5.

Hoffmann, L., Bock, N., & Rosenthal von der Pütten, A. (2018). The peculiarities of robot embodiment (EmCorp-Scale): Development, validation and initial test of the embodiment and corporeality of artificial agents scale. In *Proceedings of the 2018 ACM/IEEE international conference on human-robot interaction, Chicago, Illinois* (pp. 370−378).

Ho, C. C., & MacDorman, K. F. (2010). Revisiting the uncanny valley theory: Developing and validating an alternative to the Godspeed indices. *Computers in Human Behavior, 26*, 1508−1518.

Ito, T. A., & Urland, G. R. (2003). Race and gender on the brain: Electrocortical measures of attention to the race and gender of multiply categorizable individuals. *Journal of Personality and Social Psychology, 85*, 616−626. https://doi.org/10.1037/0022-3514.85.4.616.

Jian, J.-Y., Bisantz, A. M., & Drury, C. G. (2000). Foundations for an empirically determined scale of trust in automated systems. *International Journal of Cognitive Ergonomics, 4*, 53−71.

Johnson, K. L., Iida, M., & Tassinary, L. G. (2012). Person (mis)perception: Functionally biased sex categorization of bodies. *Proceedings of the Royal Society, Biological Sciences, 279*, 4982−4989. https://doi.org/10.1098/rspb.2012.2060.

Kamide, H., Mae, Y., Kawabe, K., Shigemi, S., Hirose, M., & Arai, T. (2012). New measurement of psychological safety for humanoid. In *Proceedings of the seventh annual ACM/IEEE international conference on human-robot interaction* (pp. 49−56).

Kervyn, N., Yzerbyt, V., & Judd, C. (2010). Compensation between warmth and competence: Antecedents and consequences of a negative relation between the two fundamental dimensions of social perception. *European Review of Social Psychology, 21*, 155−187.

Lee, S., Lau, I. Y., Kiesler, S., & Chiu, C.-Y. (2005). Human mental models of humanoid robots. In *Proceedings of the 2005 IEEE international conference on robotics and automation* (pp. 2767−2772).

Little, A. C., Jones, B. C., & DeBruine, L. M. (2011). Facial attractiveness: Evolutionary based research. *Philosophical Transactions of the Royal Society B: Biological Sciences, 366*, 1638−1659. https://doi.org/10.1098/rstb.2010.0404.

MacDorman, K. F., Vasudevan, S. K., & Ho, C. C. (2009). Does Japan really have robot mania? Comparing attitudes by implicit and explicit measures. *AI & Society, 23*, 485. https://doi.org/10.1007/s00146-008-0181-2.

Mori, M. (1970/translated in 2012). The uncanny valley. *Energy, 7*, 33—35.

Nomura, T., Kanda, T., Suzuki, T., & Kato, K. (2004). Psychology in human-robot communication: An attempt through investigation of negative attitudes and anxiety toward robots. In *Proceedings of the 2004 IEEE international workshop on robot and human interactive communication, Kurashiki, Okayama Japan*.

Nomura, T., Suzuki, T., Kanda, T., & Kato, K. (2006). Measurement of negative attitudes toward robots. *Interaction Studies, 7*, 437—454.

Nunnally, J. C. (1978). *Psychometric theory* (2nd ed.). New York: McGraw-Hill.

Pan, M. K. X. J., Croft, E. A., & Niemeyer, G. (2018). Evaluating social perception of human-to-robot handovers using the robot social attributes scale (RoSAS). In *Proceedings of the 2018 ACM/IEEE international conference on human-robot interaction, Chicago, Illinois* (pp. 443—451).

Prentice, D. A., & Carranza, E. (2002). What women and men should be, shouldn't be, are allowed to be, and don't have to be: The contents of prescriptive gender stereotypes. *Psychology of Women Quarterly, 26*, 269—281. https://doi.org/10.1111/1471-6402.t01-1-00066.

Quinn, P. C., Yahr, J., Kuhn, A., Slater, A. M., & Pascalis, O. (2002). Representation of the gender of human faces by infants: A preference for female. *Perception, 31*, 1109—1121.

Ramsey, J. L., Langlois, J. H., & Marti, N. C. (2005). Infant categorization of faces: Ladies first. *Developmental Review, 25*, 212—246. https://doi.org/10.1016/j.dr.2005.01.001.

Rosenberg, S., Nelson, C., & Vivekananthan, P. (1968). A multidimensional approach to the structure of personality impressions. *Journal of Personality and Social Psychology, 9*, 283—294.

Rudman, L. A., & Glick, P. (2008). *The social psychology of gender: How power and intimacy shape gender relations*. New York, NY: Guilford Press.

Sanders, T. L., Schafer, K. E., Volante, W., Reardon, A., & Hancock, P. A. (2016). Implicit attitudes toward robots. *Proceedings of the Human Factors and Ergonomics Society - Annual Meeting, 60*, 1746—1749. https://doi.org/10.1177/1541931213601400.

Schillaci, G., Bodiroza, S., & Hafner, V. V. (2013). Evaluating the effect of saliency detection and attention manipulation in human-robot interaction. *International Journal of Social Robotics, 5*, 139—152.

Schmitz, M. (2011). Concepts for life-like interactive objects. In *Proceedings of the fifth international conference on tangible, embedded, and embodied interaction, New York, NY* (pp. 157—164).

Schneid, E. D., Crawford, M. T., Skowronski, J. J., Irwin, L. M., & Carlston, D. E. (2015). Thinking about other people: Spontaneous trait inferences and spontaneous evaluations. *Social Psychology, 46*, 24—35.

Sebo, S. S., Traeger, M., Jung, M., & Scassellati, B. (2018). The ripple effects of vulnerability: The effects of a robot's vulnerable behavior on trust in human-robot teams. In *Proceedings of the 2018 ACM/IEEE international conference on human-robot interaction, Chicago, Illinois* (pp. 178—186).

Simon, M. (May 17, 2018). *The Wired guide to robots: Everything you wanted to know about soft, hard, and nonmurderous automatons*. Retrieved from https://www.wired.com/story/wired-guide-to-robots/.

Snyder, M., Tanke, E. D., & Berscheid, E. (1977). Social perception and interpersonal behavior: On the self-fulfilling nature of social stereotypes. *Journal of Personality and Social Psychology, 35*, 656−666. https://doi.org/10.1037/0022-3514.35.9.656.

Strasser, E., Weiss, A., & Tscheligi, M. (2012). Affect Misattribution Procedure: An implicit technique to measure user experience in HRI. In *2012 7ᵗʰ ACM/IEEE international conference on human-robot interaction (HRI), Boston, MA* (pp. 243−244). https://doi.org/10.1145/2157689.2157776.

Stroessner, S. J., & Benitez, J. (2019). The social perception of humanoid and non-humanoid robots: Effects of gendered and machinelike features. *International Journal of Social Robotics, 11*, 305−315.

Torta, E., van Heumen, J., Cuijpers, R. H., & Juola, J. F. (2012). How can a robot attract the attention of its human partner?: A comparative study over different modalities for attracting attention. In *4th international conference on social robotics (ICSR 2012), Chengdu, China* (pp. 288−297).

Waytz, A., Epley, N., & Cacioppo, J. T. (2010). Social cognition unbound: Insights into anthropomorphism and dehumanization. *Current Directions in Psychological Science, 19*, 58−62.

Weiss, A., & Bartneck, C. (2015). Meta analysis of the usage of the godspeed questionnaire series. In *Proceedings of the IEEE international symposium on robot and human interactive communication (RO-MAN2015), Kobe, Japan* (pp. 381−388).

Willis, J., & Todorov, A. (2006). First impressions making up your mind after a 100-ms exposure to a face. *Psychological Science, 17*, 592−598.

Yagoda, R. E., & Gillan, D. J. (2012). You want me to trust a ROBOT? The development of a human−robot interaction trust scale. *International Journal of Social Robotics, 4*, 235−248.

Złotowski, J. A., Sumioka, H., Nishio, S., Glas, D. F., Bartneck, C., & Ishiguro, H. (2015). Persistence of the uncanny valley: The influence of repeated interactions and a robot's attitude on its perception. *Frontiers in Psychology, 6*, 883. https://doi.org/10.3389/fpsyg.2015.00883.

Chapter 3

Robotics to support aging in place

George Mois[1], Jenay M. Beer[2]
[1]*School of Social Work, University of Georgia, Athens, GA, United States;* [2]*Institute of Gerontology, University of Georgia, Athens, GA, United States*

Chapter outline

Introduction

Robots are increasingly becoming a part of our everyday lives—from the Roomba vacuum cleaner robot to manufacturing robots to cars that are increasingly automated. One exciting application of robotics is in health care and the home. This application is of increasing importance, as the proportion of older adults in our population increases. There are many older adults in need of help with daily tasks than human caregivers to provide such assistance. Robotics can fill this health-care gap and help older adults to age in place by increasing wellness, providing rehabilitation, and assisting with activities of daily life by compensating for functional age-related declines. There are many tasks that robots could be developed to assist older adults with. Today, there are three main categories of robots that can assist older adults to age in place. There are social companion robots, such as Paro, and tele-operated robots, such as telepresence. Finally, there are (semi-) autonomous assistive robots, such as the Roomba. These robots can assist older adults with a range of daily activities, such as fetching items, helping around the house, providing support in disease management, and facilitating social connectivity. However, for robots to be truly effective in helping older adults age in place, it is important to consider how these machines will fit into older adults' daily lives. To this end, the purpose of this chapter is to (1) provide an overview of the role robotics may play in aging in place; (2) categorize the types of robots that can support aging in place; (3) identify ways in which robots could assist with activities of daily living (ADLs), instrumental activities of daily living (IADLs), and enhanced activities of daily living (EADLs); and finally (4) discuss adoption and ethical considerations in applying robots to support aging in place.

Who are older adults?

Aging is a normal part of life and everyone begins aging from the moment they enter the world at birth. The most common way to describe aging is chronological age, or someone's legal age. An adult is typically defined as an older adult when they have reached the chronological age of 65 years (Czaja & Lee, 2007; Erber, 2005). Chronological age alone does not determine how an individual feels or how they can function. Functional age is an alternative way to describe the aging process (McFarland, 1997, p. 186), measured by older adults' ability to perform their roles in their daily life (Rogers, 2015). For example, an older adult aged 70 years, who has difficulty walking, has dementia, and lives in a nursing home, will have a different functional age compared to an older adult aged 80 years who exercises daily and lives independently. Recognizing these distinctions is helpful in the development of services and technology to help promote healthy aging. Functional age can provide a more accurate account of the abilities and needs of an older adult; however, chronological age remains a marker that guides service provision (North & Fiske, 2012; Rogers, 2015).

Understanding the aging process, from both chronological and functional perspective, is essential as more adults are entering older age at a faster pace than ever before in history. In the United States, the population of older adults is estimated to grow to 83.7 million by 2050 (Bardic, 2015). Moreover, older adults aged 85+, also known as the oldest old, are becoming the fastest growing segment of the population (Meyer, 2012). Contributing factors to this accelerated growth are advances in medicine and the birth influx between 1946 and 1964, which gave rise to the baby boomer generation (Kleyman, 2017; Mellor, Mellor, & Rehr, 2005). As the number of older adults continues to grow, it is vital to address the biological, psychological, and social age-related changes and challenges that may hinder some older adults' ability to age in place (Black, Dobbs, & Young, 2015; see Table 3.1). Assistive technology, such as robotics, has potential to provide many older adults the functional support they need to age in place.

TABLE 3.1 Dimensions of functional aging.

Dimension	Description	Changes and characteristics	Citation
Biological aging	Age-related changes in physiological functions over time.	*Changes:* Circulatory system, digestive system, musculoskeletal system, respiratory system, urogenital system, nervous system, and sense organs. *Characteristics:* These changes occur involuntarily.	Gilbert (2017), Goncalves Damascena et al. (2017), Mellor et al. (2005), Saxon, Perkins, and Etten (2015)
Psychological aging	Age-related changes in cognitive functioning over time.	*Changes:* Memory, perception, reasoning, and understanding. *Characteristics:* Changes occur involuntarily and may be episodic in nature.	Goncalves Damascena et al. (2017), Małgorzata and Rafał (2014), Mellor et al. (2005), Rogers (2015), Timiras (2003), Trafialek (1997), Victor (2005)
Social aging	Views of both individuals and society about the aging process; this dimension is socially constructed and conditioned, based on societal and familiar customs	*Changes:* Family role, social interaction, social involvement, social settings, and work role. *Characteristics:* Changes can be influenced by both biological and psychological dimensions of aging.	Black et al. (2015), Heaven et al. (2013), Małgorzata and Rafał (2014), Pinto and Neri (2017)

Aging in place

Before further discussing robotic supports to assist older adult with daily activities, first it is important to understand the benefits of aging in place (Table 3.2). The preferred living arrangement for most older adults is aging in place (Markides & Gerst-Emerson, 2014). Aging in place is defined as the "ability to live in one's home and community safely, independently, and comfortably, regardless of age, income, or ability level" (Kim, Gollamudi, & Steinhubl, 2017). In fact, 92% of older adults aged 65—74 years and 95% of those aged 75+ state that they would want to remain in their own home (Dye,

TABLE 3.2 Overview of the benefits of aging in place.

	Benefit	Citation
Individual	*Promotes*: Mental health and personal safety; physical health well-being; stability	Andrews and Phillips (2005), Black (2008), Courtin, Dowd, and Avendano (2018), Fernández-Mayoralas et al. (2015), Marek, Stetzer, Adams, Popejoy, and Rantz (2012), Walker and Paliadelis (2016), Ávila-Funes et al. (2009)
Environmental	*Promotes*: Comfort; dignity; familiar environment; safety; social capital *Reduces*: Abuse; maltreatment	Castle (2012), Compton, Flanigan, and Gregg (1997, p. 632), Swagerty, Takahashi, and Evans (1999, p. 2804), Takayuki and Hiroshi (2012)
Community	*Promotes*: Connectedness; control; decision-making; dignity; independence; relationships	Blanchard (2013), Mahmood, Yamamoto, Lee, and Steggell (2008), Mowry, Pimentel, Sparks, and Hanlon (2013)
Cultural	*Promotes*: Cultural familiarity; cultural tradition; health; interactions *Reduces*: Depression; language isolation; risk of health conditions	Bacsu et al. (2014), Espino, Wood, Finely, Ye, and Angel (2013), Markides and Gerst-Emerson (2014), McFarland (1997, p. 186)
Socioeconomic	*Promotes*: Economic viability for older adults and family *Reduces*: Strain on Medicare/Medicaid	Colombo, Llena-Nozal, Mercier, and Tjadens (2011), Eftring and Frennert (2016), Kaye, Harrington, and LaPlante (2010, p. 11), Marek et al. (2012), Wick (2017)

Willoughby, & Battisto, 2011). This inclination extends to younger baby boomers aged 50 plus who report having no intentions of altering their current living environment (Blanchard, 2013). Among the challenges faced by older adults, the availability of housing, health-care resources, and social supports to enable independence are perhaps the most pressing. Maintaining independence is an important factor in healthy aging. Healthy aging is defined as "the development and maintenance of optimal physical, mental, and social well-being and function in older adults. This will most likely be achieved when communities are safe, promote health and well-being, and use health services and community programs to prevent or minimize disease" (Wangerin et al., 2006). Providing older adults with the ability to choose their preferred living arrangement promotes independence and dignity. The benefits associated with aging in place span across individual, environmental, community, cultural, and socioeconomic factors (Black, 2008; Cutchin, 2003).

Aging in place can positively impact an individual's biological, psychological, and social dimensions of functional aging (Black et al., 2015). Older adults aging in place report higher levels of life satisfaction when compared to those living in institutionalized care (Andrews & Phillips, 2005; Marek et al., 2012). Older adults living in institutionalized care, such as assisted living or nursing homes, are more likely to experience anxiety disorders, loss of dignity, inability to forge meaningful relationships, and loss of autonomy (Creighton, Davison, & Kissane, 2016; Moore, 2005; Walker & Paliadelis, 2016). Moreover, weakening family and social ties are linked to a decrease in the quality of life of older adults (Fernández-Mayoralas et al., 2015). Lower social engagement and isolation among older adults in institutionalized care also show increased cognitive and functional decline (Fernández-Mayoralas et al., 2015). Older adults aging in place show lower rates of depression and decreased activity in daily living assistance (Courtin et al., 2018).

Looking beyond individual benefits, aging in one's own home provides older adults with the safety of a comfortable and familiar environment. Although institutional facilities may seem like ideal living spaces, with facilities designed specifically with the older adult in mind, reports of maltreatment and abuse raise concerns. The World Health Organization reports that mistreatment has been identified in every country where older adult institutional facilities exist (Krug, Dahlberg, Mercy, Zwi, & Lozano, 2002). Forms of maltreatment and abuse observed in institutionalized care include physical, psychological, medication, and material exploitation (Castle, 2012). A large number of abuse and maltreatment in institutionalized care often goes unreported due to fear, lack of awareness about what abuse is, and insufficient procedures to aid with the reporting process (Compton et al., 1997, p. 632; Swagerty et al., 1999, p. 2804).

Aging in place gives older adults a sense of security as they are able to live in a safe and familiar environment; all while enabling them to conserve their social capital and community relationships developed over the span of a lifetime. Specifically, aging in place enables older adults to remain within their community, which they are acquainted with, throughout the aging process. Aging in place promotes social capital, a sense of connectedness and interdependence, which enhances over time, promoting interaction and collaboration (Blanchard, 2013). Furthermore, older adults aging in place are able to maintain relationships with family, friends, and community, which have been built over long periods of time (Mahmood et al., 2008). These relationships for many older adults give meaning and support a higher quality of life (Mowry et al., 2013).

Additionally, aging in place allows older adults to remain in an environment which enables the maintenance of cultural traditions, provides cultural familiarity, and promotes healthy aging. Culture surrounds all groups of people and shapes the aging process as it influences older adults' experiences, expectations, and concerns (Bacsu et al., 2014). The inability to age in place requires older adults to readjust to a new care facility and also its culture (McFarland, 1997, p. 186). Furthermore, the culture within institutional facilities often mimics the culture of the majority population rather than that of residents from minority groups (McFarland, 1997, p. 186). There is a gap in the availability of quality and culturally appropriate nursing homes (Markides & Gerst-Emerson, 2014). Minority older adults, residing in institutionalized care, report higher rates of depression and cognitive impairment and are more likely to have diabetes and stroke, than their white counterparts (Espino et al., 2013, p. 840). Furthermore, they face challenges maintaining cultural values due to the pressure of having to readjust to outside cultures. However, minority older adults aging in place are able to maintain their cultural social roles and not have to experience language isolation, enabling the older adult to continue using their native language and limit cultural disintegration (Markides & Gerst-Emerson, 2014).

Lastly, aging in place can reduce the financial strain, as it remains the most economical option for older adults, positively influencing the psychological and social dimension of aging. Cost of noninstitutionalized long-term care is on average $928 versus $5,243 per month for institutionalized care (Kaye et al., 2010, p. 11). Cost for assistance with activities of daily living, such as bathing, toileting, transferring, and feeding, is much higher for older adults living in institutionalized care, thus creating financial challenges for older adults, their families, and the health system. Out-of-pocket cost for care in a nursing home per person per year can rise upwards of $47,000, and $82,000 for specialized long-term care (Hurd, Michaud, & Rohwedder, 2017; Wick, 2017). According to the "Older Americans: Key Indicators of Well-Being (2012)," approximately one-fifth of all nursing home bills are paid either primarily or entirely out of pocket. Although there may be more cost-effective facilities, a decline in nursing home costs often result in a decline in quality of care (Marek et al., 2012). These costs also place a strain on programs like Medicare and Medicaid, as expenses can spike up to $19,000 a year (Marek et al., 2012). Medicaid and Medicare expenses were $1591.61 lower per month for those aging in place (Marek et al., 2012). Therefore, it is important to note that the financial strain of institutionalized care can create tremendous challenges for older adults, their family, and the public assistance system.

Emergence of robotic technology to support aging in place

The benefits of aging in place are clear. However, aging in place can sometimes pose a challenge for some older adults. Challenges that can accompany longevity may include declining functional abilities, cognitive decline, and perceptual capabilities, which may result in difficulty maintaining independence and allow aging in place. Concerns that emerge for older adults aging in place are emotional and physical isolation; physical dangers due to home design; lack of transportation; and difficulty noticing changes in nutrition, health, and hygiene (Phillips, 2018).

Over the past several decades, these challenges have fueled the advancement of home-based assistive technology specifically designed to aid in aging in place (Beer, Mitzner, Stuck, & Rogers, 2015; Kwon, 2017). Assistive technology is defined as "any item, piece of equipment, product system, or service whether acquired commercially or off the shelf, modified, or customized, including any tool or services that may help, to perform, or better fictional capabilities of individuals" (Piau, Campo, Rumeau, Vellas, & Nourhashemi, 2014, p. 102). One of the significant areas of assistive technologies, that hold the potential to support aging in place, is robotics. Robots are defined as "an autonomous system which exists in the physical world, can sense its environment, and can act on it to achieve some goals" (Matarić, 2007).

Robots are still in the early stages of commercial development. However, with computational and mechanical advancements, robots will continue to evolve (Matarić, 2007). With these advancements, robots will begin to be adopted in the homes of older adults to assist with activities of daily living and instrumental activities of daily living (Beer et al., 2015; Smarr et al., 2012). There is a growing trend in robotic systems being developed with the older adult in mind, specifically for the purpose of helping maintain independence (Forlizzi, DiSalvo, & Gemperle, 2004; Pedersen, Reid, & Aspevig, 2018). Such robots hold the potential to aid older adults' age in place, reduce healthcare needs, provide everyday assistance, and promote social interaction (Beer et al., 2012). They can provide support for care at home and in the community, while being cost-effective (Katz, 2015). There are a number of different terms and classifications used to describe robots that are potentially beneficial for older adults. To provide consistency between terms for this chapter, we categorize robot types as the following: social companion robots, assistive robots, telerobots, telepresence robots, and socially assistive robots (SARs). These types of robots serve both independent and shared functions. In Fig. 3.1, we depict the relationship between robot types. For details regarding definitions and functions of these categories of robots, refer Table 3.3.

The role of robots within the context of aging is to help alleviate the challenges encountered by older adults due to diminishing physical and psychological health (Tiberio, Cesta, Cortellessa, Padua, & Pellegrino, 2012, p. 833). To live independently, people must be able to successfully perform a wide range of tasks related to maintaining daily functions. These activities can be described in three broad classes: (1) ADL (Lawton, 1990; Lawton, Brody, Plys, & Kluge, 2016), (2) IADL (Lawton et al., 2016), and (3) EADL (Rogers, Meyer, Walker, & Fisk, 1998, p. 111). ADLs are the activities an individual does everyday without the need of assistance, such activities include bathing, brushing teeth, and rising from bed (Webb, Titus, Nadorff, Cui, & Fiske, 2018). IADLs are normal, daily tasks, which include meal preparation, banking, housekeeping, laundry, financial transactions, and shopping (Lawton

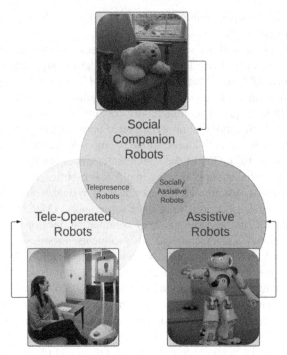

FIGURE 3.1 Shared and independent functions of robot types.

et al., 2016; Tomioka, Kurumatani, & Hosoi, 2017). EADLs include participation in social and enriching activities, such as learning new skills and
engaging in hobbies (Smarr et al., 2014).

As discussed previously, age-related declines in physical, perceptual, and
psychological abilities can make the execution of these tasks difficult for some
older adults. Physical limitations such as motor impairment and difficulty
balancing were identified as the cause of nearly 40% of the challenges faced
by community-dwelling older adults in carrying out everyday tasks (Rogers
et al., 1998, p. 111; Smarr et al., 2014). These limitations can present in each
across ADL, IADL, and EADL (Fausset, Kelly, Rogers, & Fisk, 2011; Seidel
et al., 2009). Perceptual declines in vision and hearing are common among
older adults and continue to diminish with age (Heine & Browning, 2015;
Nirmalasari et al., 2017). Older adults experiencing dual sensory loss, which is
the loss of both vision and hearing, can experience greater difficulty in performing ADL, IADL, and EADL (Davila et al., 2009).

Furthermore, cognitive declines among older adults aging in place can
have a negative impact on their ability to perform ADL, IADL, and EADL
(Rogers et al., 1998, p. 111; Seidel et al., 2009). This effect is also reciprocal,
older adults who experience a decline in ADL, IADL, and EADL functioning

TABLE 3.3 Definitions and functions of robots for aging in place.

Type of robot	Definition (s)	Functions	Citations
Social/companion robots	A social robot is an autonomous machine that engages in social interactions with humans and/or other social agents using a set of social behaviors and rules that have been assigned, learned, or being learned through their own experiences.	• Change behaviors • Combine social and technical features simultaneously • Communicate verbally • Engage • Exchange emotions • Relate to humans • Serve as partners or assistant • Therapeutic aids	Breazeal (2002), Campa (2016), Dautenhahn (1997, p. 417), De Carolis and Cozzolongo (2007, p. 805), Eftring and Frennert (2016), Fong, Nourbakhsh, and Dautenhahn (2003, p.143), Kidd, Taggart, and Turkle (2006, p. 3972), Shishehgar, Kerr, and Blake (2018)
Assistive robots	An assistive robot is a type of robot that has the capability to assist a human with general or specific needs such as recovery, learning, training, rehabilitation, or daily tasks in both home and care facilities.	• Assist human user • Assist with home tasks: getting out of bed, brushing teeth, eating, bathing, dressing, toileting, and rehabilitation • Support mobility and provide maintenance	Beer et al. (2012, 2017), Bemelmans, Gelderblom, Jonker, and de Witte (2011), Evaluating older adults' interaction with a mobile assistive robot (2017, p. 840), Feil-Seifer and Matarić (2011), Feil-seifer, Skinner, and Matarić (2007), Huschilt and Clune (2012),

Continued

TABLE 3.3 Definitions and functions of robots for aging in place.—cont'd

Type of robot	Definition (s)	Functions	Citations
Socially assistive robots	A socially assistive robot combines assistive function along with social interaction. They are autonomous, mobile, interactive machines specifically designed to help human beings with intellectual, social, and emotional care.	• Assist with intellectual, social, and emotional care • Automate physical tasks • Companion: improve the psychological status and overall well-being of the user • Rehabilitation • Service: aid with activities of daily living • Tool for diagnosis	Mohammed, Moreno, Kong, and Amirat (2015, p. 2015), Piau et al. (2014), Wu et al. (2014) Abdi, Al-Hindawi, Ng, and Vizcaychipi (2018), Bemelmans et al. (2011), Beuscher et al. (2017), Broekens, Heerink, and Rosendal (2009), Feil-Seifer and Matarić (2011), Eftring and Frennert (2016), Feil-Seifer and Mataric (2005, p. 465), Feil-Seifer, Skinner, and Matarić (2007), Forlizzi et al. (2004), García-Soler et al. (2018), Huschilt and Clune (2012), Pedersen et al. (2018), Pineau, Montemerlo, Pollack, Roy, and Thrun (2003, p. 271), Pino, Boulay,

| Telerobots (Telepresence) | A telerobot is remotely operated by a user who is not colocated with the robot. A telepresence robot provides two-way communication between two users, one of whom may be an older adult. | • Alleviate social isolation
• Connectedness: family, friends, and health providers
• Improve actual and perceived safety | Rigaud, and Jouen (2015), Smarr et al. (2014), Sparrow and Sparrow (2006), Tapus, Maja, and Scassellatti (2007), Chen, Hsu, and Lu (2013), Kristoffersson, Coradeschi, and Loutfi (2013), Pino et al. (2015), Shishehgar et al. (2018) |

are more likely to experience accelerated cognitive decline. According to a longitudinal study conducted by Rajan, Hebert, Scherr, Mendes de Leon, and Evans (2013), community-dwelling older adults experiencing difficulties with tasks related to ADL and IADL had higher rates of declining cognitive functioning (Rajan et al., 2013).

Robots hold the potential to address a wide array of these challenges and help enable older adults to age in place successfully. These challenges can be aided by robots assisting older adults with their daily tasks. Robots used by older adults can range in functionality depending on the needs of older adults. This is important because older adults aging in place often have little to no support with activities of daily living (Eftring & Frennert, 2016). Robots present an opportunity to introduce a form of support for a wide variety of ADL, IADL, and EADL which can help address concern and difficulties related to aging in place.

Robots and ADLs

The use of robots within the context of aging in place can provide assistance with a wide spectrum of ADL. Assistive robots could support older adults aging in place with a variety of ADL-related home care tasks—such as getting out of bed, brushing teeth, locomotion, and rehabilitation (Feil-Seifer et al., 2007). Majority of ADL robots are designed to provide assistance with ambulation. The primary roles of these robots are to reduce the need to move and provide support with physical movement. These types of robots include mobility devices in the form of robotic wheelchairs or walkers that can support older adults with physical movement, help older adults in avoiding obstacles, and aid with navigation (Smarr, Fausset, & Rogers, 2010). Current commercially available robots provide less support with activities such as feeding, grooming, bathing, toileting, and dressing. However, the development of robots to address these activities could be beneficial for a large number of older adults (Mitzner, Chen, Kemp, & Rogers, 2014).

Furthermore, robots can help with ADL tasks which involve reaching, fetching, and carrying objects that are heavy or out of reach. However, design functions of robots vary based on the tasks assigned to them, which can be limited depending on the size, shape, or weight, of the person or object that may be required to manipulate. Robots assisting with ADL will also need to be able to move lightweight object closer to a persons body (Mitzner et al., 2014). For example, a robot able to manipulate the weight of a person may not have the design features to allow it to pick up a toothbrush, and vice versa. Furthermore, robots need to take into account not only the individual but also their home environment. For example, a robot needs to be able to overcome navigation challenges such as narrow hallways, uneven floors, stairs, and clutter (Mitzner et al., 2014). It is important to note that the need for assistance with ADLs has been found most common among older adults residing in more advanced skilled nursing, or may require a higher level of care. Requirements to assist with these tasks tend to be more involved and require robots to carry out a multitude of complex functions. For example, dressing may require a robot to support the weight of human body, move a piece of clothing, and use sensors to provide instructions. Moreover, tasks such as grooming, bathing, and toileting can require even more advanced functions (Mitzner et al., 2014). Robots ability to address ADLs outside of ambulation requires advanced design features, thus furthering this research is crucial in assisting older adults aging in place.

The experience of older adults through the aging process can vary; therefore needs and level of accommodation to age in place differ. Assistive robots need to have the ability to adapt to the needs of the user and take into account user preference (Canal, Guillem, Torras, & Carme, 2017). With the consent of older adults, robots can help monitor, provide reminders, and aid with ADL, helping those aging in place feel safer (Pollack, 2005, p. 9), reducing undesired moves from one's own home into institutionalized care (García-Soler et al., 2018). Additionally, it is important to note that the development of robot design to aid older adults can furthermore have a tremendous impact on the well-being of their caregivers. Caregivers report that on average they provide assistance with at least three ADLs. Improving on the design of robots can help reduce caregiver burden. On average, 35% of disabled older adults receive a form of formal caregiver assistance. Moreover, approximately 50% of older adults who require assistance with more than three ADLs rely on some type of assistance from a formal caregiver (Mitzner et al., 2014).

Robots and IADLs

Some of the most challenging IADL for older adults, due to physical limitations, are housekeeping, meal preparation, transportation, and shopping. Robots addressing these needs can greatly benefit older adults wanting to age in place. Older adults residing in a private home sometimes require assistance to complete an IADL, which is often fulfilled with the help of an informal caregiver (Mitzner et al., 2014). According to a study conducted by Hopp (1999), caregivers reported that the most common IADLs they provided assistance with were running errands, transportation, housework, making phone calls, preparing meals, and assisting with medication. The use of a robot can help relieve some of the responsibilities placed on caregiver, which could help alleviate caregiver burden. Furthermore, older adults have expressed the most interest in robots which could potentially perform IADLs for them (Beer et al., 2017; Smarr et al., 2014). Robot assistance with IADLs can be organized into two categories: multipurpose or specialized robots (Smarr et al., 2010).

Multipurpose robots are developed to perform a multitude of tasks, which may include fetching and delivering items, searching for information online, preparing a meal, and providing various reminders. Moreover, these robots may assist with medication management, food preparation, shopping, monitoring user's health, and promoting healthy aging (Wangerin et al., 2006). Robots, such as Nursebot, can help provide auto reminders for older adults about events and schedules and indoor navigational support through the use of intelligent mobility platform (Matthews, 2002). These are multipurpose complex robots, which currently are not commercially readably available. However, the assistance potential of multipurpose robots can positively impact older adults' ability to age in place and promote healthy aging.

The other category of IADL robots, specialized or single-task robots, can provide assistance with only a single IADL. The Roomba, to date, is perhaps the most popular specialized IADL robot assistant that is commercially available (Roomba, 2018). This robot assists with vacuuming, using sensors and artificial intelligence to learn an environment. Assistance with home cleaning tasks, such as vacuuming, can remove the burden of having to carry out tasks that can be physically demanding. Roomba, and other robots like it, can help older adults maintain their home and age in place successfully. Developing such devices, which may one day be adopted universally have potential in alleviating the challenges older adults face in the process of aging in place. However, developing devices that are universally adopted remains a challenge in the field of robotics, thus an important area of exploration.

Robots and EADLs

Robots hold the ability to help older adults aging in place with aspects of EADLs such as hobbies, social communication, and acquisition of new skills. Service-type robots hold social functions along with that of ADLs support. The social functions enable interaction between older adult and robot. Social robots can operate as partners, peers, or assistants, meaning that they are able to exhibit flexibility and adaptability to allow social interaction with a wide range of humans (Fong et al., 2003, p. 143). EADL robots can help older adults aging in place, remain engaged, and assist with social interaction (Huschilt & Clune, 2012; Pineau et al., 2003, p. 271). Companion-type robots were designed to help improve the psychological status and overall well-being of the user (Reiser, Jacobs, Arbeiter, Parlitz, & Dautenhahn, 2013, p. 97). Furthermore, companion robots like Paro help reduce stress and encourage socialization, contributing to older adults' quality of life by supporting aging in place (Kidd et al., 2006, p. 3972; Lane et al., 2016; McGlynn, Kemple, Mitzner, King, & Rogers, 2017; Mitzner et al., 2014; Wada, Shibata, Musha, & Kimura, 2008). Along with these benefits, older adults using companion robots report decreased loneliness and engagement on emotional level (Robinson, Broadbent, & MacDonald, 2016).

Moreover, telepresence robots help promote social interaction and independent living. They enable older adults remain connected to their family, friends, health providers, and a widening array of other resources (Kristoffersson et al., 2013). Using robots to engage in enriching activities can help improve mood, decrease loneliness, alleviate stress, and increase social ties (Beer & Takayama, 2011). The presence of a robot within the context of a home can help enable older adults aging in place to remain engaged in hobbies and other activates they have engaged in throughout their life, thus promoting healthy aging.

Older adults acceptance and adoption of robots to support aging in place

Although advances in technology development and capability will lead to a market of robots to assist with ADL, IADL, and EADL tasks, a critical question remains: *Will older adults want to adopt this technology?* Our research has largely supported the fact that older adults will, in fact, hold positive attitudes toward robots into their home if the benefit of using the robot is clear (e.g., Beer et al., 2017; Smarr et al., 2014). However, robot adoption is more complicated than simply putting these robots on the market. There is a progression of technology acceptance, where a user will make adoption decisions in a series of steps, based on the theory of reasoned action by Fishbein and Ajzen (1975). Technology acceptance first begins with an attitude. For example, an older user may recognize that a home robot seems like a good idea. Next, the older adult may develop intention. In other words, they may determine that they wish to buy a home robot. Finally, this then leads to behavioral integration, and the older adult will purchase the robot and use it on a daily basis.

Using this progression model as a basis, one of the most prominent models of technology adoption is the technology acceptance model (TAM) (Davis, 1989). Research on TAM has identified two primary constructs that predict technology acceptance: perceived usefulness and perceived ease of use. Perceived usefulness is defined as the extent to which a technology is expected to improve a potential user's performance (Davis, 1989). In the case of robots for aging in place, an older adult may ask how the robot will improve his/her daily health. Perceived ease of use is defined as the amount of effort required to effectively use a technology (Davis, 1989). Does the older adult or caregiver believe that the robot will be easy to interact with? Or, does the older adult believe that the robot will be easy to learn how to use?

Both perceived usefulness and perceived ease of use have been found to be predictive of older adults' intention to use robots in the home (Ezer, Fisk, & Rogers, 2009). In fact, our own investigation of attitudinal and intentional acceptance of SARs for older adults (Beer et al., 2012, 2017, p. 335; Smarr et al., 2014) found that older adults, overall, were open to robot assistance. Older users indicated a preference toward accepting robot assistance with IADL tasks (e.g., taking their medication, reminders), more so compared to ADL (e.g., helping them to go to the toilet) and EADL tasks (e.g., companionship) (Smarr et al., 2014). In a follow-up study, we found that exposure to the robot matters. Older users' acceptance of a robot significantly increased after interaction (Beer et al., 2017). In other words, after seeing the robot in person, older adults' positive perceptions about the robot's usefulness and ease of use significantly increased. Furthermore, participants expressed interest in the robot assisting with reminders, such as taking medication (Prakash & Rogers, 2013), being reminded of appointments, and assisting with home maintenance (Beer et al., 2017).

However, application of technology acceptance theory on the adoption of robots has not been widely applied. Therefore, it is an open question regarding to what extent diffusion of innovation and TAM can explain the acceptance of telepresence robots by older adults. There are a number of considerations and challenges when applying TAM to aging in place robotics. First, most TAM research studies have primarily investigated technology adoption within the context of workplace applications (Davis, 1989; Goodhue & Thompson, 1995; Venkatesh & Bala, 2008; Venkatesh, Morris, Davis, & Davis, 2003). Robots to aid in aging in place, however, will be adopted and integrated into the home environment, becoming a part of an older adult's care plan, as well as integrating into daily functions over potentially a long-time period. While much of the research discussed in this section has focused on attitudes and intention to adopt robots, to date, few studies have investigated long-term adoption of at-home robots. Furthermore, concepts such as perceived ease of use and perceived usefulness of a robot have often been shown to be predictive of acceptance, but not diagnostic. That is, few studies have investigated *why* older users would perceive a particular robot as easy to use or useful. Lastly, the role of "costs" such as privacy or ethical concerns is not well understood in relation to technology acceptance. Thus, although it has been established that older adults hold positive attitudes toward robots to support aging in place, much research is still needed to better understand specific contexts of use and the factors that drive actual long-term adoption.

Ethical considerations for robots to assist with aging in place

As robots are increasingly applied to home settings, ethical reflection is essential (Bedaf, Gelderblom, & De Witte, 2015; Vandemeulebroucke, Gastmans, & de Casterle, 2018). Introduction of robots within the context of aging in place should be driven by the benefits they provide in assisting older adults, and no other motives (Sharkey & Sharkey, 2012). The introduction of robots with the aim to reduce the need for public and professional health-care support can have an ill effect on older adults' dignity and autonomy (Sharkey & Sharkey, 2012; Sparrow & Sparrow, 2006). The design process should incorporate the voice of older adults to assure their needs always remain the priority. Older adults should fully understand the functions of the robots they are using, including their physical capability, privacy and safety features, and social characteristics (Feil-Seifer et al., 2007; Ienca, Jotterand, VicA, & Elger,

2016; Kortner, 2016; Sorell & Draper, 2014). With the continued development of robot artificial intelligence, sensors for monitoring, and social capability, ethical considerations are becoming increasingly complex.

One area of ethical concern surrounds maintaining older adults' privacy, particularly for robots that monitor and track user behavior (Caine, Šabanović, & Carter, 2012; N. Sharkey & A. Sharkey, 2012, p. 282; Sparrow & Sparrow, 2006). For example, older adults may not realize that they are being recorded by the robot assisting them; this requires a robot to have the ability to differentiate between confidential and nonconfidential information, and not record anything that may be sensitive (Sparrow, 2002, p. 305; Sparrow & Sparrow, 2006). This ethical dilemma intensifies in the case of older adults with cognitive impairment, requiring additional effort to ensure transparency (Ienca et al., 2016). When designing robots, it is important that the user has ultimate control over the data being collected (Sharkey & Sharkey, 2012). Design considerations include privacy settings, controls, and transparency particularly when health-care information is being collected (Caine et al., 2012; Caine & Hanania, 2013; Kwasny, Caine, Rogers, & Fisk, 2008).

Privacy and safety consideration also apply to assistive robots that may physically assist with ADLs such as ambulation, rehabilitation, eating, bathing, dressing, and toileting (Beer et al., 2012; Forlizzi et al., 2004; Matarić, 2007; Mohammed et al., 2015, p. 2015). Forms of assistive robots can include aides such as wheelchairs, manipulator arms, and educational robots (Mohammed et al., 2015, p. 2015). For example, a robot that assists an older adult with bathing may also need to be able to monitor movement to inquire assistance in the case of a fall. Moreover, robots assisting with ambulation may record user location and movement, which may create a lack of privacy. Robot designers should develop switches, such as physical buttons or voice-activated interactions that allow the user to turn off the robot in case of emergency. The nature of assistive robots and their direct interaction with physical activities require design considerations that address the robots' potential to cause physical harm (Feil-Seifer & Matarić, 2011; Ienca et al., 2016; Kortner, 2016; Preuß & Legal, 2017; Sorell & Draper, 2014). For example, a large assistive robot losing power, tipping over, or experiencing sensor failure can cause physical harm to an older adult or a caregiver. Sensor redundancy may help reduce accidental failures. Moreover, incorporation of power reserves in the event of power failure can help ensure that an assistive robot is able to safely complete the tasks to which it was assigned.

Robots are not only becoming more sophisticated in their physical capability in performing tasks, but also in their ability to demonstrate social behavior, which brings about unique ethical considerations. Companion robots, such as Paro, have shown positive results in reducing stress and anxiety (Lane et al., 2016). However, an increasing amount of research is also looking at how companion social robots can facilitate more complex social engagement. For example, artificial intelligence can be used to promote naturalistic conversation between the robot and user, creating a more engaging and intelligent social interaction (Moyle et al., 2013). These functions hold the potential to engage older adults on an intellectual, social, and emotional level (Beuscher et al., 2017), fulfilling the role of a caregiver. However, relationships between older adults and their (human) caregivers consist of "caring about" and "caring for" someone; this incorporates two dimensions of care: reciprocal and technical-instrumental (Vandemeulebroucke et al., 2018). A mismatch between the robot's role and their (in)ability to care can create a disruption, which results in a loss of meaningfulness (Coeckelbergh, 2015; Parks, 2010, p. 100). The relationship which the robot should ideally have with the older adult should be a key design consideration (Sparrow & Sparrow, 2006). Older adults should not be deceived by the robots into thinking that the robot cares for them. It is crucial that there is transparency in the purpose of the robot. Furthermore, robot design should not aim to replace human interaction and assistance, as this may result in objectification, deception, and social isolation of older adults (Coeckelbergh, 2010, 2015). Designing with the aim of using robots as tools for the older adult (i.e., tools that supplement care, not replace it) can help minimize these negative effects (Coeckelbergh, 2015; Parks, 2010, p. 100; Vandemeulebroucke et al., 2018).

Finally, robots could also be used to facilitate interaction *between* people. For example, some companion and SARs have been used to encourage conversation between older adults in assisted living facilities (Broadbent, Stafford, & MacDonald, 2009, p. 319; Chang, Sabanovic, & Huber, 2013, p. 101; Kim et al., 2017; McGlynn et al., 2017; McGlynn, Snook, Kemple, Mitzner, & Rogers, 2014). Telepresence robots aim to enable communication and have much potential to keep remotely located families connected. However, for all of these types of robots, users have concerns that the robots could replace physical human contact (Beer et al., 2012; Liles, Kacmar, Stuck, & Beer, 2015; Wu, Thomas, Drobina, Mitzner, & Beer, 2017), leading to the potential of social isolation and disconnectedness from the outside world (Sparrow, 2002, p. 305). For example, the use of telepresence robots to establish virtual visits by family and friends can lead to a decrease in the number of physical visits. This can lead to relationships of trust and concern to be replaced by technical efficacy and monitoring (Sparrow & Sparrow, 2006). Health promotion and educational resources should be spent educating families about the importance of physical visits (if possible) and that such technology is only supplemental in social connectedness. Moreover, older adults should be provided with reminders about the purpose of the technology along with the importance of engagement of face to face interaction. For example, older adults and their family/friends should not be led to believe that the robot is there to replace the social interaction they should have with each other, although it may seem more convenient.

Closing

In closing, robots that can assist older adults to age in place are becoming increasingly available. The benefits of aging in place are well established, and robots have the potential to aid older adults who want or need help with maintaining their independence. Such aging in place robots take the form of companion, telepresence, or assistive robots—designed to assist older adults with biological, psychological, and social aspects of functional aging. These robots can assist older adults in performing a range of daily activities, including ADL, IADL, and EADL tasks. However, for these robots to be successful, much consideration is needed on how they will interact and be used by older adults on a daily basis. Many ethical considerations are needed to protect older adults' privacy, safety, and social engagement with robots. In this chapter, we provided a review of aging in place, how robots may fit into older adults' daily lives, and the many ethical considerations surrounding robot adoption. The field of human—robot interaction is growing, and as outlined in this chapter, there are many exciting research opportunities to better design, develop, and implement robotics to support aging in place.

References

Abdi, J., Al-Hindawi, A., Ng, T., & Vizcaychipi, M. P. (2018). Scoping review on the use of socially assistive robot technology in elderly care. *BMJ Open, 8*(2). https://doi.org/10.1136/bmjopen-2017-018815.

Andrews, G. J., & Phillips, D. R. (2005). *Ageing and place*. London: Routledge.

Ávila-Funes, J. A., Amieva, H., Barberger-Gateau, P., Goff, M. L., Raoux, N., Ritchie, K., et al. (2009). Cognitive impairment improves the predictive validity of the phenotype of frailty for adverse health outcomes: The three-city study. *Journal of the American Geriatrics Society, 57*(3), 453—461.

Bacsu, J., Jeffery, B., Abonyi, S., Johnson, S., Novik, N., Martz, D., et al. (2014). Healthy aging in place: Perceptions of rural older adults. *Educational Gerontology, 40*(5), 327—337. https://doi.org/10.1080/03601277.2013.802191.

Bardic, A. (2015). Time to rethink the boomers? *Convenience Store News, 51*(10), 136.

Bedaf, S., Gelderblom, G. J., & De Witte, L. (2015). *Overview and categorization of robots supporting independent living of elderly people: What activities do they support and how far have they developed.*

Beer, J. M., Mitzner, T. L., Stuck, R. E., & Rogers, W. A. (2015). Design considerations for technology interventions to support social and physical wellness for older adults with disability. *International Journal of AUtomation and SMart Technology, 5*(4). https://doi.org/10.5875/ausmt.v5i4.959.

Beer, J. M., Prakash, A., Smarr, C.-A., Chen, T. L., Hawkins, K., Nguyen, H., et al. (2017). Older users' acceptance of an assistive robot: Attitudinal changes following brief exposure. *Gerontechnology, 16*(1), 21—36.

Beer, J. M., Smarr, C.-A., Chen, T. L., Prakash, A., Mitzner, T. L., Kemp, C. C., et al. (2012). The domesticated robot: Design guidelines for assisting older adults to age in place. In *2012 7th ACM/IEEE international conference on human-robot interaction (HRI)* (p. 335).

Beer, J. M., & Takayama, L. (2011). Mobile remote presence systems for older adults. In *Proceedings of the 6th international conference: human-robot interaction* (p. 19).

Bemelmans, R., Gelderblom, G. J., Jonker, P., & de Witte, L. (2011). *The potential of socially assistive robotics in care for elderly, a systematic review.*

Beuscher, L. M., Jing, F., Sarkar, N., Dietrich, M. S., Newhouse, P. A., Miller, K. F., et al. (2017). Socially assistive robots: Measuring older adults' perceptions. *Journal of Gerontological Nursing, 43*(12), 35–43.

Black, K. (2008). Health and aging-in-place: Implications for community practice. *Journal of Community Practice, 16*(1), 79–95. https://doi.org/10.1080/10705420801978013.

Black, K., Dobbs, D., & Young, T. L. (2015). Aging in community: Mobilizing a new paradigm of older adults as a core social resource. *Journal of Applied Gerontology, 34*(2), 219–243.

Blanchard, J. (2013). Aging in community: Communitarian alternative to aging in place, alone. *Generations, 37*(4), 6–13.

Breazeal, C. L. (2002). *Designing sociable robots.* Cambridge, MA: MIT Press.

Broadbent, E., Stafford, R., & MacDonald, B. (2009). *Acceptance of healthcare robots for the older population: Review and future directions.*

Broekens, J., Heerink, M., & Rosendal, H. (2009). Assistive social robots in elderly care: A review. *Gerontechnology, 8*(2), 94–103. https://doi.org/10.4017/gt.2009.08.02.002.00.

Caine, K., & Hanania, R. (2013). *Patients want granular privacy control over health information in electronic medical records.*

Caine, K., Šabanović, S., & Carter, M. (2012). The effect of monitoring by cameras and robots on the privacy enhancing behaviors of older adults. In *ACM/IEEE international conference on human-robot interaction* (p. 343).

Campa, R. (2016). The rise of social robots: A review of the recent literature. *Journal of Evolution and Technology, 26*(1), 106–113.

Canal, G. A., Guillem, T., & Carme. (2017). A taxonomy of preferences for physically assistive robots. In G. Alenya & C. Torras (Eds.), (pp. 292): IEEE.

Castle, N. (2012). Nurse aides' reports of resident abuse in nursing homes. *Journal of Applied Gerontology, 31*(3), 402–422.

Chang, W.-L., Sabanovic, S., & Huber, L. (2013). *Use of seal-like robot PARO in sensory group therapy for older adults with dementia.* IEEE.

Chen, Y.-S., Hsu, Y.-L., & Lu, J.-M. (2013). *TRiC(mini)(+) − A telepresence robot for interpersonal communication for older adults.*

Coeckelbergh, M. (2010). Health care, capabilities, and AI assistive technologies. *Ethical Theory & Moral Practice, (2)*, 181.

Coeckelbergh, M. (2015). Artificial agents, good care, and modernity. *Theoretical Medicine and Bioethics, 36*(4), 265.

Colombo, F., Llena-Nozal, A., Mercier, J., & Tjadens, F. (2011). *Help wanted? Providing and paying for long-term care: OECD health policy studies.* Paris and Washington, D.C.: Organisation for Economic Co-operation and Development.

Compton, S. A., Flanigan, P., & Gregg, W. (1997). *Elder abuse in people with dementia in Northern Ireland: Prevalence and predictors in cases referred to a psychiatry of old age service.*

Courtin, E., Dowd, J. B., & Avendano, M. (2018). The mental health benefits of acquiring a home in older age: A fixed-effects analysis of older US adults. *American Journal of Epidemiology, 187*(3), 465–473. https://doi.org/10.1093/aje/kwx278.

Creighton, A. S., Davison, T. E., & Kissane, D. W. (2016). The prevalence of anxiety among older adults in nursing homes and other residential aged care facilities: A systematic review. *International Journal of Geriatric Psychiatry*, (6), 555. https://doi.org/10.1002/gps.4378.

Cutchin, M. P. (2003). The process of mediated aging-in-place: A theoretically and empirically based model. *Social Science & Medicine*, (6), 1077.

Czaja, S. J., & Lee, C. C. (2007). The impact of aging on access to technology. *Universal Access in the Information Society*, (4), 341.

Dautenhahn, K. (1997). *I could be you: The phenomenological dimension of social understanding.*

Davila, E. P., Caban-Martinez, A. J., Muennig, P., Lee, D. J., Fleming, L. E., Ferraro, K. F., et al. (2009). Sensory impairment among older US workers. *American Journal of Public Health*, *99*(8), 1378–1385.

Davis, F. D. (1989). Perceived usefulness, perceived ease of use, and user acceptance of information technology, information technology. *MIS Quarterly*, *13*(3), 319. https://doi.org/10.2307/249008.

De Carolis, B., & Cozzolongo, G. (2007). *Planning the behaviour of a social robot acting as a majordomo in public environments.*

Dye, C. J., Willoughby, D. F., & Battisto, D. G. (2011). Advice from rural elders: What it takes to age in place. *Educational Gerontology*, *37*(1), 74–93. https://doi.org/10.1080/03601277.2010.515889.

Eftring, H., & Frennert, S. (2016). Designing a social and assistive robot for seniors. *Zeitschrift Fur Gerontologie Und Geriatrie*, *49*(4), 274–281. https://doi.org/10.1007/s00391-016-1064-7.

Erber, J. T. (2005). *Aging and older adulthood.* Belmont, CA: Thomson Wadsworth.

Espino, D. V., Wood, R. C., Finely, M. R., Ye, Y., & Angel, J. L. (2013). *Characteristics of Mexican American elders admitted to nursing facilities in the United States: Data from the Hispanic established populations for epidemiologic studies of the elderly (EPESE) study.*

Evaluating older adults' interaction with a mobile assistive robot. (2017). IEEE.

Ezer, N., Fisk, A. D., & Rogers, W. A. (2009). Attitudinal and intentional acceptance of domestic robots by younger and older adults. In *Universal Access in Human-Computer Interaction. Intelligent and Ubiquitous Interaction Environments Lecture Notes in Computer Science* (pp. 39–48). https://doi.org/10.1007/978-3-642-02710-9_5.

Fausset, C. B., Kelly, A. J., Rogers, W. A., & Fisk, A. D. (2011). Challenges to aging in place: Understanding home maintenance difficulties. *Journal of Housing for the Elderly*, *25*(2), 125–141.

Feil-Seifer, D., & Matarić, J. M. (2011). Socially assistive robotics. *IEEE Robotics & Automation Magazine*, (1), 24. https://doi.org/10.1109/MRA.2010.940150.

Feil-Seifer, D., & Mataric, M. J. (2005). *Defining socially assistive robotics.* Piscataway, NJ, USA: IEEE.

Feil-Seifer, D., Skinner, K., & Matarić, M. J. (2007). Benchmarks for evaluating socially assistive robotics. *Interaction Studies*, *8*(3), 423–439.

Fernández-Mayoralas, G., Rojo-Pérez, F., Martínez-Martín, P., Prieto-Flores, M.-E., Rodríguez-Blázquez, C., Martín-García, S., et al. (2015). Active ageing and quality of life: Factors associated with participation in leisure activities among institutionalized older adults, with and without dementia. *Aging & Mental Health*, *19*(11), 1031–1041.

Fishbein, M., & Ajzen, I. (1975). *Belief, attitude, intention and behavior: An introduction to theory and research.* Reading, MA: Addison Wesley.

Fong, T., Nourbakhsh, I., & Dautenhahn, K. (2003). *A survey of socially interactive robots.*

Forlizzi, J., DiSalvo, C., & Gemperle, F. (2004). Assistive robotics and an ecology of elders living independently in their homes. *Human-Computer Interaction, 19*(1/2), 25–59.

García-Soler, Á., Facal, D., Díaz-Orueta, U., Pigini, L., Blasi, L., & Qiu, R. (2018). Inclusion of service robots in the daily lives of frail older users: A step-by-step definition procedure on users' requirements. *Archives of Gerontology and Geriatrics, 74*, 191–196. https://doi.org/10.1016/j.archger.2017.10.024.

Gilbert, S. F. (2017). Developmental biology, the stem cell of biological disciplines. *PLoS Biology, 12*. https://doi.org/10.1371/journal.pbio.2003691.

Goncalves Damascena, K., Batisti Ferreira, C., dos Santos Teixeira, P., Madrid, B., Goncalves, A., Cordova, C., et al. (2017). Functional capacity and obesity reflect the cognitive performance of older adults living in long-term care facilities. *Psychogeriatrics*, (6), 439. https://doi.org/10.1111/psyg.12273.

Goodhue, D. L., & Thompson, R. L. (1995). Task-technology fit and individual performance. *MIS Quarterly, 19*(2), 213. https://doi.org/10.2307/249689.

Heaven, B., Brown, L. J. E., White, M., Errington, L., Mathers, J. C., & Moffatt, S. (2013). Supporting well-being in retirement through meaningful social roles: Systematic review of intervention studies. *The Milbank Quarterly, 91*(2), 222–287. https://doi.org/10.1111/milq.12013.

Heine, C., & Browning, C. (2015). Dual sensory loss in older adults: A systematic. *The Gerontologist, 55*(5), 913–928.

Hopp, F. P. (1999). Patterns and predictors of formal and informal care among elderly persons living in board and care homes. *The Gerontologist*, (2), 167. Retrieved from http://proxy-remote.galib.uga.edu/login?url=http://search.ebscohost.com/login.aspx?direct=-true&db=edsbl&AN=RN060034321&site=eds-live.

Hurd, M. D., Michaud, P.-C., & Rohwedder, S. (2017). Distribution of lifetime nursing home use and of out-of-pocket spending. *Proceedings of the National Academy of Sciences of the United States*, (37), 9838. https://doi.org/10.1073/pnas.1700618114.

Huschilt, J., & Clune, L. (2012). The use of socially assistive robots for dementia care. *Journal of Gerontological Nursing, 38*(10), 15–19.

Ienca, M., Jotterand, F., VicA, C., & Elger, B. (2016). Social and assistive robotics in dementia care: Ethical recommendations for research and practice. *International Journal of Social Robotics*, (4), 565. https://doi.org/10.1007/s12369-016-0366-7.

Katz, R. (2015). Tele-care robot for assisting independent senior citizens who live at home. *Studies in Health Technology and Informatics, 217*, 288–294.

Kaye, H. S., Harrington, C., & LaPlante, M. P. (2010). *Long-term care: Who gets it, who provides it, who pays, and how much?*.

Kidd, C. D., Taggart, W., & Turkle, S. (2006). *A sociable robot to encourage social interaction among the elderly.* IEEE.

Kim, K.-i., Gollamudi, S. S., & Steinhubl, S. (2017). Review: Digital technology to enable aging in place. *Experimental Gerontology, 88*, 25–31. https://doi.org/10.1016/j.exger.2016.11.013.

Kleyman, P. (2017). The age of anti-aging: Media hype and the myth of the ageless baby boomer. *Generations, 41*(2), 41–47.

Kortner, T. (2016). Ethical challenges in the use of social service robots for elderly people. *Zeitschrift Fur Gerontologie Und Geriatrie*, (4), 303. https://doi.org/10.1007/s00391-016-1066-5.

Kristoffersson, A., Coradeschi, S., & Loutfi, A. (2013). A review of mobile robotic telepresence. *Advances in Human-Computer Interaction.* https://doi.org/10.1155/2013/902316.

Krug, E. G., Dahlberg, L. L., Mercy, J. A., Zwi, A. B., & Lozano, R. (2002). Abuse of the elderly. *World Report on Violence and Health*, 123–143.

Kwasny, M., Caine, K., Rogers, W. A., & Fisk, A. D. (2008). Privacy and technology. In *Conference on human factors in computing systems proceedings* (p. 3291).

Kwon, S. (2017). *Gerontechnology:Research, Practice, and Principles in the Field of Technology and Aging*. New York, NY: Springer Publishing Company.

Lane, G. W., Noronha, D., Rivera, A., Craig, K., Yee, C., Mills, B., et al. (2016). Effectiveness of a social robot, 'Paro,' in a VA long-term care setting. *Psychological Services, 13*(3), 292–299. https://doi.org/10.1037/ser0000080.

Lawton, M. P. (1990). Aging and performance of home tasks. *Human Factors, 32*(5), 527–536.

Lawton, M. P., Brody, E. M., Plys, E., & Kluge, M. A. (2016). Instrumental activities of daily living. Life-space mobility in a sample of independent living residents within a continuing care retirement community with an embedded wellness program. *Journal of Clinical Gerontologist, 39*(3), 210–221.

Liles, K. R., Kacmar, A., Stuck, R. E., & Beer, J. M. (2015). Smart presence for retirement community employees. In *ACM/IEEE international conference on human-robot interaction* (p. 85).

Mahmood, A., Yamamoto, T., Lee, M., & Steggell, C. (2008). Perceptions and use of gerotechnology: Implications for aging in place. *Journal of Housing for the Elderly, 22*(1/2), 104–126.

Marek, K. D., Stetzer, F., Adams, S. J., Popejoy, L. L., & Rantz, M. (2012). Aging in place versus nursing home care: Comparison of costs to Medicare and Medicaid. *Research in Gerontological Nursing, 5*(2), 123–129. https://doi.org/10.3928/19404921-20110802-01.

Markides, K. S., & Gerst-Emerson, K. (2014). Introduction: Minorities, aging, and health. In K. E. Whitfield, T. A. Baker, C. M. Abdou, & et al. (Eds.), *Handbook of minority aging* (pp. 105–109). New York, NY, US: Springer Publishing Co.

Matarić, M. J. (2007). *The robotics primer*. Cambridge, MA: MIT Press.

Matthews, J. T. (2002). Technology topics. The Nursebot project: Developing a personal robotic assistant for frail older adults in the community. *Home Health Care Management & Practice, 14*(5), 403–405.

Małgorzata, D., & Rafał, F. (2014). Biological psychological and social determinants of old age: Bio-psycho-social aspects of human aging. *Annals of Agricultural and Environmental Medicine, 21*(876253), 835–838 (876253), 835.

McFarland, M. R. (1997). *Use of culture care theory with Anglo- and African American elders in a long-term care setting.*

McGlynn, S. A., Kemple, S., Mitzner, T. L., King, C.-H. A., & Rogers, W. A. (2017). Understanding the potential of PARO for healthy older adults. *International Journal of Human-Computer Studies, 100*, 33–47. https://doi.org/10.1016/j.ijhcs.2016.12.004.

McGlynn, S. A., Snook, B., Kemple, S., Mitzner, T. L., & Rogers, W. A. (2014). Therapeutic robots for older adults: Investigating the potential of Paro. In *ACM/IEEE international conference on human-robot interaction* (p. 246).

Mellor, M. J., Mellor, M. J., & Rehr, H. (2005). *Baby boomers. [electronic resource] : Can my eighties be like my fifties?* (1st ed.). New York, NY: Springer.

Meyer, J. (2012). *Centenarians: 2010.* Washington, D.C.: U.S. Dept. Of commerce, Economics and Statistics Administration, U.S. Census Bureau.

Mitzner, T. L., Chen, T. L., Kemp, C. C., & Rogers, W. A. (2014). *Identifying the potential for robotics to assist older adults in different living environments.*

Mohammed, S., Moreno, J. C., Kong, K., & Amirat, Y. (2015). *Intelligent assistive robots : Recent advances in assistive robotics for everyday activities.* Cham: Springer.

Moore, J. (2005). Aging in place challenges assistance in IL. *Contemporary Long-Term Care,* *27*(3), 20–21.

Mowry, C., Pimentel, A., Sparks, E., & Hanlon, B. (2013). *Materials characterization activities for* *"take our sons & daughters to work day".*

Moyle, W., Cooke, M., Beattie, E., Jones, C., Klein, B., Cook, G., et al. (2013). Exploring the effect of companion robots on emotional expression in older adults with dementia: A pilot randomized controlled trial. *Journal of Gerontological Nursing, 39*(5), 46–53.

Nirmalasari, O., Simpson, A., Lin, F. R., Oh, E. S., Mamo, S. K., Nieman, C. L., et al. (2017). Age-related hearing loss in older adults with cognitive impairment. *International Psychogeriatrics,* *29*(1), 115–121.

North, M. S., & Fiske, S. T. (2012). An inconvenienced youth? Ageism and its potential inter-generational roots. *Psychological Bulletin, 138*(5), 982–997. https://doi.org/10.1037/a0027843.

Older Americans [electronic resource]: Key indicators of well-being. (2012). Washington, D.C.: Federal Interagency Forum on Aging Related Statistics.

Parks, J. A. (2010). *Lifting the burden of women's care work: Should robots replace the 'human touch'?.*

Pedersen, I., Reid, S., & Aspevig, K. (2018). Developing social robots for aging populations: A literature review of recent academic sources. *Sociology Compass, 6.* https://doi.org/10.1111/soc4.12585.

Phillips, L. U. (2018). Aging in place. In Salem Press Encyclopedia. Retrieved from: Retrieved from http://search.ebscohost.com.proxy-remote.galib.uga.edu/login.aspx?direct=true&db=ers&AN=90558240&site=eds-live.

Piau, A., Campo, E., Rumeau, P., Vellas, B., & Nourhashemi, F. (2014). Aging society and ger-ontechnology: A solution for an independent living? *The Journal of Nutrition, Health &* *Aging, 18*(1), 97–112.

Pineau, J., Montemerlo, M., Pollack, M., Roy, N., & Thrun, S. (2003). *Towards robotic assistants* *in nursing homes: Challenges and results.*

Pino, M., Boulay, M., Rigaud, A.-S., & Jouen, F. (2015). *"Are we ready for robots that care for* *us?" Attitudes and opinions of older adults toward socially assistive robots.*

Pinto, J. M., & Neri, A. L. (2017). Factors related to low social participation in older adults: Findings from the fibra study, Brazil. *Fatores relacionados à baixa participação social em* *idosos: Resultados do estudo Fibra, Brasil., 25*(3), 286–293. https://doi.org/10.1590/1414-462X201700030300.

Pollack, M. E. (2005). *Intelligent technology for an aging population: The use of AI to assist elders* *with cognitive impairment.*

Prakash, A., & Rogers, W. A. (2013). Younger and older adults' attitudes toward robot faces: Effects of task and humanoid appearance. *Proceedings of the Human Factors and Ergonomics* *Society - Annual Meeting, 57*(1), 114. Retrieved from http://proxy-remote.galib.uga.edu/login?url=http://search.ebscohost.com/login.aspx?direct=-true&db=edo&AN=ejs42102197&site=eds-live.

Preuß, D., & Legal, F. (2017). Living with the animals: Animal or robotic companions for the elderly in smart homes? *Journal of Medical Ethics: The Journal of the Institute of Medical* *Ethics, 43*(6), 407–410.

Rajan, K. B., Hebert, L. E., Scherr, P. A., Mendes de Leon, C. F., & Evans, D. A. (2013). Disability in basic and instrumental activities of daily living is associated with faster rate of decline in cognitive function of older adults. *Journal of Gerontology: Series A: Biological Sciences and* *Medical Sciences, 68*(5), 624–630.

Reiser, U., Jacobs, T., Arbeiter, G., Parlitz, C., & Dautenhahn, K. (2013). *Care-O-bot® 3 − vision* *of a Robot Butler.*

Robinson, H., Broadbent, E., & MacDonald, B. (2016). Group sessions with Paro in a nursing home: Structure, observations and interviews. *Australasian Journal on Ageing*, (2), 106. https://doi.org/10.1111/ajag.12199.

Rogers, A. (2015). *Human behavior in the social environment* (4th ed.). New York: Taylor & Francis [CAM].

Rogers, W., Meyer, B., Walker, N., & Fisk, A. D. (1998). *Functional limitations to daily living tasks in the aged: A focus group analysis.*

Roomba. (2018). Retrieved from https://www.irobot.com/For-the-Home/Vacuuming/Roomba.

Saxon, S. V., Perkins, E. A., & Etten, M. J. (2015). *Physical change and aging, sixth edition: a guide for the helping professions* (6th ed.). New York, NY: Springer Publishing Company.

Seidel, D., Crilly, N., Matthews, F. E., Jagger, C., Brayne, C., & Clarkson, P. J. (2009). Patterns of functional loss among older people: A prospective analysis. *Human Factors, 51*(5), 669–680. https://doi.org/10.1177/0018720809353597.

Sharkey, A., & Sharkey, N. (2012). Granny and the robots: Ethical issues in robot care for the elderly. *Ethics and Information Technology, 14*(1), 27–40.

Sharkey, N., & Sharkey, A. (2012). *The eldercare factory.*

Shishehgar, M., Kerr, D., & Blake, J. (2018). A systematic review of research into how robotic technology can help older people. *Smart Health*. https://doi.org/10.1016/j.smhl.2018.03.002.

Smarr, C.-A., Fausset, C. B., & Rogers, W. A. (2010). *Understanding the potential for robot assistance for older adults in the home environment.* Atlanta, GA.

Smarr, C.-A., Mitzner, T. L., Beer, J. M., Prakash, A., Chen, T. L., Kemp, C. C., et al. (2014). Domestic robots for older adults: Attitudes, preferences, and potential. *International Journal of Social Robotics, 6*(2), 229–247. https://doi.org/10.1007/s12369-013-0220-0.

Smarr, C. A., Prakash, A., Beer, J. M., Mitzner, T. L., Kemp, C. C., & Rogers, W. A. (2012). *Older adults' preferences for and acceptance of robot assistance for everyday living tasks.*

Sorell, T., & Draper, H. (2014). Robot carers, ethics, and older people. *Ethics and Information Technology*, (3), 183. https://doi.org/10.1007/s10676-014-9344-7.

Sparrow, R. (2002). *The march of the robot dogs.*

Sparrow, R., & Sparrow, L. (2006). In the hands of machines? The future of aged care. *Minds and Machines, 16*(2), 141. https://doi.org/10.1007/s11023-006-9030-6.

Swagerty, D. L., Takahashi, P. Y., & Evans, J. M. (1999). *Elder mistreatment.*

Takayuki, K., & Hiroshi, I. (2012). *Human-robot interactions in social robotics.*

Tapus, A., Maja, M., & Scassellatti, B. (2007). Socially assistive robotics [grand challenges of robotics]. *IEEE Robotics & Automation Magazine*, (1), 35. https://doi.org/10.1109/MRA.2007.339605.

Tiberio, L., Cesta, A., Cortellessa, G., Padua, L., & Pellegrino, A. R. (2012). *Assessing affective response of older users to a telepresence robot using a combination of psychophysiological measures.* IEEE.

Timiras, P. S. (2003). *Physiological basis of aging and geriatrics* (3rd ed.). Boca Raton, FL: CRC Press.

Tomioka, K., Kurumatani, N., & Hosoi, H. (2017). Association between social participation and 3-year change in instrumental activities of daily living in community-dwelling elderly adults. *Journal of the American Geriatrics Society, 65*(1), 107–113.

Trafialek, E. (1997). *Adam A. Zych: Man and old age: Essays in social gerontology* (p. 107).

Vandemeulebroucke, T., Gastmans, C., & de Casterle, B. D. (2018). *The use of care robots in aged care: A systematic review of argument-based ethics literature.*

Venkatesh, V., & Bala, H. (2008). Technology acceptance model 3 and a research agenda on interventions. *Decision Sciences, 39*(2), 273–315. https://doi-org.proxy-remote.galib.uga.edu/10.1111/j.1540-5915.2008.00192.x.

Venkatesh, V., Morris, M. G., Davis, G. B., & Davis, F. D. (2003). User acceptance of information technology: Toward a unified view. *MIS Quarterly, 27*, 425—478.

Victor, C. R. (2005). *The social context of ageing: [a textbook of gerontology]* (p. 2005). London, New York: Routledge.

Wada, K., Shibata, T., Musha, T., & Kimura, S. (2008). Robot therapy for elders affected by dementia. *IEEE Engineering in Medicine and Biology Magazine,* (4)https://doi.org/10.1109/MEMB.2008.919496.

Walker, H., & Paliadelis, P. (2016). Older peoples' experiences of living in a residential aged care facility in Australia. *Australasian Journal on Ageing, 35*(3), E6—E10.

Wangerin, B., Public, N. A., Bales, B., Banks, R., Duluth, R. C., Forsberg, M., et al. (2006). *Creating healthy Communities for an aging population.*

Webb, C. A., Titus, C., Nadorff, M. R., Cui, R., & Fiske, A. (2018). *Sleep disturbance, activities of daily living, and depressive symptoms among older adults.*

Wick, J. Y. (2017). Aging in place: Our house is a very, very, very fine house. *The Consultant Pharmacist: The Journal of The American Society of Consultant Pharmacists, 32*(10), 566—574. https://doi.org/10.4140/TCP.n.2017.566.

Wu, X., Thomas, R. C., Drobina, E. C., Mitzner, T. L., & Beer, J. M. (2017). *Telepresence heuristic evaluation for adults aging with mobility impairment.*

Wu, Y. H., Wrobel, J., Cornuet, M., Kerhervé, H., Damnée, S., & Rigaud, A. S. (2014). Acceptance of an assistive robot in older adults: A mixed-method study of human—robot interaction over a 1-month period in the living lab setting. *Clinical Interventions in Aging, 9*, 801—811, 801.

Further reading

Are robots the next eldercare trend? (2018). *Journal of Financial Planning, 31*(1), 16.

Chapter 4

Kill switch: The evolution of road rage in an increasingly AI car culture

Julie Carpenter

Ethics + Emerging Sciences Group, California Polytechnic State University, San Luis Obispo, CA, United States

Chapter outline

> *No one you have been and no place you have gone ever leaves you. The new parts of you simply jump in the car and go along for the rest of the ride. The success of your journey and your destination all depend on who's driving.*
>
> Bruce Springsteen, *Born to run* (2016)

Automated driving technologies and car design in the near future

The world of autonomous driving predicts many potential benefits from AI-guided cars: improved safety (Litman, 2019, p. 28), reduced traffic congestion (Litman, 2019, p. 28), and even lower negative stress (SMMT News, 2017) for people. Authorizing organizations that develop policy will have to adapt existing laws and create new ones to ensure the full compatibility of these vehicles with the public's expectations regarding safety, legal responsibility, and privacy. However, most of the essential technologies required for fully autonomous driving are available today and being tested in public

Living with Robots. https://doi.org/10.1016/B978-0-12-815367-3.00004-9

spaces, and some are already being deployed in commercially available vehicles. Still, the vehicles' currently limited deployment and widespread availability means there has been almost no publicly available information about the user experiences in the vehicles. Self-driving appears to be a viable near-future possibility and therefore will soon be pervasive across the everyday lives of people, but their current capabilities and limitations are unclear.

According to the Society of Motor Manufacturers and Traders (SMMT), autonomous cars can be divided into different categories of automation, with level 0 as a vehicle with no automation, while level 5 is fully automated (SMMT, 2017, "Levels of auotonomy"). In this chapter, an *autonomous* vehicle (AV) is fundamentally defined as a consumer passenger vehicle that has the capability to drive by itself. Optimistic industry observers expect there to be fully autonomously self-driving consumer car models for sale and integrated into the market by 2020 (Chuang, 2017; Garrett, 2017), although it is not certain to what extent these vehicles will be capable of self-driving in all circumstances.

Fully autonomous cars encompass a diverse set of emerging concepts that must be understood individually and as part of broader trends toward automation and technological connectivity. Combined, the technologies and conceptual changes for users are potentially revolutionary. As vehicles are imbued with increasing automation, their role in society changes, and while we can predict some trends with some accuracy, other changes to human lives will be harder to foresee. Policies and regulations can account for the uncertainties associated with some aspects of emerging technologies and ensure the rules of society follow these changes or, at a minimum, not block changes that are desirable.

The everyday human factors that will relate to understanding the interaction(s) of humans with all aspects of an automated road transport (ART) system, both from within a vehicle—when taking the role of an owner/operator and as a user sharing the road and interacting with other automated and semiautomated vehicles—will be pervasive. People will develop new relationships to cars, with rapid and widespread cultural changes. It will become increasingly important to use knowledge and theories from social-psychological and behavioral and cultural sciences to fully understand how humans interact with such systems.

With autonomous or driverless cars (terms which are used interchangeably here to mean consumer vehicles with the ability to drive without a human in the loop), everyday rituals will change, big and small. Cultural touchstones as well as the economics surrounding car ownership will change. The long-standing rite of getting a driver's license as a teenager may be replaced with other car-related rites of passage altogether as the already-complicated relationship with consumer vehicles evolves. It is likely that car purchasing criteria will also change considerably when all the variables of drivability associated with pleasure have shifted to passenger-entered concerns.

Automotive designers are already anticipating the expanded role of the car's artificial intelligence (AI) to determine what is going on outside the vehicle, as the user's role changes from driver to passenger (Jablansky, 2016). As this role changes, one popular framework of conceptualizing user experience and design in these new consumer vehicles is the idea of a car as an extension of home or workspaces (Bryant, 2015; Quoted, 2016; Sabin, 2017; Weiss, 2017).

Activities that people may want to do with their newly found commute times as passengers include everything from eating or playing video games to working or sleeping, essentially, using the car as a remote home or work. Some designers are turning to models of interactions in similar spaces as a guide for determining what people might want to do in the new role as long-term passenger, and one such existing paradigm is air travel (Hyundai, 2017; Sabin, 2017; Stoklosa, 2013).

Kota Kobayashi, leader of the Auto Digital Design team at ustwo, explained, "I started by comparing with in-flight experiences that everyone knows about. It came down to these three things: relaxation, entertainment, and productivity" (Sabin, 2017). Kobayashi further described that the differences between commercial flights and consumer car spaces means significant thoughtful adaptions between the airplane model of passenger interaction with technology and space and the merging autonomous car model. For autonomous car design, Kobayashi states that factors such as privacy, the duration of travel, and the freedom to leave the car when on-demand are what people want. In fact, he emphasizes the privacy factor by explaining, "Inside a car is a quite private, intimate space, which is different from the public space of an airplane" (Sabin, 2017).

Automotive start-up NIO was very clear with their vision:

With NIO autonomous electric vehicles, you will be as productive as you would be at your desk, or as relaxed as you would be on your couch. As the car drives, you can conduct a video conference call for work or catch up on last night's episode of *Limitless* or *Supergirl*. The vehicle's interior can be set up for a commute, a road trip, or even a nap. The car's AI system will know where you are going, what's on your calendar, and it will adjust to your needs (Weiss, 2017).

In the words of former Best Buy CTO Robert Stephens, "The minute you realize you can be in this thing and surf your email and not touch the car that will be awesome" (Keen, 2013). Since passengers will not necessarily need to be engaged with the act of driving, redesigned interior spaces of cars will suit the changed needs of people with things like reconfigured seating, built-in tables, or similar useable "furniture," and built-in touch screens with Wi-Fi, synced with smart homes and the Internet of Things (IoT) to access entertainment or work media while commuting.

Richard Bush, an automotive consumer expert from the UK-based company Car Keys, indicated there is a clear industry trend toward designing autonomous car interiors as home and workspaces (Weiss, 2017). While some autonomous concept cars showcase very futuristic features they predict consumers will want when they are no longer tasked with a driving duty, one idea that is revisited across companies and models is the idea of the car space as an extension of a space people associate with privacy, or, conversely, spending time with other people in a space designed specifically to support the user's entertainment and work in addition to transportation. The conventional forward-facing seating arrangements of consumer vehicle interiors will change significantly in the coming years. Bush confirmed, "In its place sits a much more open, living room–style layout. The two seats for the driver and passenger no longer need to stay glued to the windscreen, allowing them to swivel around and entertain their guests, friends, and children" (Weiss, 2017).

Kill switch

In engineering and manufacturing, a *kill switch* is intended as a safety measure incorporated into a design specifically with the purpose of giving ultimate user control via a mechanism that will completely and efficiently stop the mechanical or other automated processes of a system. In 2017, as part of a framework for suggested ethical design and engineering practices put before the European Commission, European lawmakers proposed that all robots have kill switches (Kottasova, 2017) integrated into their design. The idea of human control over AI is an important one in terms of physical safety, and in terms of emotional reassurance for the users. Until AI systems are refined and we as consumers become accustomed to riding in AVs, the idea of a kill switch may allay common user fears about AIs vulnerabilities, such as its potentially inadequate decision-making abilities, or susceptibility to hacking.

Thus, from the user's point of view, the ability to ultimately control the vehicle may seem like a reasonable safety measure. Yet, this effort to mitigate human fear may become an irrelevant feature as AI becomes increasingly better at navigating in lieu of human decision-making in all sorts of conditions, and the human-made parts of the environment evolve to meet the needs of these new vehicles, with modified roadways, garages, and other aspects of an ART system. One of the intrinsic benefits of AI controlling a vehicle is, theoretically, the very absence of human emotion in the decision-making processes associated with driving.

The *trolley problem* is a well-known thought experiment that asks someone to consider what they would do if they were presented with the choice of controlling a runaway trolley on a track that could hit five people, or be diverted to hit one (Foot, 1967). The trolley problem setup famously portrays the difficulties weighing ethical risks and how it takes a nuanced understanding of human ethical dilemmas to even consider the consequences of choices about control, underscoring the potential pitfalls of flawed AI decision-making. How would AI in a vehicle handle a similar real-life dilemma? A device like a kill switch may be the override needed in many such situations and one of several redundant safety measures.

However, what about a scenario where the human driver intends to override the system or is driving manually, but the AI senses it can make a "better" decision in terms of safety? One such situation might be in the case of aggressive and erratic driving by a human. In this context, should the AI have the privilege of its own kill switch, able to override the human controls?

Consider the proposed benefits of the AI system, integrated with cameras and sensors and intelligence so that it can be able to drive as well as a human (or better), and without impinging on human labor or having the flaws associated with human driving. If the car has the intelligent advantage via technology, but humans are still ultimately depended upon as the ones to carry out ethical standards, control of the car in these dire circumstances will become a significant issue.

Road rage

Conceptually, the term *road rage* has classically encompassed not only strong negative emotion but the acts provoked by these negative feelings. Road rage is closely associated with intense feelings of frustration at conditions, events, and specific people (Automobile Association, 1996). Therefore, the traditional concept of *road rage* refers to the actions, behaviors, and emotions of the primary actor driving a nonautonomous vehicle, the driver in control of the car's actions. The term encompasses a variety of aggressive behaviors by the driver where his or her actions are antagonistic and even vengeful beyond the perceived offense committed by the victim(s). These behaviors range from shouting at another driver to wielding or using a weapon—including the vehicle—to cause fear and/or pain to the victim, or damage their own car. Therefore, as a working definition for this chapter, *road rage* may be described as a system of thoughts, emotions, and behaviors that happen in response to a perceived threat or provocation while driving and that purposefully endangers and/or threatens others.

Many situational factors may converge to create an environment conducive to road rage incidents. Factors identified as contributing to road rage incidents vary from a stressful number of miles driven per day to frustration at roads congested with traffic (Lupton, 2002; Smart, Stoduto, Mann, Adlaf, & December, 2004; Szlemko et al. 2008) to drug and alcohol use (Yu, Evans, & Perfetti, 2004), and a driver's sense of anonymity (Ellison-Potter, Bell, & Deffenbacher, 2001; Szlemko, Benfied, Bell, Defenbacher, & Troup, 2008). Psychological influences that can contribute to road rage include depression (Yu et al., 2004), a person's tendency to displace anger and attribute blame to others (Lawton and Nutter, 2002), and high levels of perceived general negative stress (Lupton, 2002).

The predicted benefits of self-driving cars have also run the gamut, including new democratic models of shared car ownership, reduced personal costs, expanding the freedom of movement for people who otherwise may not have been able to drive (Overly, 2017). While AVs may deliver on all or some of these claims, there will still be multiple hurdles to a transition and normalization of these new vehicles in society, not the least of which will be refining traffic and road systems to efficiently manage vehicles of varying intelligence and autonomy for some years. The early days of integrating semiautonomous and autonomous vehicles with traditional cars on roads will cause some challenges of the type that will not necessarily eliminate every possible trigger of negatively stressful situations while in a vehicle, autonomous or not. For example, during the transition era of including fully autonomous cars into culture, traffic congestion may increase due to unforeseen use patterns of roads/highways (Overly 2017; SMMT "News" March 30, 2017). Furthermore, as with other aspects of robotics being assimilated into the world beyond industrial situations, there will be little true understanding of how the new cars will impact peoples' everyday lives until they are used "in the wild."

Of course, manufacturers are already designing autonomous cars with all the user experience concerns of traditional road rage in mind (Connelly, 2016; Jaffe, 2014; Roberts, 2015). Because of the likelihood that traditional road rage will still manifest and inhabit a world alongside the new user experiences in AVs, it is worth proposing research from many different perspectives rooted in areas of expertise such as engineering, user experience, psychology, design, and human–robot interaction, among others. One such lens for examining the user experience in autonomous car riding is by using the framework of a set of variables such as user personality traits for testing situational reactions and behaviors. As the paradigm shifts for the role of humans as drivers to the role of passengers in autonomous cars, Elbanhawi, Simic, and Jazar (2015) called the feelings surrounding this shift the *loss of controllability*. Personalities and situations that emphasize this paradigm shift and loss of controllability for the driver/passenger are areas of tension worth studying closer for their impact on the user experience in AVs.

Another research and theory-building approach is to view situation-centered aggressive driving examples with different contextual variables, such as user frustration levels, environmental cues, and vehicle features and capabilities. Then, there is also a specialized area of situation-centered research that examines vehicle characteristics and the influence they have on the aggressive behaviors of the driver. For example, a driver's perceived anonymity—as behind tinted car windows—elicits more aggressive driving behaviors (e.g., sudden acceleration) (Ellison-Potter et al., 2001). Therefore, design concepts that encourage a sense of "privacy"—like creating car interiors with cues and affordances to treat the space as an extension of the user's home—must address a balance between the idea of user seclusion and their concealment from others, and furthermore, how these different concepts may be associated with negative behaviors encouraged by the user's perceived anonymity while in the vehicle.

Chris Urmson, the head of Google's self-driving car program, has said, "The hope is you get to the point [in a driverless car] where you're on your phone or reading your book or talking to a loved one instead [of being anxious]. So, the priority moves to your interaction in life from how you're lane-changing on the freeway. I guess if you can make that time in the vehicle more meaningful and useful, maybe you don't worry as much about the time you're spending in it" (Jaffe, 2014). Whereas other forms of transportation that may have historically allowed for similar behaviors (such as train travel or other public transport) because they relieve the user of the task of driving, people create very different behavioral and social associations between public and shared spaces (e.g., a bus) versus a privately owned space. With the overall shift for the users from driver to passenger in mind, this chapter takes a path toward examining the situation-centered approach of identifying future iterations of road rage, with a focus on the user experience in autonomous cars.

New road rage: home away from home

The concept of a car's interior space will change to fit its new role as a space used not just for transportation but as a space for rest, entertainment, or work. One way to examine how people will interact with and relate to cars in a new way, beyond ownership or transportation or even as symbols of freedom or personal identity, is the space of study around the concept of human *territoriality* behaviors. Furthermore, in the framework of examining road rage through the lens of territoriality, the scope should necessarily narrow to a primary actor or actors within the vehicle first engaging in aggressive behaviors, so territoriality in terms of individual or small groups, rather than larger sets of participants.

A *territory* may be defined as a space used, controlled, marked/personalized, and defended by an individual or groups. The control that people attempt to enforce over their territory is a type of social regulation behavior through defining bounded areas of ownership. Territorial behaviors are part of how society functions, by marking spaces for needs like privacy or specific uses, and for establishing relationships such as ownership of a particular thing or space. In other words, the basic concept of territoriality is central to human culture and is used to regulate many social interactions. The value in territoriality behaviors is the establishment of some agreed upon spaces for specific functions or activities. Additionally, privacy is safeguarded in this protected or guarded personal space or *territory*. The result of successful territory defense is, of course, the creation of a safe space from others who are deemed unknown and/or dangerous.

However, feelings surrounding the ownership aspects of territory can also elicit negative individual or group behaviors and attitudes based on their perception of control and ownership (Gifford, 2007) of the space and any violation of those boundaries.

Altman and Chemers (1984) proposed territory and *territorial response* can be defined by these characteristics:

1. A place or object that is controlled and owned on a temporary or permanent basis.
2. The place or object may be small or large.
3. Ownership is by a person or group.
4. The territory can serve any of several functions, including social (status, identity, family, stability) and physical functions (child-rearing, food regulation, food storage).
5. Territories are often personalized or marked.
6. Defense may occur when territorial boundaries are violated. (pp. 121−122).

From this list, it is possible to make some additional conclusions. The concept of *territoriality* is

- highly place-specific;
- socially structured, constructed, supported, and maintained;
- within small, in-person groups of people interacting in the same space, or at least between people acknowledging the perceived boundaries of the owned space or thing;
- dependent upon temporal duration of owner(s) in the space.

Using this framework of understanding spaces then, it is possible to view even traditional cars as things people include in their territorial behaviors.

Altman and Chemers (1984) further explain that territorial behaviors have two main functions:

(1) Establishing, maintaining, and expressing personal identity of the "owner" or owners
(2) To regulate social interactions between people. As to the former, distinguishing a car as unique from similar models via articles like bumper stickers, custom designs, placing stuffed animals on the dashboard, and decorating the rearview mirror can all be examples of expression of the owner's personal identity. The latter point emphasizes the evolution of human territorial behaviors as a way of regulating social interaction. The creation of territorial boundaries and the related behaviors are a way of managing aggressive activities by requiring things like planning and anticipating the behavior of others.

Certainly, not all territories are valued the same by people. Individuals are not likely to regard a shared public space such as a retail store or train station in the same way as their own home.

Territorial behavior has been described as a typology of three nondiscrete categories: primary, secondary, and public (Altman, 1975; Altman, Vinsel, & Brown, 1981). In this model, *primary territories* are private places where the owner has exclusive rights to use or share the space. The classical example of a primary space is the home, a space easily personalized. *Secondary territories* are identified as semipublic spaces where someone interacts with familiar and/ or geographically close people such as friends, acquaintances, or neighbors, regularly. If the secondary territory is not personalized by the regular users, conflicts over ownership of that space may arise. An example of a secondary territory might be a local pub, or a private club. The category of *public territory* is a space where (almost) any person may be allowed access if they follow the norms of the territory; an example of a public territory is a public park.

The relationship between territoriality and emotion is an important one. Often, behaviors associated with territoriality are closely linked with emotions such as anger and fear, connected to the actions that surround establishing, distinguishing, and protecting or preserving territory, such as marking and defending them. Territorial boundaries that are violated can lead to feelings of loss, invasion/victimization, or other states of being that may seem to extend beyond any material value of the actual territory, underscoring the emotional connection to the space (Altman & Chemers, 1984). Therefore, understanding the emotions surrounding territorial behaviors and conditions that incite and/or support them is important to help people in the autonomous car industry understand why users might defend territories, or when, or even how they define territorial boundaries initially, and what might constitute a threat to that territory. Focusing research on analyzing these lived situations in autonomous car interaction experiences can lead to developing targeted interventions for reducing high-risk autonomous car user behaviors such as overriding AI systems for aggressive or retaliatory purposes at other people on the road.

People intuitively understand that owning a car is more than a series of economic or practical decisions, but also an emotionally invested set of experiences that have to do with the complexities of using a space that is associated closely with the ideas of freedom, control, independence, privacy, power, protection, and self-expression while also entrenched in cultures around the world as symbols of freedom, fashion, and sexual virility (Gartman, 2004; O'Connell, 1998; O'Dell, 1997; Sandqvist, 1997; Urry, 2000). Certainly, like a great deal of other consumer products, cars are marketed and designed to evoke emotional states such as excitement and desire, and to entice people to purchase them in the first place (Desmet, Heckert, & Jacobs, 2000; Haug, 1986), and want to associate them with their own personal identity (Belk, 1992). Using territoriality behaviors as a framework for understanding how people interact with their cars acknowledges the way people feel about their time in a car, which can give insights into the cause of their actions. Neglecting a significant component of how people interact with vehicles—their emotions—is the same as ignoring a substantial part of peoples' relationship with cars, which is not only meaningful to the user but also influences a series of endless personal decisions made about car ownership and driving.

Reducing dangerous driving cannot be achieved by simply shifting all or the bulk of the driving to AI because no technology can eliminate the real world factors in an endless variety of user experiences and situations on the road, some of which will lead to passenger frustration. As Fraine, Smith, and Zinkiewisz (1999) stated, "....people will frequently become impatient, intolerant, and angry" when their preferred path is obstructed (e.g., when a tree falls in the road). Cars are not only viewed as a means of transportation but also are associated with the user's "unimpeded progress" (Fraine et al., 1999), and those impediments can come in many unpredictable forms. To improve user experiences and general road safety, it is therefore imperative to investigate the new overall relationships of user to autonomous cars, and how people interact with them in their new role as passenger. Undoubtedly, it will take years of shifting culturally to the use of cars with different levels of autonomy as the dominant choice in consumer vehicles. In these culturally formative years, human drivers will share the road with autonomously driven vehicles, and it is likely this intermingling of human-centered versus AI-centered driving will create unanticipated challenges for car design, policy and law development, safety standards reviews, and city and road planning. It is not too early to begin investigating the possible consequences (as well as benefits) of unleashing autonomous cars into a market that is culturally unprepared in many ways.

In that case, many questions for possible inquiry into this specific user experience emerge. While traditional road rage may manifest in driver-centered decisions such as aggressive driving, what dangerous or negative behaviors (if any) will emerge among users as a recognizable pattern (like the actions of road rage) when people in an autonomous car are not actively engaged in driving? What, if anything, will trigger expressions of anger or frustration related to interactions in transit via an autonomous car? What will these new expressions of road rage look like, if aggressive driving is taken out of control of the users via an AI-controlled user kill switch? What situations would be acceptable to people for a car to ever take control away from a human?

When discussing autonomous cars as a context for interactions and a medium for design, the concept of territoriality behaviors associated with autonomous cars fits closely with ideas around emotional attachment to products and place. Historically, cars have been studied as possible vectors of emotional attachment for a user to a *product* rather than a place (Kressmann et al., 2006), or similarly, as a *possession* that is owned (Gatersleben, 2007; Oliver & Westbrook, 1993). Peoples' relationships to cars has been framed commonly as a consumer product; however, as discussed in this chapter, human interaction with cars is about to change significantly, so this model may be revised accordingly to offer place attachment in tandem with product attachment to adjust as a framework of understanding user interactions with a car as a work or living space and therefore, potentially considered a primary territory as well.

Product attachment investigates the existence of any emotional ties between a person and a thing or an object or product. Emotional attachment is a construct focused on a person's relationship with a thing that person believes is special, unique, has endured over time, and the need to remain in close physical proximity to that object (Ainsworth & Bell, 1970; Ainsworth, Blehar, Waters, & Wall, 2015; Bowlby, 1980). Attachment differs from other consumer behavior constructs—like territoriality—because it focuses on the consumer's relationship with a specific object. It is complementary to the notion of territoriality because of an overlap in similar emotions and behaviors related to the territory or object of attachment, such as an extension of personal identity, a relationship that exists over a period of time (not a fleeting interaction), a sense of shared history, and a sense of displacement, discomfort, or loss when separated from that space or thing or person (Ainsworth & Bell, 1970; Ainsworth et al., 2015; Bowlby, 1980; Carpenter, 2016).

When a person has deemed an object to be irreplaceable, it has a meaning for the owner not present in similar objects even if they are structurally identical. For example, many people own the same model of car released in the same year and manufactured at the same plant, but an owner may get emotionally attached to their specific car even if it is mechanically identical to all the other cars in that model's fleet. Reasons for this user attachment are linked with factors also present in aspects of determining territorial behaviors, such as marking behavior. For example, in the process of developing emotional attachment to a thing, users customize their cars with unique identifiers to distinguish their car from identical models, and acting as an extension of the owner's identity through self-expression, as with items like bumper stickers (Belk, 1988). There is a close relationship between territoriality and attachment.

People can become emotionally attached to a product irrespective of its intended function (Carpenter, 2016), which also makes it useful for examining a rapidly changing technology, like car autonomy. It is important to distinguish this concept further because *place attachment* is the emotional connection people develop for specific places. Attachment to place has often looked at human relationships with private residences or geographically bounded communities and environments (Devine-Wright, 2009; Hidalgo & Hernandez, 2001). A commonality across attachment theory has generally been an agreement that a main characteristic of the concept of attachment is the desire to maintain physical proximity to the object of attachment (Ainsworth & Bell, 1970; Ainsworth et al., 2015; Bowlby, 1980).

Models of attachment to place are concerned with the meaningfulness of the environment to a person or group, the social and individual human—place interactions and experiences that precede the development of this meaning, and the patterns of behaviors that emerge as part of this bond. Territorial behaviors are focused on access and control of the specific space in question; it is a system of beliefs and behaviors that are more than instinct and has very specific goals, such as keeping the territory as a safe space. Although territoriality is concerned with a particular bounded environment whereas attachment is focused on a thing/object outside the self, it is clear that both attachment and territorial functioning involve similar processes for user involvement, and the two concepts share a similar function for people safeguarding their personal safety, although perhaps in different ways.

There is an intersection of attachment and territoriality factors in user experiences with cars that already exists in the common relationship between owner and traditional car:

- Duration of time spent in the car; a sense of shared history with that specific vehicle.
- Marking the car as a belonging; believing the car is unique among similar cars.
- Deeming the car a place that affords privacy, safety, an extension of home or self; feeling the car is a safe haven and offers security.
- Defending the car when it is impeded, intruded, or encroached upon; separation distress when physical proximity to the car is inhibited or prevented (e.g., car is in an accident).

If the car is perceived as primary territory, then intrusions into it as a territory or another impedance of its use will be viewed very negatively, and it is likely a strong defense or series of defensive behaviors will follow. The theory of a car space as primary territory implies that people view people in other cars as a sociological *other* (Mead, 1934; Okolie, 2003). It is possible, then, that further research will reveal that mitigating territorial behaviors through design may reduce user aggressive tendencies.

Killer app

The idea of an AI kill switch for human control of a car is complicated in its ethical considerations. While it is possible that an autonomous car may be kitted with ways of gauging a user's mental and emotional state via various biofeedback (and even mood predictive) sensors, at best this is a technical intervention, not a solution to the actual issues of human behaviors associated with road rage.

Like some other technologies, autonomous cars are both mediums of social relations and produce social relations. While territoriality behavior research has been used as a lens for traditional automobiles, it is likely that new concepts for car interiors and the roles of the users will change significantly as cars turn to more autonomous processes, relieving the driver of many of the cognitive and social responsibilities of driving. Yet the changing role of the user in the driving process does not remove the human factors altogether, meaning there is still room for disruption in transportation situations, and these will sometimes elicit user frustration, anger, or other negative stress-related feelings and emotions that could further translate to aggressive behaviors.

Szlemko et al. (2008) have provided research about user perceptions of the nonautonomous car as primary territory, predicting the supporting users' territorial behaviors and the link to attachment theory as a closely related concept to user perceptions about their car as a defendable place.

While these premises have not been tested in longitudinal research situations with autonomous cars to date, this chapter has presented an initial attempt at building a framework for understanding these concepts of territoriality, emotional attachment, and user experience in relation to the new iterations of car roles and designs, although certainly more work is required. Additionally, the possibility of new ways of manifesting user aggressive behaviors raises design questions about the use of kill switches, whether for the user or the car's AI. Major ethical and practical challenges are at stake when discussing an AI kill switch for users who would require the car's AI to have a flawless understanding of human experience and the ability to apply rules and actions in this vein when discussing the AI-triggered kill switch for erratic user driving.

Moreover, including a mandatory human-controlled kill switch for the AI in a consumer vehicle depends upon the human will to resist obstructing the AI controlling the driving, and controlling aggressive driving behaviors. While these possible scenarios raise a multitude of new questions and issues, it is a set of potentially common circumstances worthy of further consideration.

Acknowledgments

Thank you to Dr. Patrick Lin and the Ethics + Emerging Sciences research group at California State Polytechnic in San Louis Obispo, CA, for their continued encouragement. This material is based upon the work supported by the National Science Foundation under Grant No. 1522240. Any opinions, findings, and conclusions or recommendations expressed in this material are those of the author and do not necessarily reflect the views of the National Science Foundation.

References

Ainsworth, M. D. S., & Bell, S. M. (1970). Attachment, exploration, and separation: Illustrated by the behavior of one-year-olds in a strange situation. *Child Development*, 49—67.

Ainsworth, M. D. S., Blehar, M. C., Waters, E., & Wall, S. N. (2015). *Patterns of attachment: A psychological study of the strange situation.* Psychology Press.

Altman, I. (1975). *The environment and social behavior: Privacy, personal space, territoriality and crowding.* Monterey, CA: Brooks/Cole.

Altman, I., Vinsel, A., & Brown, B. B. (1981). Dialectic conceptions in social psychology: An application to social penetration and privacy regulation. In *Advances in experimental social psychology* (Vol. 14, pp. 107—160). Academic Press.

Altman, I., & Chemers, M. M. (1984). *Culture and environment*. Monterey, CA: Brooks/Cole.

Automobile Association (AA). (September, 1996). Road rage. UK: Transport Research Laboratory.

Belk, R. W. (1988). Possessions and the extended self. *Journal of Consumer Research, 15*(2), 139—168.

Belk, R. W. (1992). Attachment to possessions. In *Place attachment* (pp. 37—62). Boston, MA: Springer.

Bowlby, J. (1980). *Attachment and loss* (Vol. 3). New York: Basic Books.

Bryant, R. (November 20, 2015). Bored drivers can snooze at the wheel in Volvo's Concept 26 self-driving car. *Dezeen*. Retrieved from https://www.dezeen.com/2015/11/20/volvo-concept- 26-self-driving-autonomous-car-transport-design/.

Carpenter, J. (2016). *Culture and human-robot interaction in militarized spaces: A war story*. UK: Francis & Taylor.

Chuang, T. (March 26, 2017). The first self-driving car will debut in three years, but will you want to buy the first one? *The Denver Post*. Retrieved from http://www.denverpost.com/2017/03/26/self-driving-car-debut/.

Connelly, K. (June 25, 2016). *Look, no hands! On the autobahn in Audi's driverless car*. The Guardian. Retrieved from https://www.theguardian.com/technology/2016/jun/25/look-no-hands-on-the-autobahn-in-audis-driverless-car.

Desmet, P. M., Hekkert, P., & Jacobs, J. J. (2000). When a car makes you smile: Development and application of an instrument to measure product emotions. In *NA-advances in consumer research* (Vol. 27).

Devine-Wright, P. (2009). Rethinking NIMBYism: The role of place attachment and place identity in explaining place-protective action. *Journal of Community & Applied Social Psychology, 19*(6), 426—441.

Elbanhawi, M., Simic, M., & Jazar, R. (2015). In the passenger seat: Investigating ride comfort measures in autonomous cars. *IEEE Intelligent Transportation Systems Magazine, 7*(3), 4—17.

Ellison-Potter, P., Bell, P., & Deffenbacher, J. L. (2001). The effects of trait anger, anonymity, and aggressive stimuli on aggressive driving behavior. *Journal of Applied Social Psychology, 31*, 431—443.

Fraine, G., Smith, S., & Zinkiewicz, L. (2000). The private car: A home on the road?. Paper presented at the third national conference on injury prevention and control, Brisbane, 9—12 May 1999 In R. McLure (Ed.), *Readings in injury prevention and control: Proceedings of the third national conference on injury prevention and control* (pp. 63—66). Brisbane: Centre of National Research on Disability and Rehabilitation Medicine.

Foot, P. (1967). *The problem of abortion and the doctrine of double effect*. Oxford Review, Number 5.

Garrett, O. (March 3, 2017). 10 million self-driving cars will hit the road by 2020; Here's how to profit. *Forbes*. Retrieved from https://www.forbes.com/sites/oliviergarret/2017/03/03/10-million-self-driving-cars-will-hit-the-road-by-2020-heres-how-to-profit/#5aa8593c7e50.

Gartman, D. (2004). Three ages of the automobile the cultural logics of the car. *Theory, Culture & Society, 21*(4—5), 169—195.

Gatersleben, B. (2007). Affective and symbolic aspects of car use. In *Threats from car traffic to the quality of urban life: Problems, causes and solutions* (pp. 219—233). West Yorkshire, UK: Emerald Group Publishing Limited.

Gifford, R. (2007). *Environmental psychology: Principles and practice*. Victoria, BC: Optimal Books.

Haug, W. (1986). *Critique of commodity aesthetics: Sexuality and advertising in capitalist society*. Minneapolis, MN: University of Minnesota Press.

Hidalgo, M. C., & Hernandez, B. (2001). Place attachment: Conceptual and empirical questions. *Journal of Environmental Psychology, 21*(3), 273–281.

How will the interior of driverless cars look? Experts weigh in. (May 12, 2016). Quoted. Retrieved from https://www.thezebra.com/insurance-news/2912/what-will-the-interior-of- driverless-cars-look-like/.

Jablansky, J. (December 16, 2016). Mercedes-Benz chief design officer explains the future of autonomous vehicles. *Architectural Digest.* Retrieved from http://www.roadandtrack.com/new- cars/future-cars/a30235/with-self-driving-cars-its-the-interior-that-matters/.

Jaffe, E. (May 30, 2014). *Will self-driving cars have road rage?* CityLab. Retrieved from https://www.citylab.com/life/2014/05/will-self-driving-cars-have-road-rage/371709/.

Keen, A. (May 15, 2013). *The future of travel: How driverless cars could change everything.* CNN Business Traveler. Retrieved from http://www.cnn.com/2013/05/14/business/bussiness-traveller-futurecast-driverless-car/.

Kottasova, I. (January 12, 2017). Europe calls for mandatory "kill switch" on robots. *Money.* Retrieved from http://money.cnn.com/2017/01/12/technology/robot-law-killer-switch-taxes/.

Kressmann, F., Sirgy, M. J., Herrmann, A., Huber, F., Huber, S., & Lee, D. J. (2006). Direct and indirect effects of self-image congruence on brand loyalty. *Journal of Business Research, 59*(9), 955–964.

Lawton, R., & Nutter, A. (2002). A comparison of reported levels and expression of anger in everyday and driving situations. *British journal of psychology, 93*(3), 407–423.

Litman, T. (2019). *Autonomous vehicle implementation predictions.* Victoria Transport Policy Institute.

Lupton, D. (2002). Road rage: Drivers' understandings and experiences. *Journal of Sociology, 38*, 275–290.

Mead, G. H. (1934). *Mind, self and society* (Vol. 111). Chicago: University of Chicago Press.

O'Dell, T. (1997). *Culture unbound: Americanization and everyday life in Sweden.* Lund, Sweden: Nordic Academic Press.

Okolie, A. C. (2003). Identity: Now you don't see it; now you do. In an Introduction to the Special Issue. *Identity: An International Journal of Theory and Research, 3*(1), 1–7.

Oliver, R., & Westbrook, R. (1993). Profiles of consumer emotions and satisfaction in car ownership and usage. *Emotion, 6*, 12–27.

Overly, S. (April 5, 2017). The unexpected ways our lives will change when cars drive themselves. *The Washington Post.* Retrieved from https://www.washingtonpost.com/news/innovations/wp/2017/04/05/the-unexpected-ways-our- lives-will-change-when-cars-drive-themselves/.

O'Connell, S. (1998). *The car and British society: Class, gender and motoring, 1896–1939.* Manchester, UK: Manchester University Press.

Roberts, J. (February 16, 2015). *What happens when a self-driving car meets a road rage driver?.* Retrieved from https://theconversation.com/what-happens-when-a-self-driving-car-meets-a-road-rage-driver-37150.

Sabin, D. (March 18, 2017). Autonomous cars will be "private, intimate spaces": Yes, designers are talking about how to facilitate car sex. *Inverse.* Retrieved from https://www.inverse.com/article/29214-autonomous-car-design-sex.

Sandqvist, A. (1997). *The appeal of automobiles: Human desires and the proliferation of cars.* Stockholm: Communications Research Board.

Smart, R., Stoduto, G., Mann, R., & Adlaf, E. M. (December, 2004). Road rage experience and behavior: Vehicle, exposure, and driver factors. *Traffic Injury Prevention, 5*(4), 343–348.

Society of Motor Manufacturer's (SMMT). (March 30, 2017). Connected & autonomous vehicles will improve quality of life for 6 in 10 people with limited mobility, finds new study. In *News.*

Retrieved from https://www.smmt.co.uk/2017/03/connected-and-autonomous-vehicles- will-improve-quality-of-life-for-six-in-10-people-with-limited-mobility-finds-new-study/.

Society of Motor Vehicles (SMMT). (2017). *Levels of autonomy (scale)*. Retrieved from https:// www.smmt.co.uk/industry-topics/technology-innovation/connected-autonomous-vehicles/.

Springsteen, B. (2016). *Born to run*. New York, NY: Simon & Schuster.

Stoklosa, A. (December 11, 2013). Not even flying is better": Rinspeed introduces autonomous car interior for less attentive future. *Car and Driver*. Retrieved from http://blog.caranddriver.com/not-even-flying-is-better-rinspeed-introduces-autonomous-car- interior-concept-for-a-less-attentive-future/.

Szlemko, W. J., Benfied, J. A., Bell, P. A., Defenbacher, J. L., & Troup, L. (2008). Territorial markings as a predictor of driver aggression and road rage. *Journal of Applied Social Psychology, 38*(6), 1664–1688.

Urry, J. (2000). *Sociology beyond societies: Mobilities for the twenty-first century*. London: Routledge.

Weiss, C. C. (March 27, 2017). Eve *"vision car" opens new door on autonomous car design*. New Atlas. Retrieved from http://newatlas.com/nio-eve-autonomous-car/48585/.

Will cars of the future be portable living spaces?. (January 24, 2017). Hyundai.news. Retrieved from https://www.hyundai.news/eu/technology/will-cars-of-the-future-be-portable-living- spaces/.

Yu, J., Evans, P. C., & Perfetti, L. (2004). Road aggression among drinking drivers: Alcohol and non-alcohol effects on aggressive driving and road rage. *Journal of Criminal Justice, 32*(5), 421–430.

Further reading

Belk, R. W. (2004). *Men and their machines. ACR North American Advances*.

Millennials embrace ride-hailing for pave a new path for mobility. (November 16, 2016). ReportLinker. Retrieved from http://www.reportlinker.com/insight/mobility-services.html.

Sharkin, B. (2004). Road rage: Risk factors, assessment, and intervention strategies. *Journal of Counseling and Development, 82*, 191–198.

Shumaker, S. A., & Taylor, R. B. (1983). Toward a clarification of people-place relationships: A model of attachment to place. In N. R. Feimer, & E. S. Geller (Eds.), *Environmental psychology. Directions and perspectives* (Vol. 2, pp. 19–25). New York: Praeger.

Sundstrom, E., & Altman, I. (1989). Physical environments and work-group effectiveness. *Research in Organizational Behavior, 2*, 175–209.

Swan, M. (2015). Connected car: Quantified self becomes quantified car. *Journal of Sensor and Actuator Networks, 4*(1), 2–29.

Chapter 5

Development and current state of robotic surgery

Rana Pullatt[1], Benjamin L. White[2]

[1]Department of Surgery, Medical University of South Carolina, Charleston, SC, USA; [2]General
Surgery, Medical University of South Carolina, Charleston, SC, USA

Chapter outline

Introduction

If you undergo a surgical procedure in the health-care systems of today's world, it is entirely plausible, and becoming increasingly likely, that your surgeon will perform the operation with the assistance of robotic technology that, even in its relative infancy, confers major advantages to both the surgeon and the patient. What does it actually mean to undergo a robotic surgery? Perhaps fueled by imagery from science fiction, there seems to be a pervasive public misunderstanding regarding robotic surgery and what is currently possible. The results of an interesting survey published in 2016 in the journal *Surgical Endoscopy* showed that nearly 25% of nonphysician responders and 5% of physicians believed that the robots perform operations autonomously. While such a possibility is not outside the realm of the imaginable, and the idea of incorporating machine learning offers hope for future feasibility, the reality is that the robotic surgical system of today is simply a tool at the disposal of the modern surgeon, albeit an incredibly powerful one. We believe the more accurate term is robotic-*assisted* surgery, which more poignantly describes the relationship between the surgeon who remotely controls the movements from the surgeon console and the robotic platform that interprets, scales, and performs the movements in the operative field. While our surgical robots are not yet operating

Living with Robots. https://doi.org/10.1016/B978-0-12-815367-3.00005-0

independently of the surgeon, setting this as the benchmark for what impresses us does a disservice to the immeasurable complexity of the technology currently in use, and lessen its impact on the field. In short, the robotic platforms we use today are already making us better surgeons, augmenting our technical performance in ways that are difficult to overstate.

The origins of robotic surgery date to the early 1980s, as experimental robotic systems with applications in neurosurgery and orthopedics found niches and laid the foundation for newer robots, first for maneuvering and driving laparoscopic cameras, and eventually fully integrated operative systems similar to what is still in use today. The development of robotic technology including microelectronics, computing, sensors, and digital imaging and displays occurred synchronously and in parallel with the advent of laparoscopy, which revolutionized surgery with minimally invasive "keyhole" operative technique that confers innumerable benefits to patients and surgeons over traditional open surgeries.

While traditional laparoscopy was refined and widely adopted in the late 1980s and early 1990s, innovators were already at work developing new and exciting uses for robotic surgical technology that progressed from purpose-driven applications like patient positioning and voice command camera operation to the immensely beneficial master—slave operating platforms still in use today. Robotic surgery, most notably the *da Vinci* platform, evolved to address several of the key problems with laparoscopic surgery and improve even further on the surgeon-augmenting capability of performing complex operations through small incisions in previously challenging to access areas of the body. The details of these differences and the advantages of robotic-assisted surgery over traditional laparoscopy will be covered further in this chapter.

The current state of robotic surgery represents the aggregate of centuries of growth in surgical and general medical knowledge, development of surgical technology and minimally invasive techniques, and the advent of computer and robotic technology capable of augmenting surgeon performance. While a successful operation still requires the knowledge, expertise, and skill sets of the surgeon to ensure a good outcome, current robotic-assisted surgical technology confers innumerable benefits over traditional, open, and even modern minimally invasive operative techniques that represent the standard of care, and the future endeavors offer even more exciting potential. However, to fully appreciate the benefits of robotic-assisted surgery, it is critical to understand how surgery has changed, and the series of revolutionary technological advancements that brought us to where we are today.

The hand of the surgeon

The surgical treatment of disease dates to the earliest recorded human history. The nature of our biology and the pathology that afflicts us require that the treatment of certain diseases and conditions be performed not with medicines, alterations in lifestyle, or pleas to the heavens for reprieve, but with the physical manipulation of the body and the tissues that comprise it. Beginning during the European enlightenment, within the last several hundred years, surgery has evolved from the days of the barber surgeon and rudimentary, fruitless, and often horrifyingly painful procedures to an era in which the practice of surgery has been fully incorporated into a scientific discipline, modernized and mastered. With a background of knowledge of anatomy, physiology, and pathology, and the judgment and skills acquired over a minimum of 20,000 h of supervised postdoctoral training, surgeons of various disciplines can remove a tumor from any part of the body, repair the arteries of a bleeding wounded soldier, operate on a fetus in the womb, transplant living organs, alter anatomy to effect massive weight loss, or replace a joint that has lost its function. While in many cases surgery can definitively cure what nonsurgical treatments can only manage, this is not without risk.

The hand of the surgeon is hard, but healing.
Walter Map, 11th century Welsh monk

Even within the broader field of medicine, surgery is quite unique. In consenting to undergo an operation, the patient entrusts the surgeon to perform a treatment that, unlike the counsel or prescription of a physician, requires physically altering or removing one or multiple parts of the body. Even in the most extreme versions of medical therapy, chemotherapeutic drugs that alter cell physiology and are designed and made to destroy cells from within, the prescriber is divorced from the actual mechanism of action and the physical delivery of the treatment. A medicine is *given* from a physician *to* a patient; an operation is *performed* by a surgeon *on* a patient and is therefore not immune to the faults and limitations of the human. The process of obtaining informed consent prior to any operation mandates a discussion regarding not only the benefits of the planned procedure but also the alternatives and the risks involved. Surgery causes pain. Unintentional consequences are far too common. Operations can be unsuccessful or aborted for a litany of reasons. In the worst circumstances, surgeries can maim, debilitate, and kill. Accepting these risks is the cost of the promise for potential gain.

For millennia, the performance of surgery and the success of its outcomes have been limited to the amalgamation of the patient's individual circumstance and the surgeon and his acquired knowledge, experience, judgment, and technical ability. Put succinctly, the success or failure, cure or ongoing affliction, and in many cases life or death of the patient, rest solely in the hands of the surgeon. Physical and mental attributes like eyesight, natural tremor, rest, and level of focus are immutable factors in the technical success of an operation, yet vary wildly from surgeon to surgeon, and sometimes even day to day in an individual. Experience, operative judgment, and ability to improvise and adapt to complications or unusual circumstances are all hard to objectively measure, and yet carry enormous implications of surgical outcomes.

Centuries of surgical innovation

In the last several decades, broad technological advancements and adaptations of those technologies within the field have pushed the boundaries of what is possible in surgery. The incorporation of technology has allowed surgery to advance beyond its historical constraints, and feats previously impossible to imagine have become routine. From the simplest problem-based solutions like methods to monitor and augment patient temperature intraoperatively with the growing understanding that this plays in issues like drug metabolism, blood clotting, and wound healing to population-based system-wide solutions to problems like morbid obesity and its associated comorbidities with the advent of bariatric surgical procedures, technology has revolutionized the care provided to patients. Standards of care have been rewritten. Entire industries have evolved to develop, refine, and support new technologies that have extended the field of surgery to allow new techniques and innovative procedures that augment the capabilities of the surgeon to deliver care to his patients. A heightened understanding of the impossible complexity of human physiology driven by research and the scientific method, coupled with the availability of new technology developed in the private and military sectors, has driven the development of new and incredible changes to the practice of surgery.

Although innovation and scientific progress have been at the heart of the field of medicine since its modernization, most notably with radiographic imaging, asepsis, and anesthesia credited with revolutionizing the field of surgery in the mid-19th century and allowing for the development of many of the operations still done today, the technical aspects of the actual performance of surgery remained largely unchanged between the 1850s and the 1970s. Surgeries were performed by direct visualization via large, open incisions. Recovery was long and painful, hospital stays long and fraught with risk of hospital-acquired infections, certain areas of the body were still considered inaccessible, and tissue damage and scarring were accepted as necessary evils in the delivery of care. Around the turn of the century, hospitals and surgery were in a place that would be recognizable today. Open operations were being performed under general anesthesia, liberating the field of surgery from the horrifying pain its subjects previously endured. Yet even then, the groundwork was being laid for laparoscopic and other minimally invasive surgical techniques that would reduce bleeding, minimize tissue damage, reduce post-operative pain, shorten length of hospitalization, and ultimately eventually replace open operations as the accepted standard of care.

In many cases, as in the aforementioned examples, the incorporation of medical technology has bridged the gap between knowledge or acknowledgment of a problem and the delivery of clinical patient care, but some advances have even allowed for the evolution of surgical care beyond the limitations of human capability. No more apparent is this improvement in the delivery of care to patients as a direct result of surgeon-augmenting technological advances than with the concept of minimally invasive surgery. Endoscopy, from the Latin *endo-*, within, and *-scopy*, to observe, is the use of an instrument to see inside a hollow organ or body cavity, extending the human eye to diagnose and treat within organs and areas previously inaccessible, or only accessible with major operations. Endoscopy is now ubiquitous in modern medicine, with broad applications spanning medical and surgical sub-specialties including esophagogastroduodenoscopy and colonoscopy to view and manipulate the upper and lower GI tracts, laparoscopy and thoracoscopy to view and operate within the abdomen and chest, bronchoscopy to see within the upper and lower airways, cystoscopy and hysteroscopy to view within the urinary and female reproductive systems, and arthroscopy to see within joints. Although endoscopy was considered experimental and had very limited applications for much of its history until the 1970s and 1980s, an examination of its pioneers and sequential advancements, each building upon the last, reveals a common spirit of curiosity and innovation shared with the robotic surgeons of today and serves to illuminate the immutable forward trajectory of the field.

While physicians and surgeons for centuries have imagined peering inside the human body, the origins of genuine endoscopy can be traced to the mid-1800s. German physician Adolph Kussmaul, revered for additions to multiple fields in medicine, is credited with the first attempt at gastroscopy, peering within the stomach of a living patient, in 1868. Prior to the advent of electricity, he used the rays of a lamp reflected down a series of lenses within a rigid metal tube to peer down the esophagus and into the stomach of a local famous sword swallower. Subsequent development of electric light allowed others to experiment and advance the technology toward clinical applications. One major early limitation was thermal injury on the tissues being examined caused by the light source. This was overcome first in 1877 by German urologist Maximillian Nitze with an innovative solution. He placed a super-heated platinum wire within the quill of a goose feather, sheathed within a metal tube containing lenses for magnification of the view, and cooled with a continuous flow of ice water. This instrument gained popularity with many diagnostic clinical applications that allowed the field of urology to modernize ahead of its time. This early cystoscope was borrowed and adapted by others for varying purposes in other fields of surgery and served as the earliest laparoscope to view structures within the abdomen. While peering inside the GI tract, bladder, and airways provided early physicians with new techniques for diagnosis and eventually for the performance of minor procedures, it was the advent and growth of minimally invasive surgery that would revolutionize the field of surgery and serve as the foundation for the development of current robotic-assisted surgical platforms.

Laparoscopy, commonly referred to as keyhole surgery, traces its earliest uses to the beginning of the 20th century, when prominent European surgeons began using the aforementioned cystoscope and endoscopes in novel ways. In 1910, Swedish physician Hans Christian Jaceobaeus published the first reports of diagnostic laparoscopy and thoracoscopy on humans, inserting the cysto-scope into the abdomen and chest to explore and aid in diagnosis. As word of his successes spread, many more began adopting and refining this technique across many surgical specialties. Gynecologists in particular found laparos-copy very useful not just for diagnosis, but for therapeutic purposes as well. French surgeon Raoul Palmer, who lived and practiced in Paris in the 1930s–1940s, was among the first to publish papers on laparoscopy and is credited with several advancements that are still widely used by minimally invasive surgeons today, most notably the use of the Veress needle to establish pneumoperitoneum, and the use of carbon dioxide rather than oxygen to insufflate the abdomen.

Inspired by Palmer's work, German gynecologist Kurt Semm pushed the field even further in the 1960s and 1970s, both in scope of work and inventions such as the electronic insufflator, and new techniques such as intracorporeal suturing. He is credited with developing multiple gynecologic laparoscopic surgeries, as well as the first laparoscopic appendectomy. Despite these incredible advancements that serve as the foundation for the basis of modern surgical technique, Semm was sharply criticized by his contemporaries, many of whom considered laparoscopic surgery experimental, even as far as calling it unethical. Nevertheless, laparoscopy spread around the world, and surgeons learned and got more comfortable with the technique, and eventually applied it to their own specialties.

Arguably the seminal moment in laparoscopic surgery was the invention of the charge-coupled device, or CCD, that allowed for video display and rapidly spread across all forms of endoscopy. In the operating room, this change meant that instead of the surgeon looking through the laparoscope eyepiece, now the surgeon and entire surgical team could see the same image clearly displayed in monitors set up around the room. Following this, the laparoscopic revolution began in earnest. In 1985, German surgeon Erci Muhe performed the first laparoscopic cholecystectomy (gallbladder removal); yet, like his pre-decessors, his accomplishment was vilified. The following year a pair of American surgeons in Marietta, Georgia, performed the first such case in the United States. Rapid acceleration in the technique's acceptance began. At the American College of Surgeons clinical congress in 1989, laparoscopic cho-lecystectomy was a featured exhibit, prompting enormous demand from sur-geons around the world for training in the new technique. Even the lay public saw the benefits of smaller incisions, faster recovery, fewer complications, and less pain, all of which laparoscopy promised over open surgery. Manufacturers of cameras and laparoscopic instruments struggled to keep up with demand, and in certain cases paid for surgeons to attend training courses in an economically driven effort to fan the flames of revolution. New applications for laparoscopy developed rapidly, including appendectomy, hernia repair, colon resections, stomach and esophageal surgeries, bariatric surgeries, and many more.

By the late 1990s very few abdominal operations had not been at least attempted with laparoscopic technique, and in fact a large percentage of open surgeries had been outright replaced as the standard of care by laparoscopy. While every operation has been individually studied and analyzed for open versus laparoscopic techniques, it is now generally acknowledged that the latter confers major advantages at minimum in terms of decreased hospital length of stay and fewer overall complications, and in certain operations even decreases procedure-related mortality. This understanding that less invasive procedures are better for patients continues to drive development of new medical technologies across all fields to push minimally invasive techniques to new limits.

Emergence of surgical robots

In the midst of the laparoscopic revolution in surgery, its successor was already well into development. The integration of robotic technology and minimally invasive surgery was on the minds of innovators as early as the late 1970s, who envisioned using emerging computer technology to make surgical procedures stable, accurate, and replicable, and augment the surgeon's technical performance. One of the key features of all robotic surgical systems to date has been stability and the elimination of tremor and unwanted movement, which improves surgical precision. Credited with being the first surgical robot in clinical use, the *Arthrobot*, developed in 1984 by the University of British Columbia's biomedical engineers James McEwen and Geof Auchinleck and orthopedic surgeon Brian Day, was a robotic arm attached to the patient's lower leg that upon voice commands would move the patient's leg to various positions. This allowed Dr. Day to focus entirely on the operation while the robot manipulated the joint, effectively taking the place of a surgical assistant who can fatigue over time. With voice recognition technology from Toshiba, a hydraulic arm, and controlled with two IBM computers, *Arthrobot* assisted in over 250 knee surgeries, beginning in March of 1985 and ultimately "retiring" in 1988 after a disappointing lack of academic or commercial interest. Sadly, *Arthrobot* was lost to history not only figuratively, but physically lost sometime around 2000.

Arthrobot, 1984; eldiario.es.

Nearly simultaneously, radiology researcher Yik San Kwoh of Memorial Medical Center in Long Beach, California, developed a software program to integrate CT imaging with an industrial robotic arm called the PUMA, built by Unimation, one of the first robot-producing companies in the world. The PUMA, an acronym for *programmable universal manipulation arm*, when synced with CT images was able to localize and calculate the exact angle, depth, and trajectory to biopsy lesions deep within brains. Whereas biopsying these lesions with open surgery required larger resections of skull and put the patient at risk for injuring blood vessels and adjacent brain tissue, the PUMA selected a precise path, stable platform for taking the biopsy, and remarkable accuracy that require only a tiny burr hole and reduced risks inherent in human error. This technique decreases complications and shortens length of stay following this procedure. Prior to performing the first procedure on a human in April 1985, Dr. Kwoh and the team of neurosurgeons practiced with PUMA by localizing small BBs within watermelons with pinpoint accuracy. Unimation was subsequently acquired by Westinghouse, who ceased production of the PUMA for medical purposes. However, this robotic-assisted adaptation of stereotactic biopsy inspired the development of several competitors, some of which are still used today. Additional early surgical robots in the late 1980s included the PROBOT, developed in England and used to perform transurethral prostate surgery, and ROBODOC, used by orthopedic surgeons to bore out femurs to accommodate hardware during hip replacements. ROBODOC, developed by Integrated Surgical Supplies in Sacramento, California, with collaboration from IBM research became the first surgical robot to be widely accepted and used, primarily in Europe. These early adaptations of robotics to the field of surgery are noteworthy for their innovation, but none had any real widespread use or long-lasting impact. What they did accomplish was professional and societal acceptance of the use of robots in surgery, and they drew the attention of powerful and well-funded organizations.

Dr. Kwoh and his PUMA 200.

The US military and NASA had interest in developing a system for telepresence surgery, or the ability to operate on soldiers, or astronauts in space, from a remote location. The idea of telemanipulation was not a new one, robotic arms controlled from remote locations had been used in industry for decades, primarily for dangerous work, like the handling of hazardous materials. The translation of that idea to surgery would ideally reduce battlefield mortality by immediately connecting wounded soldiers on the front lines to surgeons located remotely who could treat their injuries. Research on this concept was funded and carried out in parallel by multiple entities with various NASA contracts, NIH grants, and funding from the Pentagon's Defense Advanced Research Projects Agency (DARPA). Up to this point, robotic surgery had many exciting possible applications, but no genuine direction. The various systems previously described all had very specialized uses that precluded their gaining widespread adoption. Government funding began to focus surgical robotics work in the late 1980s and happened to coincide with the explosive growth of laparoscopy, punctuated by Dr. Mouret's laparoscopic cholecystectomy presentation at the American College of Surgeons meeting in 1989—the future of robotic surgery was clearly in augmenting and improving minimally invasive surgery.

To that end, the leading experts in the field began narrowing their focus on building robotic systems that could be controlled remotely, and simultaneously address some of the technical limitations of laparoscopy. Borrowing from earlier work in surgical robots that permitted stability and reduced motion, one of the first areas addressed was the handling of the laparoscopic camera, and the development of systems to obviate the need for a human assistant to hold and direct the camera to maintain the field of view. A group at the IBM Watson Research Center in New York led by Russell Taylor, who also contributed greatly to the ROBODOC, developed new robotic programming language and advanced automation of robotic motion. In collaboration with Johns Hopkins surgeon Mark Talamini, they developed the Laparoscopic Assistant Robotic System (LARS), which functioned as a "third hand" for the surgeon, holding the laparoscopic camera and controlled with a joystick. One key component of LARS was the development of Remote Center of Motion (RCM), a technical feature of robotic surgery wherein which there is a fixed point in space around which a mechanism can move, effectively functioning as a joint but without having to be physically fixed. RCM is one of the key components of the robotic systems still used today.

Another limitation of laparoscopy is the two-dimensional projection on the viewing monitors, which eliminates depth perception, a key ability of any surgeon to understand relationships of objects in three-dimensional space. Phil Green and the team at the Stanford Research Institute (SRI) in Menlo

Park, California, collaborating with Army surgeon John Bowersox and surgeons at Stanford University developed their telepresence surgical system, the first to use integrated stereoscopic three-dimensional viewing. Their controlling computer system also eliminated the fulcrum effect, or motion reversal, that comes with operating through the abdominal wall with rigid instruments in laparoscopy wherein which the surgeon must move their hand to the left, for example, in order for the instrument tip to move to the right. Eliminating the fulcrum effect makes robotic surgery far more intuitive for the surgeon and contributes to the shortened learning curve compared to laparoscopy.

While this still has yet to be achieved, they also made the first attempts at giving the surgeon haptic feedback, or the ability for the surgeon to feel how gently or tightly their instrument is gripping something. Restoring haptic feedback, translating the sense of touch through a surgical instrument, is considered by many robotic surgeons to be the "Holy Grail" in robotic surgery. Inspired by the DARPA vision for telesurgery, MIT professor Kenneth Salisbury and his Ph.D. candidate student Akhil Madhani were experimenting with haptics and developed a prototype called the "Black Falcon," a new robotic surgical arm. The key feature of the Black Falcon was the control mechanism, a separate hand piece manipulated remotely while viewing the slave arm on a monitor with images transmitted by a laparoscopic camera. This controlling hand piece was a major step forward in providing partial haptic feedback and set the industry standard in haptics for decades.

A key advantage of robotic surgical instruments is the degree of dexterity afforded to the surgeon that mimics, and in some ways exceeds, the dexterity of the human hand. Laparoscopic instruments have four degrees of motion: they can move in/out, left/right, up/down, and roll along their long axis, in addition to opening and closing of the instrument tip. This development occurred in parallel between groups in Europe and the United States. Gerhard Beuss and his team at the University of Karlsruhe developed a prototype called ARTEMIS, the robotic arm of which was equipped with additional joints near the instrument tips that afforded additional degrees of motion. Concurrently, MIT trained engineer Hari Nayar and his team at the NASA Jet Propulsion Laboratory in Pasadena, California, collaborated with a company founded by ophthalmologic surgeon Steve Charles called MicroDexterity Systems, Inc. to develop their robot-assisted microsurgery (RAMS) platform, a six-degree-of-freedom telemanipulator that they envisioned being used to perform microsurgery that restored the surgeon's full dexterity, and was also the first to sense and filter out tremor between the surgeon and the end of the robotic instrument, in a sense pushing even beyond the limits of human dexterity.

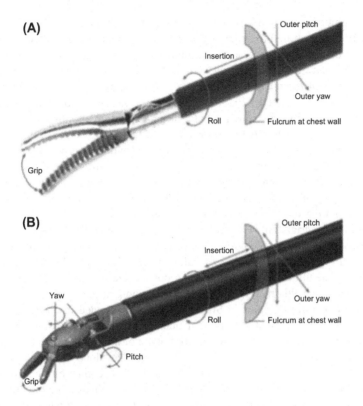

Two additional joints at the end of robotic instruments (below) afford additional dexterity and degrees of motion compared to laparoscopic instruments (above). *Image from Intuitive Surgical.*

By the early 1990s, the critical elements of robotic telesurgery— stable operating platforms; 3D optics; remotely manipulated robotic arms with dexterous operating tools; and the computer technology to sense, coordinate, and control them— were all in place. What followed was an engineering and legal arms race between two rival companies to realize the vision of a fully integrated robotic telesurgical system. The two rival variants of the same concept would push one another over the next decade toward the production and approval of commercially available products until a legal battle over patents led to their eventual merger.

From the lab to the operating room— ZEUS versus da Vinci

In 1992, University of California-Santa Barbara Ph.D. candidate Yulan Wang utilized grants from DARPA and a NASA backed contract from the JPL with the intent of furthering the military's goal of remote surgery, developing a surgical assistant for operating the laparoscope, similar to Russell Taylor's LARS, that he called AESOP, for Automated Endoscopic System for Optimal Positioning. Wang's company Computer Motion, Inc. patented AESOP and developed a product that would lead Computer Motion to become the preeminent commercially viable robotic surgery company in the 1990s. AESOP was modified to drive the laparoscopic camera manipulated by voice commands and approved for use on humans by the FDA in 1994. Computer Motion began acquiring proprietary technology and filed patents on multiple components of robotic surgery and began developing their integrated robotic surgical system dubbed ZEUS, a three-armed OR table-mounted system in which two surgeon-controlled robotic arms and a third holding the AESOP optics system, operated by the surgeon located in a workstation comprising the manipulator instruments and a monitor, viewed while wearing a pair of 3D glasses. Among its many achievements, the ZEUS control system was able to take surgeon movements and scale them down, making it ideally suited for very fine and microsurgical work. In 1995, a ZEUS prototype was demonstrated, and the following year it began testing on animal models and worked toward human trials. In 1998, ZEUS was used to complete the first completely endoscopic robotic procedure in Cleveland, OH, assisting gynecologic surgeons during the reconnection of a fallopian tube. Computer Motion set about achieving the ultimate goal before being commercially viable, FDA approval; they would lose this race to their only major competitor.

Up the California coast in Silicon Valley and founded in 1995 by physicians Frederick Moll and John Freund, and electrical engineer Robert Younge, Intuitive Surgical, Inc. was building a prototype of its own. After acquiring the requisite capital, the company licensed the SRI-developed technology, purchased the patent for Black Falcon, and established collaboration with MIT and IBM. Infatuated with Leonardo da Vinci and his renaissance era drawings of primitive robots, the first two prototypes of their acquired patented robotic elements were named "Lenny" and "Mona," their third and final prototype nickname "da Vinci" stuck, and in 1997 they debuted the robotic system that would come to dominate robotic surgery and effect change across the entire field. At the time of its introduction, da Vinci was the most sophisticated robotic surgery platform to date, and though there have now been multiple iterations, the basic design has remained largely unchanged.

The da Vinci system is composed of three component parts, the vision cart, the patient cart, and the surgeon console. The vision cart houses the camera equipment, a screen showing the same display that the surgeon is seeing, and various housings for energy equipment and accessories used during surgery. The camera used with da Vinci has two visual feeds, one for each of the surgeon's eyes. The vision cart receives the inputs from the camera, integrates them, magnifies them up to 10×, and sends them to the surgeon console and to monitors around the room. This high-definition, magnified, three-dimensional image is a remarkable improvement over laparoscopic camera technology and greatly exceeds the limits of human eyesight. Even more remarkable when considering that this is done through a 1-cm incision, and the surgeon is seated across the room. The enhanced, and remarkable stable, vision system is one of the key features that spurred the original growth in use of da Vinci in gynecology and urology, whose procedures take place in extremely narrow, tight areas in the pelvis.

The patient cart is a hulking three (current models now have four)-armed platform that is positioned directly over the patient on the operating room table. One of these arms holds the camera, and the other arms can be set up to hold dozens of different instruments manipulated remotely by the surgeon, including a variety of graspers, energy devices, staplers and more, each with the aforementioned "wristed" instrument tips that afford incredible dexterity. Each arm has multiple articulating joints that allow the robot to be positioned in a variety of different ways, affording complete flexibility in setting up the arms to be used in innumerable operations, regardless of patient positioning. Each arm is quickly attached to a trocar, a hollow metal tube just like those used in laparoscopic surgery. Instruments are attached to a housing on the robotic arm that controls their movements, then passed through the trocar, and positioned within the patient. The instruments themselves can be rapidly exchanged during an operation by an assisting surgeon or a surgical nurse. Sensors in the arms are able to identify the instrument's location in space prior to removal, allowing instruments to be taken out and replaced with new ones in the exact same location within the patient, virtually eliminating the risk of inadvertently injuring structures that are out of view during instrument exchange, a not uncommon complication of laparoscopic surgery. The arms rotate around a remote center of motion (RCM), pioneered with the LARS system, located at the fulcrum of the trocar. This minimizes trauma to the patient's abdominal or chest wall. While operating, the instruments follow the exact movements of the surgeon's hands from the operating console, measure, and track the surgeon's hand movements 1300 times per second, and are able to filter out even microscopic tremor, making the robotic instruments more stable, more dexterous, and more precise than human hands. The patient cart, particularly current iterations, genuinely conforms to preconceived ideas of what robotic surgery *should* look like, but it is critical to remember that the robotic arms are under complete control of the surgeon.

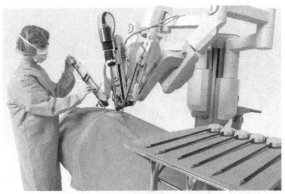

Demonstration of instrument exchange on the da Vinci, Intuitive Surgical.

The third component, the surgeon console, is the major distinguishing feature of da Vinci from ZEUS. The console consists of three major parts, all integrated and in-line, in front of which the surgeon sits. The top portion is the visual housing. The surgeon looks into a viewfinder that receives input from the vision cart and gives the surgeon a three-dimensional reconstructed field of view that confers impossibly accurate depth perception. On the heads-up display, the surgeon can also see the instruments that are currently in use, and lights flash on those instrument icons when they are being used, to deliver electrocautery, for example. One of the many safety mechanisms built in to da Vinci, a sensor acknowledges when the surgeon is looking into the console and activates the instruments; if the surgeon takes his head out of the console, the arms will not move, thereby preventing inadvertent injury to the patient.

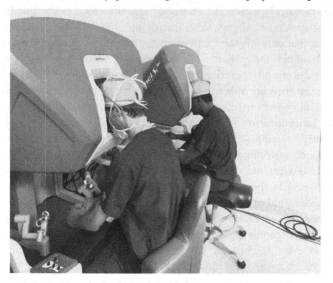

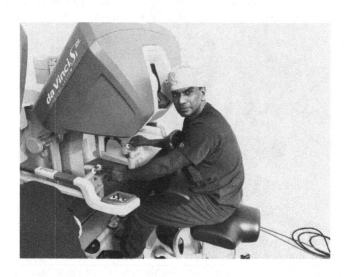

Directly underneath and in-line with the optics display are the master controllers, a pair of arms jointed much like the human arm with wrists, elbows, and shoulders. The arms are mounted to the console and controlled by placing two fingers of each hand, typically the thumb and first finger, into velcro straps. With an array of gyroscopes, sensors, and accelerometers, the arms are incredibly responsive to the surgeon's controls and move with a fluidity that is difficult to describe any way other than that it just feels *good*. A very intuitive design, the surgeon moves the controllers as their own hands would move performing the operation, and da Vinci scales, filters, and transmits these motions to the instruments inside the patient. Each controller can be pinched between the fingers, opening and closing the instruments with a calculated and measured degree of force. The controllers also have a clutch function, which when utilized freezes movement inside the patient and allows the surgeon to return the master controllers to a more ergonomic location if the performance of the surgery has required wide motions or overextension of the wrist.

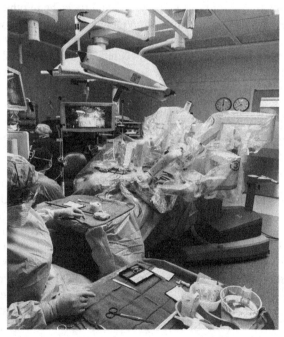

The last portion is the footboard, which has multiple pedals for using functions of various instruments, for switching control between arms, and for steering the camera, which is positioned with the master controllers while deploying a pedal. The stereoscopic 3D vision and in-line arrangement of the surgeon's hands and eyes give the sense of standing directly in front of the patient while operating, a true telepresence. The entire arrangement is very ergonomic for the surgeon. In stark contrast to laparoscopy wherein the surgeon must assume sometimes very awkward positions, stand for hours at a time, and apply torque against the abdominal wall while manipulating instruments, being able to sit comfortably and control the entire operation from the same position is enormously beneficial to the surgeon in individual cases and probably more importantly over the duration of a career.

While "Mona" was tested in Belgium in 1997, reportedly being used to perform cholecystectomy and Nissen fundoplication, the first fully realized da Vinci platform was delivered to Leipzig University Heart Center in Germany in 1998, where a team of cardiothoracic surgeons used da Vinci to perform robotic-assisted coronary artery bypass surgeries. In 2000, Intuitive Surgical was given FDA approval for laparoscopic and thoracoscopic operations, and the era of da Vinci in the United States began. The first models were sold at a cost of just over $1 million. Despite multiple efforts at marketing da Vinci for use in heart surgery, it found its niche in other areas. The earliest reported case series using da Vinci were published by urologists performing robotic-assisted prostate surgery, an area where this technology proved immediately and immensely beneficial. The next group of surgeons to identify benefits of robotic surgery was gynecologists, who began performing robotic-assisted hysterectomy. These two procedures proved to have fewer complications, decreased hospitalization, and better surgical outcomes compared to open and traditional laparoscopic approaches, and these early successes facilitated the early growth and spread of da Vinci systems across US hospitals.

While da Vinci was finding its footing, Computer Motion's ZEUS was being tested in new and exciting ways, and eventually gained FDA approval in October 2001 with 25 of its systems in place in US hospitals and 24 systems abroad. It debuted at a cost of $975,000, in an effort to undercut its competition. Just one month before its approval, in September 2001, ZEUS was used to realize one of the original dreams of telepresence, in what remains one of the most remarkable feats in medical history. With collaboration between European research powerhouse IRCAD, Computer Motion, and France Telecom, French Surgeon Jacques Marescaux performed a robotic-assisted laparoscopic cholecystectomy on a 68-year-old patient in Strasbourg, France, while seated at a ZEUS console in New York City, NY. After months of preparation and practice runs, the 48-min-long procedure, called "Operation Lindbergh," was made possible with the use of specially provided high-speed fiber optic connection, with virtually no delay between the surgeon commands in New York and the robotic arms operating in France. While this sort of application is not widely used today, this operation proved feasibility and carries massive implications for future uses of robotic technology including battlefield surgery, remote "digital consultations," and improving third-world access to surgeons.

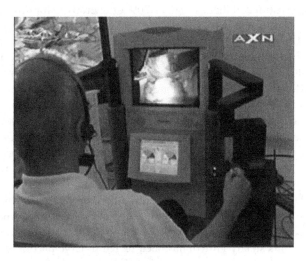

Dr. Marescaux in NYC performs the "Lindbergh Operation," removing the gallbladder of a patient in France in 2001.

Public demonstrations of the capabilities of these systems took place, with surgeons peeling grapes and making paper airplanes on daytime talk shows. Surgeons, hospitals, and patients took notice; the era of robotic surgery had arrived. In the midst of all of the development, early distribution, and excitement over this new technology, Computer Motion and Intuitive Surgical were embroiled in a massive legal dispute. Suits and countersuits between the two rival companies over proprietary technology and alleged patent infringements impaired progress in the field. After years in courts without any resolution, the two merged in March of 2003, with the more valuable Intuitive absorbing Computer Motion. According to a press release at the time, Computer Motion shares were converted to 0.52 shares of Intuitive for a total value of the combined company of 32%. At the time, shares of Intuitive Surgical were valued at $2.80. Both companies knew what was at stake, and the future potential of their products; in October 2018, shares of Intuitive are trading for $554. With the market consolidated and virtually all of the patents on requisite technology to develop robotic surgical systems owned by Intuitive, ZEUS was discontinued and da Vinci began to flourish.

Growth, ongoing development, and current issues in robotic surgery

Data and evidence regarding the safety and efficacy of operations performed with da Vinci began accumulating, and surgeons and hospitals took notice. By 2007, it is estimated that as high as 70% of operations for prostate cancer were performed robotically. With uses in urology, gynecology, general surgery, GI surgery, thoracic surgery, cardiac surgery, and others, nearly 4,500 da Vinci robots have been installed, and the United States healthcare system is the major driving force in the application and progress of robotic surgery. 67% of all da Vinci robots are in the United States, performing 79% of all robotic surgeries worldwide. One in four American hospitals has at least one da Vinci robotic system. According to Intuitive, 877,000 robotic-assisted operations were performed with its systems in 2017, 2,400 operations every single day using this single piece of technology, a year-over-year increase of 16%. Looking back further, it is impossible to ignore the growth of robotic surgery as more and more indications and applications are being explored. Using the last 10 years of available data published by Intuitive Surgical in annual SEC filings, the total number of worldwide procedures has increased by an astonishing 545% since 2008, and the trajectory is quickening. This steady growth has been fueled in large part in recent years by growing applications in general and cardiothoracic surgery, in addition to steady rates of use in the fields of urology and gynecology, which were early adopters of robotic technology. As more surgeons gain experience with the benefits conferred by the robotic surgery, and more robotic surgical systems become commercially available in the coming years, it can be safely assumed that the trend will continue. Ongoing developments and improvements to da Vinci are largely responsible for the ongoing growth and discovery of new applications, but this has also been bolstered by strong branding and marketing employed by Intuitive. Surgeons are eager to use the robot for more cases, and a wider array of procedures, in part due to patient demand that is driven by a marketing strategy employed by Intuitive that has been coined "indirect-to-consumer" marketing. In contrast to pharmaceutical companies that advertise their medicines on television or in magazines, Intuitive provided hospitals that purchased da Vinci with strategy on marketing their hospital over local competition, including press releases announcing the availability of robotic surgery, and help with advertising these services in local radio, Internet, and social media avenues. In this way, Intuitive's brand is built largely by the hospitals that purchase their robots. In turn, patients who hear or read about robotic surgery will subsequently seek out hospitals or even individual providers who perform robotic-assisted operations.

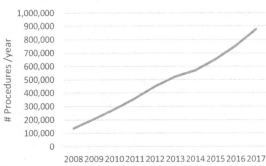

Even after its consolidation of the market, Intuitive continued to make improvements and adjustments to da Vinci that have spurred the growth into increasingly more surgical procedures. Several iterations of da Vinci have been introduced since its inception, with additional features including a third surgical arm, changes to the patient cart to make docking and undocking more streamlined, and the addition of a second console used for training or a co-surgeon. With the third arm, the surgeon can rapidly switch between three different surgical instruments with the simple push of a pedal on the footboard of the console, allowing increased dexterity and improving exposure. In many cases, the use of the third arm precludes the need for an assistant at the bedside to also have a laparoscopic instrument inside the patient for the purposes of grasping, holding, and providing exposure for the operating surgeon. With three surgical arms and an arm for the camera, da Vinci gives the surgeon four hands to work with, conferring complete control over aspects of the operation that in open or laparoscopic surgery must be ceded to an assistant. While some have suggested that in surgical training centers this may impair the ability of the trainee to learn how to perform operations, the introduction of the second console with the da Vinci Si launch in 2009 obviated this concern. Previously, robotic surgeries were taught by the operating surgeon while the assisted stood either at the patient's bedside, assisting and exchanging instruments, or by standing next to the surgeon console, watching the operation on a monitor. With the second console, complete or partial control of the operation can be ceded to the training surgeon. Control of individual arms can be changed between consoles easily and fluidly, and tools like markup of the heads-up display can be used to direct and instruct the training surgeon. This method of training, along with da Vinci's highly instinctive design, has been shown to reduce the learning curve of minimally invasive operations, particularly among surgical novices, suggesting that new surgeons can become proficient with robotic-assisted operations, even without having learning laparoscopy. The most recent iteration of da Vinci is the Xi, a sleek and modern interpretation with overhead mounted arms and a slimmer frame making it easier to dock and position, as well as the ability to integrate with operating room tables, so that the patient positioning can be changed during the course of the operation without having to reposition the robot. da Vinci Si and Xi both cost between $2–2.5 million.

da Vinci Xi, Intuitive Surgical.

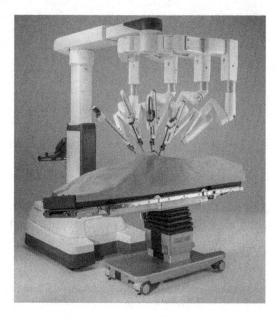

In 2011, Intuitive released a system for performing single-site endoscopic operations, a technique that had already seen some use in the world of laparoscopy. The concept is that through a single incision, multiple laparoscopic instruments can be used, offering a more cosmetically sensitive alternative to multiport endoscopic operations. The technique was applied to many operations including colon and kidney resections and some stomach surgeries, but really excels in operations confined to one area of the abdomen, such as cholecystectomy and hysterectomy. The da Vinci single-site system utilizes a single flexible molded plastic dumbbell-shaped flange that spans the abdominal wall and is inserted through a 5-cm incision, usually centered around the navel. Through the flange, a camera trocar and two curved instrument trocars are inserted. The truly novel development with this system is the use of semi-rigid operating instruments that seat to the robot just like the normal instruments and course through these curved trocars, where they are more rigid at the ends. While there is still limited mobility and the matter of tight working space similar to laparoscopic single site surgery, the use of da Vinci mitigates some of the physical stress on the surgeon and makes this technique feasible.

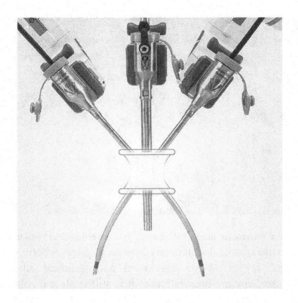

Da Vinci single-site curved trocars, Intuitive surgical.

Additional recent innovation has come in the realm of imaging technology incorporated into the robotic system. Even with the standard da Vinci camera, the combination of the length and reach of the arm, up to 10× high-definition magnification, the stable operating platform, and direct surgeon control allow the surgeon unique control and a degree of precision and accuracy that far exceeds laparoscopy. On the leading edge of this vision technology is the use of fluorescent near-infrared imaging. Following injection of an inert dye that has been used in ophthalmology for decades, the dye binds to proteins in the blood. Newer iterations of the robotic camera can then emit an infrared laser and can then detect, and with proprietary software colorize and display this fluorescent imaging. A simple tap of a fingertip from the surgeon console can switch between white light and fluorescent imaging. The implication of this is that anatomic structures including blood vessels and bile ducts can be more easily and reliably identified, preventing inadvertent injuries and potentially devastating complications. In this sense, the robotic technology augments and extends the limits of the human eye.

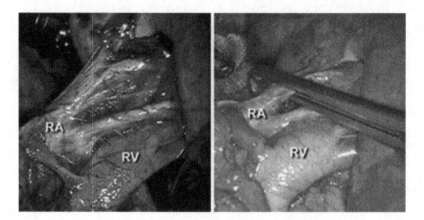

Demonstration of fluorescent imaging differentiating between different vascular structures.

While its popularity and influence continue to grow, robotic surgery is not without staunch critics. While the visual and technical advantages over traditional laparoscopy are unquestioned, it is still unclear if robotic surgeries have changed outcomes at all. One of the commonly repeated critiques of robotic surgery is that it is a "solution searching for a problem," and there are many valid points to be made. Lingering technical criticisms, steep learning curve for both surgeons and OR staff, direct-to-consumer marketing, outcome equivalence, and major economic concerns are pervasive counterarguments to the fervent growth of robots in the operating room.

The most thoughtful critiques come from within the field of surgery itself, where data- and evidence-based medicine is revered and new therapies or technologies must be compared to the current standard of care. One of the largest metaanalyses of trials comparing robotic surgery versus traditional laparoscopy to date confirms that while robotic surgery has been shown to decrease intraoperative bleeding and need for blood transfusion, and there are many operation-specific outcome benefits, as of today, there is no definitive advantage with robotic surgery when comparing overall complication rate, hospital length of stay, or major outcome measures. Most of the published literature regarding long-term outcomes is in the field of urology, where robotic-assisted prostatectomy is considered by many to be the standard of care. The data comparing robotic-assisted and laparoscopy, however, have largely been equivocal when considering oncologic outcomes, postoperative functional outcomes, and quality of life measures, which when combined with the increased operative time and increased cost of robotic surgery leaves critics skeptical of any real advantage. Other studies comparing the two techniques in rectal cancer resections have had similar results, only showing benefit with robotic-assisted technique in surgeons with extensive robotic experience.

This highlights two more important critiques of robotic surgery that are generally linked, the learning curve for surgeons and staff and increased operative time. While many have attempted to study the learning curve for robotic surgery, that is to say, how many of a certain operation one must do to be considered proficient, the conclusions have varied wildly, from 30 cases to 1000. This question is inherently difficult to answer and difficult to replicate methodology, given that one person's perception of proficiency may vary wildly from another's. While it is generally accepted that laparoscopic operations have a longer learning curve than open surgeries, given the technical limitations and requisite mastery of technology in addition to the anatomy and operative steps, we do not feel that this constitutes an effective rebuke of robotic-assisted surgery. In fact, there is emerging data suggesting that achieving proficiency with endoscopic surgical skills is quicker with the robot, particularly among novices, as mentioned earlier in this chapter. The bottom line is that robotic surgery is easier to learn than laparoscopy; the lack of fulcrum effect, the fluidity of motion, tremor reduction, the in-line ergonomics, and the effectual telepresence of the optics combine to make a platform that just *makes sense* to the user. One recent study has even suggested that robotic surgery eliminates hand dominance, with their subjects showing no difference in speed or precision with their nondominant hand using a da Vinci simulator, whereas they showed disparate performance in similar laparoscopic observation. While it is easy to understand that experienced laparoscopic surgeons transitioning to robotic technique will require time to learn the finer points of its setup and use, this does not constitute a significant limitation, and furthermore, the widespread availability of simulation should allow for the requisite practice without jeopardizing patient care. Once proficiency is achieved there should be no difference in the time of the actual performance of the operation, and studies in the early 2000s showed this.

Where robotic surgery does add time to the total length of the operation, however, is in the preoperative setup and positioning of the robot. The length of time from patient arrival in the room to incision is longer in robotic surgery compared to open or laparoscopic, notably because the robot takes extra time to drape, instruments to be set up, the room to be arranged, and the patient positioned appropriately. This is understandable, particularly with early iterations of da Vinci that were bulkier, more difficult to drape and move, and surgical teams were trying to learn and adopt this new technology. However, the effect of experience on this has been well studied, with good evidence that with experience, preoperative setup time drops considerably, with as few as 30 cases to gain proficiency. This has led to the suggestion and development of dedicated robotic surgical teams, which in our own experience has proven to be an immensely valuable asset and shortens not only setup and docking time, but makes the entire operation proceed more fluidly and efficiently.

One of the most pervasive criticisms of robotic surgery is the economic concern. The current hardware alone costs between $2–2.5 million, depending on the particular system. Furthermore, maintenance on the systems is estimated at around $100,000 annually, and the instruments used with the robotic surgery platform have a limited number of uses and therefore must be replaced regularly, at much higher frequency, and much higher cost, than traditional laparoscopic instruments or open surgical instruments. One longitudinal study at Stanford University determined a per-case increased cost of $2700 per robotic-assisted operation. Particularly in an era where efforts to reign in health-care costs and provide value in health-care delivery, a strong argument could be made that until significant outcome advantages can be seen in the literature, robotic surgery will remain a novelty. However, this seems to be a very superficial take on the issue. Operative costs are but a fraction of the total charges billed to a payer, with hospital charges making up the majority of the total cost. The implication is that shorter postoperative hospitalization is more cost-effective overall, even with higher operative costs. This too has been borne out in the literature, with direct comparisons between robotic and laparoscopy showing shorter length of stay postoperatively translates to lower overall costs. The cost savings between inpatient and outpatient surgeries is even wider, and with more applications of minimally invasive technology, more and more operations that previously required hospitalization will be performed on an outpatient basis. Further, the costs of da Vinci amortized over time, with the initial investment being mitigated with operative volume. Another consideration in this discussion is the limited competition in the field, largely due to the innumerable patents held by Intuitive. As Intuitive's patents expire, new competitors will be eager to take a piece of their over $60 billion market cap. The availability of viable competitors will drive costs down, narrowing the differential that currently exists between laparoscopic and robotic surgical costs. Simply put, considering only the surgical charges as opposed to the total cost of hospitalization and ignoring the evidence showing shortened length of stay for robotic-assisted operations is incredibly short-sighted and fails as a meaningful critique of robotic surgery.

Despite its criticisms, we maintain that robotic surgery is the future of the field. The current state of robotic-assisted surgery is one of major technological achievement, rapid growth, and yet still unmet potential. While it has been well established in the training paradigms of urology and gynecology residency for years, and therefore more common among current practicing physicians in those specialties, anecdotally the large majority of general and thoracic surgeons do not use the robot even when available at their institutions. However, this may be beginning to change, as young and training surgeons see the advantages conferred by a system that marries the benefits of minimally invasive surgery and effectively maintains the technical advantages of open operations and receive early experience with it. Robotic surgery curriculums are being developed at training programs with collaboration from Intuitive, whereby new surgeons entering practice will be credentialed to operate on da Vinci and offer patients this technique.

On the horizon

One of the persistent limitations and major criticisms of da Vinci among surgeons is the lack of haptic feedback. The consequence of the absence of haptics is that if you cannot feel how hard you are holding or retracting tissue, inadvertent injury can occur. Unfortunately, applying force-feedback to the master controllers to simulate haptic feel has proven to be a difficult feat of engineering, and no real solutions have materialized. The surgeon must instead rely on visual cues, constantly watching and being mindful of how much tension *appears* to be being put on whatever is being grasped. Although this sensory substituted feedback has been shown to improve technical details like amount and consistency of tension applied while suturing with the robot, it is believed that genuine haptic feedback would improve the experience and expand the applications of robotic surgery even further. While this requisite adaptation has not precluded the growth and widespread adoption of robotic surgery, solving the problem of limited tactile sensation would carry enormous impact, not only in surgery but across all areas where robots are employed. The potential of a successful haptic system is widely recognized, with thousands of researchers in the United States alone designing and testing systems with applications from surgery to virtual reality, video games, and industry.

Early work in force-feedback in surgical robots has proven difficult, as vibration and "rumble" feedback, similar to what is commonly seen in video game controllers, can disrupt the surgeon's precise control of the slave instruments, and have to be scaled down to a point where the sensation is more nuisance than benefit. Two alternatives in particular, with haptic feedback arrangements that more closely resemble the sensory capability of the human fingers, are in development with potential use in future robotic surgical systems. Working closely with Intuitive Surgical, preeminent researcher in the field of haptics Allison Okamura, previously of Johns Hopkins and now with Stanford's Collaborative Haptics in Robotics and Medicine (CHARM) Lab, has been publishing work on haptics in robotic surgery since the early 2000s. Her lab has developed devices that can apply graded force to deform and stretch fingertip skin to simulate kinetic touch, in what they believe is the most intuitive feedback mechanism. Also working with Intuitive, researchers at UCLA's Center for Advanced Surgical and Interventional Technology (CASIT) have developed what they call a pneumatic haptic feedback system, whereby which sensors at the working tips of da Vinci instruments transmit force information back to the master controllers, where pneumatic balloons inflate and deflate proportionally to give the sensation of resistance to the surgeon. Both are intriguing concepts, but have yet to come to fruition, at least in terms of translation from the laboratory to the operating room. There is, however, a robotic system available today that has made some improvement in this area.

Receiving its FDA approval for use in the United States in October 2017, the Senhance system, developed by Transenterix, has been available in Europe since 2010, originally sold as the ALF-X system. Its FDA approval officially ended nearly 15 years of monopolization of the market by Intuitive. The Senhance system functions like an intermediate between traditional laparoscopy and the robotic surgery archetype, da Vinci. The instruments are held by arms that dock individually, offer a stable platform much like the da Vinci, and there is a console from which the surgeon operates while seated; this is where the similarities largely end. The controllers for the arms are shaped like traditional laparoscopic instruments, and most of the instruments in use for the Senhance are not articulating but rather have the standard four degrees of motion. The surgeon looks at a monitor while wearing 3D glasses and interestingly can control the camera with eye-tracking technology, eliminating the need for a bedside assistant or for manual control. The instruments and their control deliberately maintain the fulcrum effect at the patient's abdominal wall, and the system makes use of standard laparoscopic trocars. It also uses standard laparoscopic trocars, and employs reusable instruments, conferring a key economic advantage over its industry-standard competitor. The key feature of Senhance is genuine haptic feedback transmitted through sensors on the shaft of the surgical instruments; pressure against the instruments inside the patient is recreated on the laparoscopic control handles at the console. In this manner, the haptic feedback is essentially exactly that of laparoscopy— the surgeon can feel when their instruments are pushing or touching against something. Despite this achievement, it has not been able to create grip haptics, the goal that Intuitive has been pursuing. While the Senhance is a unique alternative to da Vinci, it has yet to find any commercial success, in fact only a handful of its systems have been sold in Europe, and only two are known to be in use in the United States. While haptic feedback and restoring the surgeon's sense of touch remains a work in progress, many more companies are nevertheless eager to bring new robotic surgical systems to the market, and this competition and ongoing innovation will invariably lead to new and exciting options for surgeons and patients.

Transenterix is a small company relative to the massive Intuitive Surgical, but massive health-care and medical device players are interested in garnering a portion of Intuitive's annual over $3 billion in revenue. Medtronic, the largest medical device manufacturer in the world, with reported revenues approaching $30 billion, is well into the development of its own robotic system, that it is creating with collaboration from German robotic engineering company DLR. Rumored to have independent and highly mobile robotic arms, as well as its own form of haptics, its project titled "Hugo" is anticipated to begin human trials in 2019. Due to Medtronic's long-established relationships with hospitals across the world and the stability of a major industry powerhouse, many believe Hugo may become a viable competitor to da Vinci. Other areas of medicine and minimally invasive surgery will soon find robotic-assisted alternatives to current standards of care. Intuitive founder Fred Moll's newest venture Auris Surgical Robotics has created a robotic flexible endoscopy platform for use in locating and biopsying lung tumors by going through the mouth and traveling within tiny airways. Another mega collaboration is promising massive changes to robotic surgery. Google parent company Alphabet and Johnson and Johnson subsidiary Ethicon have teamed to create Verb Surgical, which is not only working on producing its own competitor to da Vinci but has broader aims to increase the worldwide availability of surgical robots, and to introduce the ideas of machine learning and data integration. By recording key data points and video of every procedure performed on its system, Verb posits that its robots will be able to share information acquired on tens or hundreds of thousands of similar procedures, making them the most "experienced" and qualified surgeons in the world. They foresee a time where this data-driven technology can help surgeons distinguish sick from healthy tissue, identify blood vessels and nerves before they can be inadvertently injured, or help the surgeon identify common missteps that can lead to complications. This would help reach their stated goal of "democratizing" surgery, by lending surgeons judgment and data that far exceed their own skill and experience. One can foresee, albeit far in the future and limited with the same liability constraints as self-driving vehicles or airplanes, this machine learning being translated to semiautonomous or autonomous surgical robots.

On a far more practical level, there are many more future directions in robotic surgery that are possible with existing technology. The Lindbergh operation in 2001 demonstrated proof of concept that even vastly remote telepresence surgery is feasible and safe. Despite the success of that operation, remote surgery and telepresence have not seen any genuine progress over the last two decades. Many have suggested that this technology could be used for virtual consultation, where a subspecialist could be summoned virtually to participate in an operation in a different hospital where the case may be particularly difficult, or a complication has arisen that this specialist has special expertise or knowledge in treating. This is genuinely possible even now, given adequate telecom connectivity and minor allowances in hospital credentialing. To push the concept even further, telepresence could be used to improve access to surgical specialists in the developing world, although this will require substantial changes in robotic platforms cost and distribution.

As previously established in this chapter, the history of surgery is marked with pervasive changes driven by technical innovation and scientific progress, often times initially disparaged. We posit that surgeons who ignore the benefits of robotic surgery and do not become comfortable with its use will be in the same position as our colleagues in the late 1980s and early 1990s who disregarded laparoscopy and were soon rendered irrelevant. Even with robotic-assisted surgery being relatively new, the advantages are immediately apparent to those who use it, even among very skilled laparoscopic surgeons, and there is already an enormous amount of high-quality evidence assuring its safety of use, and areas of superiority to existing standards of care. While we do not expect robotic surgery to replace laparoscopy any time soon, there is clearly space in the current practice of surgery for both techniques, and the future possibilities of robotic surgery would be unwise to ignore. Exciting future developments including machine learning, development of haptic feedback mechanisms, remote surgery, improved patient access to experts, and one day possibly autonomous surgical robots, will continue to inspire innovators in the field and push the possibilities of robotic surgery to new heights.

The immediate research in surgical robotics is application of smaller systems and integration of reliable haptic feedback, However in this era of cost-conscious medicine, the widespread adoption of surgical robotics is still hampered by the increased cost of these systems and the disposables needed for completion of the procedure. With more companies entering the surgical robotics industry, healthy competition should hopefully reduce the cost of these systems. The natural progression of surgical robotics is integration of artificial intelligence into the operating systems, currently we are still dealing with a master—slave relationship with the robot. With progression in AI it is likely that computers which are excellent at pattern recognition would be able to help surgeons prevent iatrogenic injuries by overlaying the computer's perception of surgical anatomy over what the surgeon thinks he is seeing. The patterns that the computer overlays could be a result of thousands of other surgeries performed by master surgeons all around the world which the computer can access. This could be invaluable to a surgeon who may otherwise due to human fallibility cause an iatrogenic injury. The other promise of surgical robotics is remote surgery. Ever since the first transatlantic cholecystectomy was performed by Professor Jacques Maresscaux and team, there have been instances of surgical robotics being performed remotely to telementor surgeons. This could be further developed to help patients in remote areas by offering them surgical expertise which they may have otherwise not had access to. In the distant future where space exploration becomes a reality, it is likely that a general surgeon may be the only one who travels with the team and the robot that performs surgery may just need bedside assistance or oversight while it performs neurosurgery or cardiac surgery. Evolution of robotic surgery could lead to development of truly autonomous robots which could be ingested by the patient may be able to carry out surgery inside the patient's digestive system or circulatory system. This also brings with it the ethical dilemmas of human compassion which is so important to healing clashing with the cold logical thinking of a machine. For this reason alone, I do not believe humans will ever be devolved of patient care. In conclusion, we have barely entered the era of surgical robotics and exciting developments await us.

Chapter 6

Regulating safety-critical autonomous systems: past, present, and future perspectives

M.L. Cummings[1], David Britton[2]

[1]*Department of Electrical and Computer Engineering, Duke University, Durham, NC, USA;*
[2]*Department of Mechanical Engineering and Materials Science and the Law School, Duke University, Durham, NC, USA*

Chapter outline

Introduction

Autonomous systems in the world today include self-driving vehicles, which use sensors to estimate nearby obstacles and stored mapping data in order to safely navigate to a desired destination; artificial intelligence—based financial trading systems, which track market conditions and individual stocks and make independent decisions on when to buy or sell (Maney, 2017), and even new medical devices which monitor a patient's physiological condition and alter the rate of drug delivery or direct other medical intervention without caregiver input (Schwartz, 2017).

Living with Robots. https://doi.org/10.1016/B978-0-12-815367-3.00006-2
119

Differentiated from *automated* systems that operate by clear repeatable rules based on unambiguous sensed data, *autonomous systems* take in information about the unstructured world around them, process that information to analyze possible outcomes, and use that analysis to generate alternatives and make decisions in the face of uncertainty.

While autonomous systems hold great promise including increased access to education, public health, mobility, and transportation, there are also potential negative consequences. For example, consequences may include privacy invasions by camera vision and related tracking systems, significant opportunities for abuse and manipulation of autonomous systems such as that exhibited in the 2017 US election manipulation of social media algorithms (Woolley & Howard, 2017), and threats to personal safety as seen in the recent death of a pedestrian due to self-driving car sensor blind spots (Griggs & Wakabayashi, 2018). As a result, calls for increased government regulation of autonomous systems are growing (Laris, 2018; Lietzen, 2017).

Technology regulation typically focuses on lowering risks and reducing potential negative consequences associated with an industry, activity, or product. Technology regulation could be seen as limiting the use of a technology, which could result in a decrease in innovation and incentives to invest in newer technologies (Jaffe, Peterson, Portney, & Stavins, 1995). However, competing research demonstrates that regulation can actually drive innovation and technological progress toward societal goals (Ashford & Hall, 2012). Thus, the overarching challenge of regulating emerging technologies is to design regulations that both encourage fulfillment of a technology's potential but also manage associated risks.

There are many risks associated with autonomous systems that regulators will likely not have encountered with previous technologies, or risks will be manifested in new ways. Autonomous systems require new forms of computer-based sensing, information interpretation, and action generation in ways that are not always understood even by their own programmers (Knight, 2017). The newness and unpredictability of autonomous systems means that many failure modes will be unforeseen, and therefore untested and unmanaged. Reducing the risk of human error is often cited as a main benefit of autonomous systems (Villasenor, 2014), but that is only possible if autonomous systems become more reliable than humans.

Determining whether autonomous systems meet or exceed the reliability of humans is not straightforward due to the complexities of the software that drive these systems as well as what kind of testing is needed to make such assertions. For example, one study has asserted that in order to demonstrate a driverless car is as safe as humans, at least 275 million miles must be driven, which would take possibly up to a decade under current testing protocols (Kalra & Paddock., 2016). Thus, potentially new and different reliability assessment methods are needed if technology innovations are to be realized in more expeditious time frames. Unfortunately, testing and certification of autonomous systems is still an immature field of inquiry.

Autonomous systems rely on probabilistic reasoning and significant estimation through a mathematical estimate approach called machine learning, aka deep learning. Such pattern recognition algorithms are a data-intensive approach to developing an autonomous system world model, which serves as the core set of assumptions about who, what, and where agents in the system are and what their likely next set of behaviors and actions will be (Hutchins, Cummings, Draper, & Hughes, 2015). To date, there exists no industry consensus on how to test such systems, particularly in safety-critical environments, and such approaches to computer-based reasoning have been criticized as deeply flawed (Marcus, 2018).

Given that there are new and emerging risks that must be mitigated with the introduction of autonomous systems in safety-critical environments, it is not clear how regulatory agencies could and should respond. Regulatory agencies typically struggle to keep pace with technological change, often referred to as the pacing problem (Krisher & Billeaud, 2018). The inertia created by the procedural requirements of administrative law causes agencies and regulations to lag behind technological innovation, which is especially problematic in the current climate of rapid autonomous technology development. Institutional expertise also lags as, for example, robots and artificial intelligence are introduced into industries whose traditional regulators are unfamiliar with advanced computing and need to acquire the technical knowledge needed to understand such systems (Calo, 2014).

In order to better understand how regulatory agencies of safety-critical systems could and should adapt as autonomous systems become more commonplace, we first discuss how such technologies come into existence from a systems engineering perspective. We then discuss how three different federal regulatory agencies, the Federal Aviation Administration (FAA), the Food and Drug Administration (FDA), and the National Highway Transportation and Safety Administration (NHTSA), approach regulation of new technologies in general, and more specifically their progress with automated and autonomous systems. We conclude with a comparison of the three different approaches to regulation of new technologies and discuss possible paths forward.

The systems engineering V-model

In order to understand how autonomous systems could or should be regulated, especially those in safety-critical applications, it is first important to understand how such systems come into existence, so that critical regulatory decisions can be mapped to major gateways and milestones of system development. There are many prescriptive frameworks that describe in detail how such complex systems should be engineered, including the traditional waterfall system engineering process (Blanchard & Fabrycky, 1998), the spiral model (Boehm, 1988), and the agile software model (Crowder & Friess, 2013). The systems engineering model that will be used in this discussion is the V-model since it represents a concise visual representation of the major steps in a system's development life cycle, as well as the iterative nature of the underlying processes (Mitre, 2014).

The V-model (Fig. 6.1) is a visual representation of the main steps of systems engineering, sometimes referred to as the life-cycle building blocks (Mitre, 2014). On the horizontal axis is time, indicating that the activities in each block occur in a certain order, but also overlap in time. This implies that some iteration between steps may be necessary, and that some elements of a project may proceed to the next block while others stay behind. The vertical distribution indicates the level of system decomposition, such that the lower blocks address components of a system, while higher blocks look at system definition, integration, and implementation.

As depicted in Fig. 6.1, in an ideal setting when a new system is conceived like a self-driving car, a management plan is developed that accounts for initial budgets, project timelines, and necessary personnel, which then leads to the definition of a concept of operations. A concept of operations (CONOPs) is then conducted, which generally describes how operations with a new technology should occur in order to meet some common goal or identified need. CONOPs frequently embody plans for resource allocation and scheduling (both objects and people), particularly for complex operations that involve many different entities. In the example of a self-driving car, a CONOP would lay out when, where, and under what conditions self-driving cars would

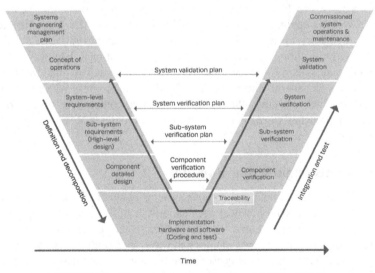

FIGURE 6.1   The systems engineering V-model (Mitre, 2014).

operate, including contingency operations and identification of relevant stakeholders like pedestrians, bicyclists, etc.

Once the CONOPs is agreed upon, then system and component requirements can be generated, which are critical in defining the design space. Good requirements are unambiguous, measurable, testable, and traceable statements that form the intermediary step between the concept of operations and detailed system design. They define the criteria that must be met by designs and implementation and then theoretically form the backbone of testing on the right side of the V-model.

System requirements typically revolve around anticipated functionalities, i.e., a self-driving car must be able to operate in rain, snow, and fog and on city and highway roads, while component requirements typically focus on lower level details such as a LIDAR (light detection and ranging) that should be able to detect a static or dynamic obstacle within 200 m of a moving vehicle.

Once the system and component level requirements are generated, then the design space can be characterized, which then results in the development of both hardware and software. The CONOPs, requirements generation, and design phases are iterative and fluid, especially in the early days of a system's development. Often design issues, such as the inability of a sensor to work in all weather conditions like LIDAR, will cause engineers to revisit the CONOPs and requirements to fill in a gap that was only revealed in the design and implementation stages. Engineers, in theory, should be able to trace design decisions back to the relevant requirements, in an effort to assure that the end product matches stakeholder needs. Traceability to requirements is a key systems engineering concept at play in the design and implementation phase.

Once initial designs are completed, verification and validation tests ensue, typically first at the component levels, i.e., testing a LIDAR first in a laboratory before it is integrated into a moving vehicle. Eventually, tests address full-scale system operation in realistic environments, like having a self-driving car drive on public roads with a safety driver behind the wheel. It is not typically feasible for engineers to test all possible scenarios faced by the system, including environmental influences, varieties of user input, and all the ways that system components might fail. Thus, engineer must develop a cost-benefit trade-off plan to determine how much testing is needed to demonstrate a system is safe enough. Of course, these test plans are heavily influenced by what, if any, testing regulations exist.

For deterministic systems, those that react in the same way to the same situation every time, comprehensive testing is much easier to achieve, and such testing is well established in current safety-critical systems such as aviation. But for autonomous systems that incorporate machine learning and other probabilistic reasoning techniques, proving that these systems will act as needed across a comprehensive set of tests, including corner cases at the limits of a system's capability, is not well established, and is still an open area of basic research (Andrews, Abdelgawad, & Gario, 2016; Cummings, 2019).

Once a system passes its final validation tests, then in theory the system is ready for large-scale operation and deployment. However, testing often reveals latent issues either in design or even perhaps a requirements gap, which then requires revisiting an earlier block as represented by the horizontal lines in Fig. 6.1 that reach back to a previous set of decisions. Thus, the design of such systems is iterative and not linear. Revisiting earlier blocks, especially those that require movement from right to left across the V, represent very costly decisions, both in time and money. Thus, companies should strive to address as many problems as possible before moving up the right leg of the V with final designs and associated testing. Uncovering design flaws at the top right of the V can spell disaster for a system, especially one with significant embedded software, which is a hallmark of autonomous systems.

Without principled and extensive testing, often software issues do not reveal themselves until the late stages of testing or even operation, sometimes resulting in fatal outcomes. The airline industry is replete with examples of latent software issues not revealing themselves until years into operations (Favarò, Jackson, Saleh, & Mavris, 2013). Medical communities (Grissinger, 2012; Leveson & Turner, 1995) and air traffic control systems (Bar-Yam, 2003) have also experienced such latent problems due to a lack of comprehensive software testing, a lack of understanding of the critical human—automation interface, and a lack of a principled systems engineering process. Most recently, a latent problem with a self-driving car's computer vision system and its inability to make a decision about the existence of a pedestrian led to the death of a pedestrian in March 2018 while Uber was conducting late-stage validation tests (Griggs & Wakabayashi, 2018).

It is important to note that the V-model systems engineering process, or really *any* system engineering process, is an ideal, best-case process. Technical risks are theoretically identified early in the process and mitigated through careful design, development, and testing, with a focus on assuring safety, reliability, or redundancy where needed. In reality, many companies do not have an adequate understanding of the risks embedded in their systems as they take shortcuts through their engineering process, for example, often not defining a clear CONOPs, not generating requirements, or skipping potentially critical testing gates. Often pressure to get a product to market motivates such shortcuts or a lack of monetary resources (extensive testing can be very expensive) or a combination of both.

For safety-critical systems like those in transportation and medicine, it is because of the propensity of some companies to take such short cuts that regulatory bodies are needed so that an independent assessment can be made as to whether such technologies are truly safe and ready for large-scale deployment. In the next sections, we will contrast and compare how three different regulatory bodies view their role in regulating aviation, medicine, and surface transportation with an emphasis on which stage of the V-model these agencies get involved in technology regulation.

The FAA approach to regulation of new technologies

Commercial passenger airline safety is at an all-time high, with an accident rate of one fatal accident for every 16 million flights as of 2017 (Shepardson, 2018). The aerospace industry has led the broader transportation industry in terms of incorporating significant automation into vehicles, with planes routinely landing themselves at hundreds of airports worldwide. Because of the routine use of advanced automation in commercial aviation, reviewing FAA regulation of aircraft safety provides a window into how one regulatory agency deals with safety-critical automation and related complex systems.

The FAA asserts that safety is its primary value in overseeing air transportation (FAA, 2018). In support of this mission that emphasizes safety first and efficiency second, the FAA insists that any aerospace company wishing access to the US national airspace first must engage in a *Partnership for Safety* Plan. This program defines the working relationship between a company and the FAA independent of any specific project, in order "to build mutual trust, leadership, teamwork, and efficient business practices (AIA, AEA, GAMA, & FAA Aircraft Certification Service and Flight Standards Service, 2017). Trust is a key element for working with the FAA, and working with them as early as possible can, in theory, help to reduce regulatory delays by identifying issues and requirements for certification of new technologies and/or procedures.

Once this partnership is established, when an aerospace company wants to develop a new aircraft, or even part of a new aircraft like an aircraft engine, the FAA's aircraft certification process begins. The most onerous regulatory certification is called a "type certification" and refers to the approval process for the design of an entire aircraft, including subcomponents like jet engines and avionics. Much like the V-model in Fig. 6.1, type certification consists of five phases: conceptual design, requirements definition, compliance planning, implementation, and post certification (AIA et al., 2017). However, this systems engineering approach to regulation is designed to structure the information flow between the company and the FAA, in effect giving both sides a script that guides the regulatory process.

The FAA's conceptual design phase consists of "familiarization meetings" between the FAA and company to discuss the new product idea and its concept of operations. The goal is to identify critical areas and difficult certification issues at the outset and to develop shared awareness of what the company hopes to achieve. A "Project Specific Certification Plan" is started during this phase, which includes a project timeline, checklists for moving on to the next phases, means of compliance, testing plans, and other project management information. In effect, the FAA uses this plan to determine how aligned a company is with a systems engineering plan.

The FAA Requirements Definition stage focuses on how a company plans to address specific regulations and methods of compliance. Specific regulations known as airworthiness standards address all safety-related aspects of an aircraft including such items as weight limits, takeoff speeds, fabrication methods, and even passenger information signs. If a new product feature is not a covered by existing airworthiness regulations, a "special condition" assessment may be needed. A special condition is a new regulation particular to that aircraft, typically developed through notice-and-comment rulemaking, which fills the gap in existing airworthiness standards. Rulemaking can be a time- and labor-intensive process, so communication between a company and the FAA at the Requirements Definition stage allows for earlier processing of a perceived need for a special condition.

The Compliance Planning phase consists of completing the Project-Specific Compliance Plan, including finalizing airworthiness standards and detailing test plans to show compliance with those standards. It is at this stage where the critical role of the designee is formalized. Under statutory authority dating to at least 1958, the FAA delegates some of its certification responsibilities to employees of those companies with an established partnership for safety plans. These employees, known as designees, theoretically provide efficient collaboration between companies and the FAA and thus reduce the regulatory footprint. The legitimacy of the designee system has not always been viewed in a positive light (Henderson, Scott, & Hepher, 2013; Koenig, 2018).

In the Implementation phase, the company works closely with the FAA/designee to ensure that certification requirements are met. Testing is an important component of this phase and tests only count toward certification if the FAA agrees prior to testing as to the purpose and scope of the tests. Thus, testing for new technologies is a mutually agreed upon plan. When all compliance activities are complete, the type certification approval can be issued. By the time a new aircraft is fully approved for commercial operation, as much as 8 years may have passed since the beginning of the type certification process (Boeing Commercial Airplanes, 2013).

The final phase, Post Certification, focuses on continued airworthiness through maintenance and operational awareness, as well as conformance to approved manufacturing processes. Any subsequent required inspections are typically carried out by company's designees and overseen by the FAA. If a safety risk is discovered post operational deployment, the FAA can implement an "Airworthiness Directive" through notice-and-comment rulemaking (14 CFR §39), which makes it unlawful to operate an aircraft unless an inspection or some other mitigating action occurs. Airworthiness directives, which happen relatively frequently, allow the FAA to manage risk and address potential threats to safety in a relatively expeditious manner.

The FAA clearly approaches regulation of aviation systems through the lens of system engineering. The FAA builds trust and confidence in those companies that wish to fly in the national airspace through an intensive relationship building process. While such a regulatory approach is comprehensive, it also can be extremely costly and add significant time to the deployment of new technologies, which is often at odds with rapid design and implementation cycle of many autonomous vehicle technologies, particularly those coming from Silicon Valley.

Indeed, the FAA's traditional and process-laden approach to regulation has caused issues for the emerging unmanned aerial vehicle, aka drone, industry. After years of delay, the FAA was pushed through industry lobbying to address the growing demand for commercial drone use and accommodate them in the national airspace (Morgan & Seetharaman, 2015). In addition to commercial applications for small drones weighing less than 55 lbs, there is currently a push to begin passenger-carrying drone operations, which would involve significantly more reliance on autonomous systems than what is in current drone systems. However, the regulatory obstacles presented by the FAA for doing so are substantial (Nneji, Stimpson, Cummings, & Goodrich, 2017), and so it is not clear how these regulatory barriers could be overcome to take advantage of what could be transformational transportation technologies.

The FDA approach to regulation of new medical devices

Medical devices are another potential outlet for autonomous technology application, including surgical robots, drug delivery systems, and artificial intelligence—based diagnostic programs. When such technology falls within the statutory definition of a medical device as an instrument, machine, or a contrivance "intended for use in the diagnosis ... cure, mitigation, treatment, or prevention of disease," it falls into the regulatory purview of the FDA (21 USC §321(h)).

Tasked to both protect the public health and advance it through innovation, the FDA's medical device evaluation program attempts to ensure the safety and effectiveness of proposed systems in treating patients without placing overwhelming regulatory obstacles in the way of device developers (Maisel, 2015). In general, the FDA requires all medical device companies to follow a set of manufacturing best practices, which also includes controls on how a device is developed. These "design controls" essentially mandate that a medical device company follows a version of a systems engineering framework that includes design planning, input, output, review, verification, validation, and transfer (21 CFR §820). Although the FDA does not directly monitor a developer's adherence to a system engineering process like the FAA does, the FDA's stance is that "Design controls increase the likelihood that the design transferred to production will translate into a device that is appropriate for its intended use" (21 CFR §820.30).

Communication between medical technology developers and the FDA begins when a medical device developer wants to start testing a new device on humans, which occurs just before the System Validation stage of the V-model in Fig. 6.1. Human trials cannot be conducted without prior FDA clearance under an Investigational Device Exemption (IDE, 21 CFR §812.1). Because a device might attack a disease or condition in a novel way as compared to a currently approved device, no standard metrics of success can necessarily apply to new medical devices, which is why an applicant must work with the FDA to determine the criteria, endpoints, and objectives of clinical trials. Compulsory meetings before clinical trials thus serve to help determine what the goals of the testing will be and also mitigate risk.

Acquiring an IDE requires meetings with the FDA and submission of significant information about the device. This information includes a device description, drawings, components, specifications, materials, principles of operation, analysis of potential failure modes, proposed uses, patient populations, instructions, warnings, training requirements, clinical evaluation criteria and testing endpoints, and summaries of bench or animal test data or prior clinical experience (Center for Devices and Radiological Health, 2001).

The FDA currently has two main regulatory pathways for placing a new medical device on the market: premarket approval (PMA) and a 510(k) clearance. PMA is the more stringent of the two and applies to devices intended to support or sustain human life or when the device presents a potentially unreasonable risk of illness or injury (21 USC §360c(a)(1)(C)). For PMA, the FDA must determine that sufficient, valid scientific evidence exists to indicate the proposed device is safe and effective for its intended use (21 CFR 814). Thus, a PMA applicant generally must provide results from clinical investigations involving human subjects showing safety and effectiveness data, adverse reactions and complications, patient complaints, device failures, and other relevant scientific information (21 CFR 814.20(6)(ii)).

In 2005, the FDA estimated that reviewing one PMA application costs the agency an average of $870,000 (Crosse, 2009). One survey of medical device companies found that it took an average of 54 months to reach approval from first communication with the FDA about a potential innovation. The same survey found that the average total costs for a medical device company from the time of product conception to approval was $94 million, although these costs cannot all be attributed to compliance activities (Makower, Meer, & Denend, 2010).

The 510(k) pathway for approval is more straightforward as it applies to moderately risky devices. Generally, developers only need to show that the new device is "substantially equivalent" to a "predicate" device already on the market. A predicate device is one that was available on the market before 1976, or any device cleared since then via 510(k). In contrast to PMA, human-subject clinical trials for safety and effectiveness are typically not required (J. A. Johnson, 2016). However, the FDA can respond to a 510(k) application by requesting additional information it deems relevant (CFR §807.100(a)(3)), and data from device testing are typically provided for agency review.

A 510(k) application is significantly cheaper for the FDA to review, at an estimated average cost of $18,200 per application (Crosse, 2009). A company's total costs from product concept to clearance is around $31 million on average with an average time of 10 months from first submission of an application to clearance (Makower et al., 2010). This faster timeline and the lower evidentiary requirements may make 510(k) appealing to device companies over PMA, but it also potentially allows them to circumvent the systems engineering process.

Similar to the FAA, the FDA is struggling to understand the impact of autonomy as it relates to medical devices in the future. While the FDA does not have much experience in regulating autonomous systems that incorporate probabilistic reasoning, it does have experience with automated medical devices that operate within well-defined feedback control loops such as the Automated External Defibrillator (AED) and automated insulin monitoring and delivery devices (FDA, 2018). Just recently the first autonomous medical device, i.e., one that leverages probabilistic reasoning, was approved by the FDA, which allows a system to autonomously detect diabetic retinopathy (US FDA, 2018). This device, developed through a relatively new FDA Breakthrough Devices Program which is another version of a 510(k) approval, is only a diagnostic device and takes no action based on the information it senses. Thus, it remains to be seen how the FDA will approach the regulation of truly closed-loop autonomous systems that leverage probabilistic reasoning to both detect and then take action based on input.

The NHTSA approach to regulation of new technologies

Federal regulation of the automotive industry falls to NHTSA, whose mission is to "save lives, prevent injuries, and reduce economic costs due to road traffic crashes through education, research, safety standards, and enforcement activity" (NHTSA, 2018). NHTSA has authority over motor vehicles and related equipment including all components, accessories, and software which impacts the safety of a vehicle. With respect to cars, trucks, motorcycles, and other motor vehicles on public roadways, NHTSA attempts to assure safety through two mechanisms: minimum safety standards and recall authority (NHTSA, 2016c).

NHTSA administers the Federal Motor Vehicle Safety Standards (FMVSS), which provides minimum safety requirements to be followed by vehicle manufacturers (49 CFR §571). Established through notice-and-comment rulemaking, the FMVSS consists of 73 separate standards grouped generally into three categories: crash avoidance, crashworthiness, and post-crash survivability. These minimum safety standards address safety-related aspects of a vehicle, including headlights, braking systems, turn signals, electronic stability control, seat belts, motorcycle helmets, bus emergency exits, flammability, and many others (49 CFR §571). The FMVSS can be very specific, dictating subcomponent requirements as well as the objective tests needed to show compliance (e.g., 49 CFR §571.104 S4.1.2). Thus, the FMVSS can essentially dictate design requirements and testing standards, which streamline the systems engineering process for automotive manufacturers at the component level.

While NHTSA sets the FMVSS compliance tests, it does not independently test vehicles for compliance before they reach the market. Instead, manufacturers must self-certify that their vehicles comply with all relevant FMVSS. Moreover, while the FMVSS address verification testing, NHTSA does not require manufacturers follow a specific certification process. Instead, manufacturers are allowed to take those actions they deem meet compliance standards (Office of Vehicle Safety Compliance, 1998). They are also expected to monitor vehicles postmarketing for any compliance concerns.

After vehicles are on the market, the Office of Vehicle Safety Compliance (OVSC) buys cars from real-world new-car dealerships and then tests 30 of the 44 testable FMVSS on these cars. Due to budget limitations, these tests are effectively quality assurance spot checks, with the majority of vehicle makes and models never tested, although OVSC prioritizes testing high-risk vehicles (Office of Vehicle Safety Compliance, 1998). According to NHTSA, instances of manufacturer noncompliance with significant safety compromises are rare (NHTSA, 2016b).

As long as manufacturers meet the FMVSS, they are not prevented or restricted in adding new features into vehicles. Thus, unlike the FAA and the FDA, when an automotive manufacturer wishes to insert a new technology in a vehicle, there is no expectation of discussions or formal notification to the regulatory body as long as the FMVSS are met. Indeed, NHTSA generally only initiates dialogue with manufacturers when a defect is suspected in a car already released to the public or when manufacturers seek an exemption to the FMVSS.

NHTSA considers a problem to be a "defect" if it "poses an unreasonable risk to motor vehicle safety" (NHTSA, 2016c). A defect determination can be made whether the cause of the defect is known or unknown. In theory, NHTSA will act on a suspected defect so long as there is a likelihood that the suspected defect could or has caused crashes, injuries, or deaths. Once a defect is identified, NHTSA notifies the manufacturer, who can then choose to remedy the defect through repair, replacement, or refund (49 USC §30120). NHTSA has the authority to carry out civil enforcement actions, like mandating a recall and can impose civil penalties if manufacturers do not comply with orders to remedy defects (NHTSA, 2016c). However, NHTSA's actual ability to investigate defects is limited, with only 20 investigators in 2017 and a budget of less than $23 million dollars to fund defect investigations for the 250 million cars on American roadways (NHTSA, 2016a).

In addition to conversations that happen between NHTSA and manufacturers over possible defects, the other event that triggers formal dialogues is requests for FMVSS exemptions. This exemption process was designed to allow automotive manufacturers the ability to conduct more streamlined development and field evaluation of new safety technologies, with an assumption that these proposed new technologies would provide equivalent or better levels of safety as compared to legacy technologies. Under this exemption process, manufacturers can sell up to 2500 cars per year for 2 years (49 USC 301). However, such requests are rare, with reportedly only eight such exemptions requested since 1994 (Fraade-Blanar & Kalra, 2017).

Of the three federal regulatory agencies facing revolutionary changes due to autonomous systems, NHTSA by far has been the agency most targeted by industry and lobbyists to relax its regulatory approach. With more than $80 billion dollars invested in the research and development of cars that are self-driving (a car that occasionally requires human intervention) or driverless (a car with no controls available to a human), the autonomous vehicle industry is anxious to realize returns on its investments and see the FMVSS as a major barrier (Kerry & Karsten, 2017). Because manufacturers are currently limited to 2500 cars per exemption, the existing exemption process is generally seen as too restrictive and major efforts are underway to remove these regulatory restrictions so that these experimental cars can be sold on the market (Fraade-Blanar & Kalra, 2017; Kulisch, 2018).

A major problem with the removal of such regulatory restrictions designed to ensure safe technologies operate on public roads is establishing whether these new autonomous vehicles (either self-driving or driverless) truly have equivalent or better levels of safety than current cars. The 2018 death of a pedestrian caused by an Uber self-driving car highlighted the brittleness of an autonomous vehicle's perception system, as well as an overreliance on human vigilance meant to prevent such engineering flaws from surfacing (Laris, 2018).

In addition, there have been numerous deaths attributed to the Tesla Autopilot system, which is a precursor technology to self-driving cars but currently sold as a driver-assist feature and not covered by the FMVSS. While NHTSA absolved Tesla of any defects in the Autopilot system after the death of a driver in Florida in 2016 (Habib, 2017), the National Transportation Safety Board (NTSB), an independent government agency responsible for determining the probable cause of transportation accidents, found that Tesla did bear responsibility in the design and marketing of the Autopilot system (NTSB, 2017). Additional NTSB and NHTSA investigations are currently underway for another Tesla Autopilot-related fatality in California in 2018.

As a result of these fatalities and other problems exhibited by autonomous cars, many have called for the development of new testing protocols such as computer vision tests to ensure these new and unproven technologies are ready for the myriad of conditions they could face in different environments (Claybrook & Kildare, 2018; Cummings, 2019). However, it is not clear how and when such testing would be inserted into NHTSA's regulatory process, especially since it currently regulates cars *after* they have been sold on the market. Thus, regulation occurs in the operations and maintenance block in Fig. 6.1 and not in the testing blocks like what occurs for the FDA and FAA.

To better elucidate how the different agencies can both learn from one another but also recognize where true regulatory innovation is needed, the next section compares and contrasts the three different agencies' approach to regulation, with specific focus on regulation for automated and autonomous technologies.

Lessons learned across aviation, automotive, and medical device regulation

Given that the FAA, FDA, and NHTSA are all agencies that regulate safety-critical systems, it is instructive to compare how these agencies go about their approval processes and also examine some of their past difficulties to shed light on how they are likely to deal with autonomous systems in the future. To this end, the following sections compare when the three agencies intervene in the regulatory process, how they have dealt with past automation surprises, and how a bias toward regulating technologies based on equivalence could set a dangerous precedent.

Point of first contact

FAA, FDA, and NHTSA clearly have very different approaches in regulating new technologies; however, they all, in principle, share the same primary mission which is to promote safety. As illustrated in Fig. 6.2, one of the major differences in their approaches to new technology regulation is the point of first contact between manufacturers and the regulatory agencies, which is

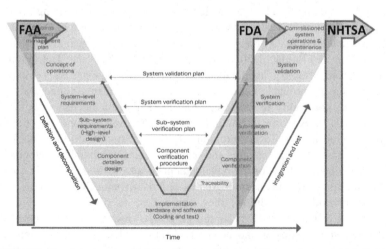

FIGURE 6.2 Regulatory agency first formal point of contact with manufacturers. *FAA*, Federal Aviation Administration; *FDA*, Food and Drug Administration; *NHTSA*, National Highway Transportation and Safety Administration.

overlaid on the V-model from Fig. 6.1 to gain a better understanding of both the time and engineering maturity stage differences.

The timing of these regulatory interventions should be viewed through the lens of how the notion of *safe enough* has developed in each of the agencies over time. Political and public discourse has significantly shaped each agency's culture, and often major events in an agency's history often shape new policy. Moreover, each agency has had very different experiences and timelines in terms of dealing with advanced computer systems, which will be discussed below.

The FAA, as depicted in Fig. 6.2, is the earliest intervening agency in terms of advancing new technologies, especially those that affect flight safety. The FAA's early intervention in the systems engineering process of a technology and continuous relationship building with aerospace companies, while time consuming and expensive, also helps companies to avoid major postmarket problems. This approach, which often takes longer than companies would like, has led to continued decreasing accident rates, with 2017 as the safest year on record for commercial air travel (Shepardson, 2018).

In contrast to the FAA, the FDA only becomes involved in medical device regulation once the system test validation stage is reached, as seen in Fig. 6.2. The FDA's middle ground approach likely reflects the nature of regulating potential life-or-death medical devices but also an understanding that many medical devices are eliminated internally due to a lack of funding or poor bench testing results. The FDA regulatory process also adheres to a systems engineering process which helps to mitigate the risk, especially for unproven technologies. However, as will be discussed in more detail in the following section, allowing companies to bypass a more rigorous systems engineering approach by claiming equivalence to an existing technology moves the point of contact to the right. This movement allows companies to bypass more expensive test and evaluations and shifts the burden of testing from the company to the public.

Lastly, when looking at the motor vehicle regulatory process, NHTSA has almost no involvement in a manufacturer's systems engineering process and only actively regulates technologies after problems emerge postmarket. Clearly the primary advantage to this approach is that it allows companies to get technologies to market faster and more cheaply. Whether this is an effective regulatory approach in terms of safety is a debated topic, especially as systems in cars grow more complex. While annual motor vehicle fatality rates steadily fell from the late 1970s, reaching their lowest point in 2011, they have been trending upward since that time (NSC, 2018), suggesting that the current status quo is not sufficient.

One example of how increasing complexity in automotive designs is at odds with current postmarket regulatory practices is the Toyota unintended acceleration problem in the 2009–10 timeframe. During this time period, at least 89 people were killed when Toyota cars reportedly accelerated in an uncontrollable manner, causing catastrophic accidents (Associated Press, 2010). In 2011, NTHSA and the US Department of Transportation absolved Toyota of any technical liability for these instances and instead blamed drivers (US DOT, 2011).

However in 2013, Toyota paid $1.6B to settle a class action lawsuit over these incidents (Trop, 2013, p. B3). Then a few months later, a jury found Toyota responsible for two unintended acceleration deaths with expert witnesses citing bugs in the software and throttle fail-safe defects. In emails released as part of the legal proceedings, Toyota executives admitted that they were not familiar with systems engineering practices like the V-model and that considering design of fail-safe technologies "is not part of the Toyota's engineering division's DNA" (Koopman, 2014). In a related finding, in 2014, the US Department of Justice fined Toyota $1.2B for covering up known safety problems with the system which were related to mechanical issues with the mats (Douglas & Fletcher, 2014).

This case highlights that waiting to regulate until postmarket problems emerge for complex systems with embedded software is a dangerous strategy, especially when manufacturers do not understand the importance of engaging in well-established risk mitigation strategies for safety-critical systems. In the end, the cost of not regulating the insertion of advanced automated technologies in this case was many deaths and billions of dollars in settlements and fines. Unless changes are made in how NHTSA currently regulates such technologies, this problem is likely only to get worse with the introduction of autonomous cars, which are far more complex with no standards for testing or safety.

Automation surprises

Since the 1970s, commercial airline accident rates and fatalities have fallen due to improvements in air traffic control and aircraft technologies, as well as crew training. However, in the early 1990s, there was an uptick in accidents that can be partially attributed to insertion of new automated flight control technologies which caused a series of episodes often termed as "automation surprises" (Sarter, Woods, & Billings, 1997). More specifically, these accidents were caused by a disconnect in the design of the advanced automation and pilot interfaces, with a series of airline accidents worldwide caused by pilot misunderstanding of what new advanced fly-by-wire technologies were doing (Ben-Yosef, 2005). This phenomenon is termed "mode confusion," which indicates that an operator does not realize what mode the automation is in and may take counterproductive actions as a result (Bredereke & Lankenau, 2002).

Significant research into this phenomenon followed this realization and resulting improvements have been made in aviation human–automation interfaces, as well as improved training. However, mode confusion continues to be a problem even in commercial airline operations today. Given that accident rates have decreased despite continued problems with mode confusion, one could argue that the FAA's early and frequent interactions with industry have provided checks and balances to this emergent problem, despite the fact that the FAA has not issued any specific regulations to guard against mode confusion.

The FDA has similarly struggled with understanding the impact of a similar phenomenon in the medical devices they regulate. One such example is the da Vinci robotic surgical assistant, which allows surgeons to remotely manipulate very small surgical tools through teleoperation. Such systems are automated and not autonomous, meaning that the computer only translates a surgeon's commanded inputs into specific actions, and no probabilistic reasoning occurs.

In addition to the significant number of technical and engineering problems with the da Vinci, research has demonstrated that almost 9% of all problems with da Vinci can be attributed to a form of mode confusion called unintended operation (Alemzadeh, Raman, Leveson, Kalbarczyk, & Iyer, 2016). Despite a significant number of lawsuits, both past and present, the FDA has not specifically addressed these mode confusion problems, which also occur in other computerized medical devices like patient-controlled analgesic pumps (Obradovich & Woods, 1997) and in radiation therapy (Leveson & Turner, 1995). Given that autonomous systems are even more difficult to understand, it is likely these mode confusion problems will lead to even more problems unless specifically acted upon by regulatory agencies.

Automation can produce additional surprises in the form of emergent latent software failures, which has been experienced by both commercial airplanes (Johnson & Holloway, 2007) and medical devices like the da Vinci (Alemzadeh et al., 2016). NHTSA is particularly susceptible to these problems since the Federal Motor Vehicle Safety Standards do not address software safety. In 2015, software bugs in general were responsible for 15% of automotive recalls, and the number of software-related components involved in recalls grew by almost 600% between 2011 and 2015 (Steinkamp, 2016). NHTSA's inexperience in understanding the systems engineering principles behind software testing and safety assurances means that NHTSA is ill-prepared to understand what safety regulations are needed for autonomous cars, which presents an exponential leap in software complexity.

Regulating technologies vis-à-vis equivalence

One commonly used regulatory tool for approving technologies that are deemed low risk is to provide exemptions and expedited approval processes. As discussed previously, the FDA has attempted to streamline the regulatory process of medical devices by providing a shorter and cheaper path to market though the 510(k) process for technologies deemed to be of lower risk. A key element of such approvals is the fact that new technologies can be shown to be equivalent to existing technologies in some way. This test of equivalence is not clearly defined and can vary widely across devices, and this practice has recently been widely criticized.

An example of one such decision for an automated medical device is the approval process for the da Vinci surgical robot (Rabin, 2013). The da Vinci received approval in 2000 from the FDA through the 510(k) process (Jones, 2000), claiming equivalence to existing laparoscopic surgical technologies. In 2014, Intuitive, the manufacturer of da Vinci, earmarked $67 million dollars for settlements for over 3000 product liability claims (Baron, 2017).

The substantial settlements which are ongoing with at least 52 pending lawsuits across 22 states suggest that the FDA failed to accurately assess the risk of this new technology, which clearly was not low. As discussed in the previous section on automation surprises, technology with embedded software, even if it performs the same function as an analog device, cannot be considered equivalent because of the unique and opaque nature of software code. If and when true autonomy is inserted in the da Vinci or other robotic surgery systems, it is not clear whether the FDA will understand the substantial increase in risk or continue to let manufacturers use the less rigorous 510(k) process which only requires limited testing, effectively allowing manufacturers to bypass well-established systems engineering practices.

Autonomous technologies are new and unproven, with no accepted software testing practices. Even the Department of Defense is struggling to determine what processes and technologies are needed to test autonomous systems (Ahner & Parson, 2016). Given the significant unknowns and the fact that these are safety-critical systems, it seems as if the "precautionary principle" (Wiener, 2017) should prevail. Where the risks of a new technology are unproven or unpredictable, the precautionary principle suggests (or in alternative formulations, demands) that technology be banned from public use until scientific methods show that the risks are acceptably low. When the risks include long-term, irreversible damage, of the three regulatory approaches featured here, it appears that the FAA's approach is the most precautionary.

This is not to say that the FDA and NHTSA should necessarily adopt those practices of the FAA, but rather that these and other agencies need to work together to define an approach to the regulation of autonomous systems. If a technology is truly low risk, then perhaps NHTSA's postmarket approach and even the FDA's 510(k) approach is warranted. But all agencies need to recognize that autonomous systems are not equivalent to any systems on the market and new regulatory approaches to these high risks, probabilistic reasoning safety-critical systems are needed.

Conclusion

When considering three different regulatory agencies (FAA, FDA, NHTSA) that certify technologies in safety-critical systems, the FAA's approach to regulation is the most conservative and precautionary in nature, in that a new product is not allowed to be put to real-world use without extensive review and testing. NHTSA's approach is exactly the opposite, namely that it assumes a new technological feature on a car is safe enough to put on the market unless shown to pose an unreasonable risk after introduction into the marketplace. The FDA is somewhere in the middle, as it leans more toward the precautionary approach by requiring extensive testing for new medical devices unless equivalency can be shown with an existing device, in which case a more limited premarket review is applied.

Past history of regulation of advanced automated safety-critical systems, specifically the da Vinci and the Toyota unintended acceleration case studies, demonstrate that the FDA and NHTSA approaches to regulation may not accurately assess the risk to public safety particularly for embedded software systems. While aviation has not been immune to similar problems, the FAA's precautionary regulatory process has provided a layer of safety checks and balances not afforded by other expedited or postmarket regulation approaches.

Given that autonomous systems will be much more difficult to assess in terms of risk to the public than previous automated technologies, regulatory agencies need to reassess when and how they make their first points of contacts with manufacturers of autonomous systems, as well as understanding the importance of tracking a company's use of established systems engineering practices that help to reduce risk. Moreover, these agencies need to realize that because of the complexities of probabilistic reasoning software that are at the heart of autonomous systems, traditional approaches to regulation may not support their overall mission of public safety.

To this end, new regulatory approaches are needed that likely involve not just reassessing current practices but also incorporate expertise from a larger group of stakeholders. In order to develop a set of regulatory best practices that permit innovation while ensuring public safety for autonomous systems, regulatory agencies will need to include company representatives like software engineers, much like the FAA currently does for its type certifications. In addition, because of the nascent and unproven nature of autonomous technologies, these regulatory agencies should routinely call on academics and government experts from places like federally funded research and development centers (FFRDCs) as independent reviewers.

Autonomous systems across medicine and transportation have the potential to usher in a new age of personalized services, which could dramatically improve the quality of life for a broad cross section of society. However, autonomous systems represent a significant increase in system complexity, with engineers and computer scientists still struggling to understand their own creations in this space. Given that there is no consensus on how to test embedded probabilistic reasoning in autonomous software systems to ensure equivalent or better levels of safety, it seems prudent that regulatory agencies, at this point in time, should take a more precautionary approach until more confidence is gained, especially for application in safety-critical systems.

Acknowledgment

This chapter was supported in part by the US Department of Transportation and the University of North Carolina's Collaborative Sciences Center for Road Safety (CSCRS).

References

Ahner, D. K., & Parson, C. R. (2016). *Workshop report: Test and evaluation of autonomous systems. Wright-Patterson AFB.* OH: US Air Force.

AIA, AEA, GAMA, & FAA Aircraft Certification Service and Flight Standards Service. (2017). *The FAA and industry guide to product certification.* Washington DC: US Department of Transportation.

Alemzadeh, H., Raman, J., Leveson, N., Kalbarczyk, Z., & Iyer, R. (2016). Adverse events in robotic surgery: A retrospective study of 14 Years of FDA data. *PLoS One, 11*(4). https://doi.org/10.1371/journal.pone.0151470.

Andrews, A., Abdelgawad, M., & Gario, A. (2016). World model for testing autonomous systems using Petri nets. In *Paper presented at the IEEE 17th international symposium on high assurance systems engineering (HASE), Orlando, FL.*

Ashford, N. A., & Hall, R. P. (2012). Regulation-induced innovation for sustainable development. *Administrative & Regulatory Law News, 21*(3).

Associated Press. (2010). Sudden acceleration death toll rises. *New York Times,* B2.

Bar-Yam, Y. (2003). When systems engineering fails — toward complex systems engineering. In *Paper presented at the 2003 IEEE international conference on systems, man and cybernetics, Washington DC.*

Baron, E. (2017). Robot-surgery firm from Sunnyvale facing lawsuits, reports of death and injury. *The Mercury News.*

Ben-Yosef, E. (2005). *The evolution of the US airline industry: Theory, strategy and policy.* New York: Springer US.

Blanchard, B. S., & Fabrycky, W. J. (1998). *Systems engineering and analysis* (3rd ed.). Upper Saddle River, NJ: Prentice Hall.

Boehm, B. (1988). A spiral model of software development and enhancement. *Computer,* 61−72.

Boeing Commercial Airplanes. (2013). *Certifying boeing airplanes.*

Bredereke, J., & Lankenau, A. (2002). A rigorous view of mode confusion. In *Paper presented at the SafeComp, Bremen, Germany.*

Calo, R. (2014). *The case for a federal robotics commission.* Retrieved from Washington DC.

Center for Devices and Radiological Health. (2001). *Early collaboration meetings under the FDA modernization act (FDAMA); final guidance for industry and for CDRH staff.* Washington DC: Department of Health and Human Services.

Claybrook, J., & Kildare, S. (2018). Autonomous vehicles: No driver...no regulation? *Science, 361*(6397), 36−37. https://doi.org/10.1126/science.aau2715.

Crosse, M. (2009). *Shortcomings in FDA's premarket review, Postmarket surveillance, and inspections of device manufacturing establishments.* Washington DC: Government Accounting Office.

Crowder, J. A., & Friess, S. A. (2013). *Systems engineering agile design methodologies.* New York: Springer.

Cummings, M. L. (2019). Adaptation of licensing examinations to the certification of autonomous systems. In H. Yu, X. Li, R. Murray, S. Ramesh, & C. J. Tomlin (Eds.), *Safe, autonomous and intelligent vehicles* (pp. 145−162). Basel, Switzerland: Springer International Publishing.

Douglas, D., & Fletcher, M. A. (2014). Toyota reaches $1.2 billion settlement to end probe of accelerator problems. *Washington Post.*

FAA. (2018). *Mission*. Retrieved from https://www.faa.gov/about/mission/.

Favarò, F. M., Jackson, D. W., Saleh, J. H., & Mavris, D. N. (2013). Software contributions to aircraft adverse events: Case studies and analyses of recurrent accident patterns and failure mechanisms. *Reliability Engineering & System Safety, 113*, 131–142.

FDA. (2018). *FDA approves automated insulin delivery and monitoring system for use in younger pediatric patients* [Press release].

Fraade-Blanar, L., & Kalra, N. (2017). *Autonomous vehicles and federal safety standards: An exemption to the rule?*. Retrieved from Santa Monica, CA.

Griggs, T., & Wakabayashi, D. (2018). How a self-driving Uber killed a pedestrian in Arizona. *New York Times*.

Grissinger, M. (2012). Misprogramming patient-controlled analgesia levels causes dosing errors. *Pharmacy and Therapeutics, 37*(2), 74–75.

Habib, K. (2017). *Investigation: PE 16-007. (PE 16-007)*. Washington DC: US Department of Transportation.

Henderson, P., Scott, A., & Hepher, T. (2013). *Insight: Will dreamliner drama affect industry self-inspection?* Reuters.

Hutchins, A. R., Cummings, M. L., Draper, M., & Hughes, T. (October 26-30, 2015). Representing autonomous systems' self-confidence through competency boundaries. In *Paper presented at the 59th annual meeting of the human factors and ergonomics society, Los Angeles, CA*.

Jaffe, A. B., Peterson, S. R., Portney, P. R., & Stavins, R. N. (1995). Environmental regulation and the competitiveness of U.S. Manufacturing: What does the evidence tell us? *Journal of Economic Literature, 33*(1), 132–163.

Johnson, J. A. (2016). *FDA regulation of medical devices*. Congressional Research Services.

Johnson, C. W., & Holloway, C. M. (2007). The dangers of failure masking in fault-tolerant software: Aspects of a recent in-flight upset event. In *Paper presented at the 2nd Institution of Engineering and Technology International Conference on System Safety, London*.

Jones, U. (2000). *FDA clears robotic surgical system*.

Kalra, N., & Paddock, S. M. (2016). *Driving to safety: How many miles of driving would it take to demonstrate autonomous vehicle reliability?*. Retrieved from Santa Monica, CA http://www.rand.org/pubs/research_reports/RR1478.html.

Kerry, C. F., & Karsten, J. (2017). *Gauging investment in self-driving cars*. Retrieved from Washington DC.

Knight, W. (April 11, 2017). The dark secret at the heart of AI. *MIT Technology Review*.

Koenig, D. (2018). *US watchdog criticizes FAA oversight of American Airlines*. Associated Press.

Koopman, P. (Producer). (July 18, 2014). A case study of Toyota unintended acceleration and software safety [presentation]. Retrieved from https://users.ece.cmu.edu/~koopman/toyota/koopman-09-18-2014_toyota_slides.pdf.

Krisher, T., & Billeaud, J. (June 22, 2018). *Police: Backup driver in fatal Uber crash was distracted*. Associate Press.

Kulisch, E. (March 16, 2018). Lobbying push targets holdouts on autonomous vehicle bill. *Automotive News*.

Laris, M. (2018). Fatal Uber crash spurs debate about regulation of driverless vehicles. *Washington Post*.

Leveson, N. G., & Turner, C. S. (1995). An investigation of the Therac-25 accidents. In D. J. Johnson, & H. Nissenbaum (Eds.), *Computers, ethics & social values* (pp. 474–514). Upper Saddle River, NJ: Prentice Hall.

Lietzen, I. (2017). *Robots: Legal affairs committee calls for EU-wide rules* [Press release].

Maisel, W. (2015). *Robotic assisted surgical devices workshop keynote*. Silver Spring, MD: Department of Health and Human Services. Retrieved from http://www.fda.gov/MedicalDevices/NewsEvents/WorkshopsConferences/ucm435255.htm.

Makower, J., Meer, A., & Denend, L. (2010). *FDA impact on U.S. medical technology innovation: A survey of over 200 medical technology companies.* Retrieved from Stanford, CA.

Maney, K. (2017). Goldman sacked: How artificial intelligence will transform wall Street. *Newsweek Magazine.*

Marcus, G. (2018). *Deep learning: A critical appraisal.* arXiv.

Mitre. (2014). *Systems engineering guide.* Retrieved from McLean, VA.

Morgan, D., & Seetharaman, D. (2015). Industry lobbyists take aim at proposed FAA drone rules. *Technology News.*

NHTSA. (2016a). *Budget estimates fiscal year 2017.* Washington DC: US Department of Transportation.

NHTSA. (2016b). *Federal automated vehicles policy:accelerating the next revolution in roadway safety.* Washington DC.

NHTSA. (2016c). *NHTSA enforcement guidance bulletin 2016–02: Safety-related defects and automated safety technologies.* Washington DC: Federal Register.

NHTSA. (2018). *NHTSA's core values.* Retrieved from https://www.nhtsa.gov/about-nhtsa.

Nneji, V., Stimpson, A., Cummings, M. L., & Goodrich, K. (2017). Exploring concepts of operations for on-demand passenger air transportation. In *Paper presented at the AIAA aviation, Denver, CO.*

NSC. (2018). *NSC motor vehicle fatality estimates* [Press release].

NTSB. (2017). *Highway accident report: Collision between a car operating with automated vehicle control systems and a tractor-semitrailer truck near Williston, Florida, May 7, 2016. (NTSB/HAR-17/02 PB2017-102600). Washington DC.*

Obradovich, J. H., & Woods, D. D. (1997). Users as designers: How people cope with poor HCI design in computer-based medical devices. *Human Factors, 38*(4), 574–592.

Office of Vehicle Safety Compliance. (1998). *Compliance testing program.* Washington DC: US Department of Transportation.

Rabin, R. C. (March 25, 2013). Salesman in the surgical suite. *New York Times.*

Sarter, N. B., Woods, D. D., & Billings, C. E. (1997). Automation surprises. In G. Salvendy (Ed.), *Handbook of human factors and ergonomics* (pp. 1926–1943). New York: Wiley.

Schwartz, A. (2017). Hybrid closed-loop insulin delivery systems for type 1 diabetes come of age. *Stanford Medicine News.* Retrieved from https://med.stanford.edu/news/all-news/2017/04/hybrid-insulin-delivery-systems-for-type-1-diabetes-come-of-age.html.

Shepardson, D. (January 1, 2018). *2017 safest year on record for commercial passenger air travel.* Reuters.

Steinkamp, N. (2016). *2016 automotive warranty & recall report.* Retrieved from.

Trop, J. (2013). *Toyota will pay $1.6 billion over faulty accelerator suit.*

US, D. O. T. (2011). *U.S. Department of transportation releases results from NHTSA-NASA study of unintended acceleration in Toyota vehicles* [Press release].

US FDA. (2018). *FDA permits marketing of artificial intelligence-based device to detect certain diabetes-related eye problems* [Press release].

Villasenor, J. (2014). *Products liability and driverless cars: Issues and guiding principles for legislation.* Retrieved from Washington DC.

Wiener, J. B. (2017). Precautionary principle. In L. Krämer, & E. Orlando (Eds.), *Principles of environmental law.*

Woolley, S. C., & Howard, P. N. (2017). *Computational propaganda worldwide: Executive summary.* Working paper 2017.11. Retrieved from Oxford, UK: comprop.oii.ox.ac.UK.

Chapter 7

The role of consumer robots in our everyday lives

Heather C. Lum

Embry-riddle Aeronautical University, Daytona Beach, FL, United States

Chapter outline

Robotics in the consumer sector has been dominated primarily by cleaning devices, starting in 2001, when British manufacturer Dyson had an unusual innovation: a robotic vacuum. Turn it on, and let it sweep up dust, dirt, and debris. Dyson never launched the vacuum, as it thought the price would not be well received, and companion robots were still science fiction. Meanwhile, the first Roomba (vacuuming robot) by iRobot was introduced a year later in 2002, and now up to 23% of households vacuum their floors with a robot (medium.com, 2018). Dyson later joined in, and today, there are many different robotic vacuums with improved technology at various prices. The field of robotics is currently undergoing a paradigm shift in which we are going "from the factory into service and our homes" (Castelo & Schmitt, 2017). A new generation of robots that operate in service applications, domestic environments, entertainment domain, or even within the human body is being developed in public and corporate research laboratories all over the world. These robots will change the way we grow up, play, teach, work, pursue our lifestyle, entertain ourselves, interact with machines, animate our surroundings, get old, care, or alleviate handicaps.

With acceptance of robot vacuums in people's homes, there is growing demand for personal robots to aid in a variety of tasks. It could be that Rosie, the robot maid from *The Jetsons* cartoon, has been engrained as the

Living with Robots. https://doi.org/10.1016/B978-0-12-815367-3.00007-4

prototypical representation of what a robot should do. However, the consumer robot market is changing as well as our expectations of what their roles are in our homes and beyond. Consumer robotics is shifting from a phase of being largely dominated by cleaning robots to one where robotic personal assistants or family companions are becoming the norm. Indeed, these robots are transforming into interactive connected devices. Worldwide sales of consumer robots reached $3.8 billion in 2016, and the market will continue to grow strongly over the next few years, while providing significant opportunities for new industry participants as well (medium.com, 2018). This is a market with very high potential in value and volume. Today, China is the fastest-growing robotics market, followed by Japan and the United States. As the opportunities are numerous, more and more entrepreneurs are jumping into the market to take advantage of the popularity for consumer robots. In fact, it is this entrepreneurial innovation that is fueling the demand for robotics. Research from the International Federation of Robotics (2018) states that startups less than five years old already make up 15% of all companies engaged in the services robotics market. A lot of investment is pouring in, only adding to the number of companies in this space. What is even better for investors and entrepreneurs is the fact that robotics is no longer just for the luxury market or limited to certain industries. It is a global opportunity ripe for innovation in the areas of education, entertainment, health care, and defense. In this chapter, we will examine the role of robots in our everyday lives, particularly robots whose purpose is as companions to us. We will dive in to the perceptions and uses of these robots, whether they are effective in their roles, a history of how companion robots have come to be and are transforming into, and will first start by defining what companion robots actually are and what they are not.

What are companion robots?

A 2017 report by P&S Market Research (2017) projected that the global personal robot market would reach $34.1 billion by 2022. While cleaning robots still hold the largest share of this market, demand for companion robots is also expected to grow. A companion robot is one that is capable of providing useful assistance in a socially acceptable manner. This means that a robot companion's first goal is to assist humans in some way. They may aid in social facilitation, communication engagement, and overall companionship to their user(s) (Feil-Seifer & Mataric, 2005). Robot companions are expected to communicate with the lay person in a natural and intuitive way without the need for programming or other technical knowledge. These robots are often developed to help people with special needs such as older people, autistic children, or the disabled. They usually aim to help in a specific environment: a house, a school, a care home, or a hospital (Robinson, MacDonald, Kerse, & Broadbent, 2013).

Robots at home

Within the home setting, robot companions should ideally be able to perform a wide array of tasks including educational functions, home security, diary duties, entertainment, and message delivery services. Although there are none that can currently accomplish all of the tasks, we are moving closer to that reality. Robot assistants are the primary driving force in the home setting. Assistants are robots that help you with day-to-day household tasks, making your life easier. These little in-home companions serve a variety of purposes: everything from educational assistance to schedule organization. They are designed to take the daily tasks that make your life more stressful off your hands, like trying to remember upcoming appointments or birthdays. For instance, there is a new robot on the market called Professor Einstein who engages with you, shares his passion for science, delivers brain games, and more (Gruber, 2017). While other robot assistants like Amazon Echo or Google Home focus on schedule keeping and offloading mental tasks and reminders, Professor Einstein attempts to improve and enhance cognitive functioning. Other robots like iPatrol Riley are mobile home monitoring robots that detect motion, alert users remotely, and can call the police for you. Others like Jibo helps you manage and build on the most important relationships in your life. The bot learns to recognize the faces of your family and friends, so that it can start conversations with them when they enter a room or come visit your home (Gruber, 2017). It also helps you take and share photographs to your social media accounts, so you will never forget to capture and share an important family moment again. Popularity with consumer robots in the home will continue to grow as we integrate more and more "smart" solution to make our everyday lives easier.

Robots at school

In a school setting, aside from their growing role in primary education as tools for teaching science and engineering topics, robots have been used in schools in order to encourage socialization among students (Kanda, Hirano, Eaton, & Ishiguro, 2003). Using robots to support teaching and learning, from secondary school to undergraduate courses to graduate education, has become a popular research topic in recent years (Klassner, 2002; Klassner & Anderson, 2003). Weinberg and Yu (2003) describe three factors (unique learning experience, cost, and plug-and-play feel) to demonstrate that robots will successfully support education. First, robots are the physical embodiment of computations and provide unique experiences for the learner. They provide a wide design space for students to explore, to make hypotheses about how things work, and to conduct experiments to validate their beliefs and assumptions. Students can receive strong, visceral feedback from physically experiencing their work. The second factor described by Weinberg and Yu is cost. Over the last decade, the cost of computation has dropped exponentially. As a result, robot controllers have been designed and marketed at prices that are accessible to schools with even modest budgets (Marin, Mikhak, Resnick, Silverman, & Berg, 2000). The third important factor is the plug-and-play feel of the new robot platforms. The multidisciplinary nature of robots has previously relegated their study to larger research institutions that have the range of prerequisite knowledge for engineering complex systems. Robot controllers, such as the Handy Board and the Mindstorm RCX, have mitigated this need by making it relatively simple to plug in motors and sensors and use well-known or simple programming environments. The development of educational robots is still in the initial stages. As robot technologies develop, the use of robots to support teaching and learning has gained popularity. Over the past decade, researchers have provided substantial evidence that the robot is a great teaching aid for mathematics and science (Chang, Lee, Chao, Wang, & Chen, 2010). Furthermore, educational robots are helpful to students in developing collaboration and problem-solving abilities.

Robots in care facilities

In care facilities such as nursing homes or hospitals, robots are used to aid in physical therapy, as daily life assistants who engage as cognitive aides and as companions to help reduce stress and depression. The rising number of older people is an increasing concern because of the predicted strain on health-care services. Two current demographic trends in industrialized countries are the decrease in rates of childbirth and the great increase in life expectancy (Doi, Kuwahara, & Morimoto, 2017). These tendencies have deep societal implications, creating a growing proportion of elderly people. The more people get older, the more they are likely to need medical, social, and personal care services. At the same time, there is a smaller proportion of young people to support these needs. As a consequence, a more supporting environment has to be envisioned in order to reduce the individual and community burden. This environment involves the implementation of robots to aid several different ways. A health-care robot is a robot with the aim of promoting or monitoring health, assisting with tasks that are difficult to perform due to health problems, or preventing further health decline. Health in this sense encompasses not just physical but mental, emotional, and psychosocial problems. Health-care robots can have many different functions and can be categorized as either rehabilitation robots or social robots. Rehabilitation robots are physically assistive devices that are not primarily communicative or perceived as social entities. Their job is to perform a physical task or make a task easier for the user. In contrast, a social robot is an easily understood and likable interface for older people to interact with and/or act as a companion. Social robots can also help a person perform a task to improve day-to-day life. Social robots can further be categorized into service-type robots or companionship robots. Service-type robots are assistive devices and are designed to support people living independently by assisting with mobility, completing household tasks, and monitoring health and safety (Broekens, Heerink, & Rosendal, 2009). The robot is classed as social because the user can interact with it and the robot can determine from the user's input how it can assist. Companion robots do not assist the user in performing any task but aim to improve quality of life by acting as a companion. Some robots provide both companionship and assistance.

Human—robot interaction

Robotic technology has begun to flourish within the past 10 years, and recently robots have begun to be used for purposes outside of industrial and manufacturing of products. Indeed, we have seen robots becoming social beings developed to be our companions, our help, our entertainment, and it is that direct contact with us, which has allowed research in this area to be ever present. This has implications for various fields of research including but not limited to robotics, engineering, psychology, computer science, and many more (Fong, Nourbakhsh, & Dautenhahn, 2003). If robots are to be used in everyday environments, they will have to encounter and interact with people. They must survive and carry out tasks in a disordered and unpredictable environment, safely and effectively.

Sociability

The sociability of robots is a more recent phenomenon, and it is becoming an increasingly important component that robots may need in order to interact in a human world. There are a number of contributions in the literature where humans and robots coexist in the same environment. These studies have frequently focused only on the safety of the human (Nomura, Kanda, & Suzuki, 2006) and have failed to take human comfort into account. Even such terms as "robotiquette" have been developed and studied in order to instill more effective human—robot interactions (Ogden & Dautenhahn, 2000). As the uses of robots become increasingly social in nature including those used as therapeutic agents, social mediators, and even model social agents (Dautenhahn, 2003), it is important that we study how these social robots may be perceived by the humans they are meant to interact with. However, human—robot interaction research is still relatively new in comparison to traditional service robotics where, e.g., robots deliver hospital meals or provide security services, application domains that require relatively minimal human—robot interaction.

Anthropomorphism

Humans have a natural tendency to respond to nonhumans in a humanlike manner. This is called anthropomorphism and is the attribution of human qualities, characteristics, or states (cognitive or emotional) placed on nonhuman entities (Guthrie, 1993), such as animals, robots, or inanimate objects. This allows humans to rationalize the entity's actions and behaviors (Duffy, 2003). There is some debate between researchers in regard to the importance of anthropomorphism on scientific research. Some suggest that anthropomorphism confounds scientific research and could potentially lead to issues of unpredictability that could compromise the design of the study (Shneiderman, 1989). Since complete removal of anthropomorphism from science is rarely possible, it is suggested that researchers should only consider anthropomorphism in order to account for its presence during assessment (Caporael, 1986). However, instead of trying to eliminate the effects of anthropomorphism on research, we need to focus on anthropomorphism directly. This will allow us to further understand the link between the human and entity during a social interaction.

The role of anthropomorphism is particularly important in consumer robotics as it directly affects how the human interacts with and perceives said robot. Our natural tendency to anthropomorphize, grounded in Theory of Mind and related psychological mechanisms, is crucial to our interactions with robots (Boden, 2006, p 69-74.). Some relatively superficial aspects of robots (e.g., physical appearance) can trigger animistic, even empathetic, responses on the part of human beings. Other factors are subtler, including various aspects of the language (if any) used by the artifice, and/or of the thinking processes apparently going on. Robotics (like AI in general) both promises and threatens to alter how people think about themselves. Unlike AI programs, robots are physical entities moving around in a physical world. This makes them more humanlike in various ways. But physicality is not the same thing as embodiment. For someone who wants to insist on a distinction between robots and humans, the fact that robots are not living things is likely to be important.

By incorporating the underlying principles and expectations people use in social interactions into human–robot interactions, we are able to facilitate rather than constrain the interaction (Duffy, 2003). There is a two-way interaction between a robot and that which it becomes socially engaged with, whether another robot or a person. It is in embracing the physical and social embodiment issues that a system can be termed a "social robot" (Duffy, 2000). A robot's capacity to be able to engage in meaningful social interaction with people inherently requires the employment of a degree of anthropomorphic, or humanlike, qualities whether in form or behavior or both. This area of research allows us to classify the anthropomorphic tendencies necessary to enhance human–robot interaction and design more effective robots necessary to meet the needs of the ever-increasing number of social robots available to the general public.

Applications of companion robots

Children

One area, where human–robot interaction has been studied is the application of robotic pets for children and how they distinguish robotic entities with live ones. One such study observed the spontaneous interaction behavior when children and adults interacted with either a Sony AIBO robotic dog or a real dog. There was no difference in amount of time before first tactile interaction with the entity or length of time spent touching the real dog versus the AIBO (Kerepesi, Kubinyi, Jonsson, Magnusson, & Miklosi, 2006). However, another study focusing on children's beliefs about robots revealed that they do indeed make a distinction between live and robotic entities (Bernstein & Crowley, 2008). After interacting with eight separate entities, two of which were robotic, the children made unique classifications for the humanoid robot and rove along the biological and intelligence characteristic spectrum. This was also true for the psychological characteristics attributed to the robotic entities when compared with the people, cat, computer, and doll. In this instance, the robotic entities were considered to have more psychological characteristics attributed to them than the computer or doll, but far less than the cat or people. Children in this study, did make unique distinctions between live, robotic, and other entity types on behavioral and psychological markers.

Another study examined the beliefs that preschool-age children had of AIBO and a stuffed animal dog. When these children interacted with either entity their beliefs about the "animal" and ways that they behaved with it were not consistent with each other. In this study, the same proportion of preschool children attributed mental states, social rapport, and moral standing to both AIBO and the stuffed animal. From the behavioral interaction, it is suggested that preschool children treated AIBO like it was more capable of making its own decisions than the stuffed dog (Kahn Jr., Friedman, Perez-Granados, & Freier, 2006). Yet another study found that when children were put in an interaction situation, they were just as likely to talk to AIBO as they were a real dog. Despite this, the children conceptualized the real dog as having more physical essences, mental states, sociality, and moral standing than AIBO (Melson et al., 2009). This suggests that while people may treat an AIBO and real dog similarly, they may have different beliefs or attributions about them.

Interestingly, although children are encouraged to take part in a wide range of robotic competitions, robots are still frequently designed from an adult perspective, ignoring children's perceptions and attitudes about robots (Druin, 1999). If successful robots are to be designed and used within educational curriculum activities, children should be at the forefront of the design course and suitable methods for obtaining children's views should be designed and utilized.

Elderly adults

The significant rate of increase of older individuals within the population has spawned a field of research looking at the potential benefits that can be achieved through human—robot interaction. Robots are now being designed specifically to meet the various care needs that attend to increased independence (Camarinha-Matos & Vieira, 1999) ranging from companionship to therapeutic assistance.

Often, the design of these specialized robots is dependent upon a specialized task (e.g., escorting people, cognitive impairment) or population (e.g., nursing home patients, dementia patients). Intelligent assistive technologies such as activity monitoring, assurance systems, compensation systems (navigational support, schedule management, activity-guidance systems), and assessment systems are being implemented in robots in order to provide assistance for daily activities for older individuals including those with cognitive impairments (Pollack, 2005). For example, Nursebot is one mobile robot that was designed to escort individuals, provide reminders of appointments and guidance to the elderly in an assisted living facility (Montemerlo, Pineau, Roy, Thrun, & Verma, 2002). Knowing that the elderly find robots to be more complicated to use and use different strategies when learning how to use a robot (e.g., elderly will ask experts for help) than younger adults (Scopelliti, Giuliani, & Fornara, 2005), designing a robot that is intuitive to use is recommended (Monemerlo, Pineau, Roy, Thrun & Verma, 2002). Further, Heerink, Krose, Evers, and Wielinga (2010) looked at how likely an elderly population is to actually use a robot. They found that elderly individuals were more likely to use socially expressive robot, more adaptive capabilities of robot influences intent to use, intent to use predicts actual use, and usefulness and attitude predict actual use of a virtual agent.

Scopelliti et al. (2005) suggest that acceptance is dependent upon both the practical benefits that robots provide as well as the cognitive, affective, and emotional components individuals have with respect to the robots. Increasing communication is the important goal for the elderly population. Elderly seem to be more comfortable and expressive in communicating with robots who are in turn socially communicative with them (Heerink, Krose, Evers, & Wielinga, 2006; Looije, Neerincx, & Cnossen, 2009).

Arras and Cerqui (2005, p. 605) suggested that among all age groups, older adults had the best image of robotics and were the most inclined to believe that robotics could somehow contribute to their personal happiness. In addition, they were the group that was most likely to believe in a robot for helping them regain independence at performing their daily tasks. However, they did not want to depend on robots, for fear that it might lead them to have fewer social contacts. In the study by Ezer, Fisk, and Rogers (2009), the older adults reported more willingness than younger adults to have robots perform critical monitoring tasks that would require little interaction between the robot and the human. The particular limitations and unique needs of the elderly population need to be considered by designers when creating robots to aid in their everyday tasks.

Perceptions of robots and conclusion

The arrival of robots in our daily life has been anticipated long before they finally set foot into our homes. The mere existence of robots does not come as a surprise to the man in the street. But going further, how far is he or she ready to accept a robot in his or her daily life? One of the main challenges when designing robots will be people's acceptance of robots sharing their daily lives.

But what do we know exactly about how this new kind of machine is perceived? In order to develop robots for personal use, the answers to some questions are still lacking. For instance, what are current perceptions of robots by the general public and what influences this? Do people actually need robots and what for? What sort of appearance and interaction modality is most desirable? There have been only a few large-scale studies exploring social perception and acceptance of robots. In Japan, Nomura studied robots' effect on humans (2006). He developed a psychological scale to measure the negative attitudes toward robots and anxiety evoked in human–robot interaction. He designed several questionnaire-based studies gathering up to 2300 answers. He mainly showed that people's assumptions about robots influence their attitudes toward them. In Switzerland, Arras and Cerqui (2005) carried out a large-scale survey including more than 2000 people. They investigated questions related to the image of robotics, the potential acceptance of robots in daily life, and appearance preferences. The study showed that 70% of people have a neutral image of robotics, and 71% stated that they could imagine living with robots on a daily basis. This survey also showed that almost half of the sample would not like to have a robot with a humanoid appearance.

Robots will some day be part of our everyday lives. Robotics research is advancing to the point where we can begin building robots to act as partners with us in domains such as education, health care, household work, entertainment, and scientific research. What does it mean for a robot to act as a partner rather than as a tool? In general, we would expect the robot to act and react in many respects like a human does: to understand our directions to complete a task, to guide us in learning something new, and to assist us when we need a helping hand. The enhanced social capabilities of current robots will stretch the boundaries of how firms directly interact with their consumers. Thus, the user's role in robot interaction will eventually evolve from a present research participant to a future service consumer, making it important to understand the implications of perceptions of robot interaction in a service environment, such as the value users perceive from service delivered by a robot.

When building robots to interact with people in social ways, there are many important features of the robot that must be implemented well, such as having sufficient agility to complete their tasks, being robust enough for the environments they work in, and having an appearance acceptable to their desired audience. The aspects of social robots that we are concerned with here are mainly with regard to how people perceive them. When a robot is designed to be depended on by a person for completing a task, it must be seen as trustworthy. This is not a feature that we know how to turn off or on, so it likely has to do with how the robot interacts with a person. In interactions where a person is relying on a robot for information, they must believe that the information is credible (Burgoon, Bonito, Bengtsson, Kundeberg, & Allspach, 2000). If information is being conveyed in a situation where a robot is teaching a person, then the robot must be capable of engaging the person in an interaction.

Current research consistently indicates that the way a robot interacts with the human is the most important factor in how it is perceived (Dautenhahn et al., 2005). From an anthropological perspective, human values are always embedded in technological devices. Thus, contrary to accepted ideas, technology is never neutral but rather it is a mirror of the society. From this viewpoint, robots are created according to what is important in the social group where they are built and represent a kind of externalization of human abilities. They are not the exact replication of mankind but only of some selected aspects of it. Studying these aspects shows what is considered as important. Further, robots have a very strong symbolic impact, as once robots do exist, humans redefine themselves in comparison with them. Thus, knowing more precisely what people think of robots as well as their expectations for the future of robotics gives us also a better idea about how humans describe themselves.

References

Arras, K. O., & Cerqui, D. (2005). *Do we want to share our lives and bodies with robots? A 2000 people survey: A 2000-people survey*. Technical Report.

Bernstein, D., & Crowley, K. (2008). Searching for signs of intelligent life: An investigation of young children's beliefs about robot intelligence. *The Journal of the Learning Sciences, 17*(2), 225–247.

Boden, M. A. (2006). *Robots and anthropomorphism*. Tech. Rep. WS-06-09.

Broekens, J., Heerink, M., & Rosendal, H. (2009). Assistive social robots in elderly care: A review. *Gerontechnology, 8*, 94–103.

Burgoon, J. K., Bonito, J. A., Bengtsson, B., Cederberg, C., Lundeberg, M., & Allspach, L. (2000). Interactivity in human-computer interaction: A study of credibility, understanding, and influence. *Computers in Human Behavior, 16*, 553–574.

Camarinha-Matos, L. M., & Vieira, W. (1999). Intelligent mobile agents in elderly care. *Robotics and Autonomous Systems, 27*(1–2), 59–75.

Caporael, L. R. (1986). Anthropomorphism and mechanomorphism: Two faces of the human machine. *Computers in Human Behavior, 2*(3), 215–234.

Castelo, N., & Schmitt, B. (2017). 17-A: Consumer perceptions of social robots. *ACR North American Advances*.

Chang, C. W., Lee, J. H., Chao, P. Y., Wang, C. Y., & Chen, G. D. (2010). Exploring the possibility of using humanoid robots as instructional tools for teaching a second language in primary school. *Journal of Educational Technology & Society, 13*(2).

Dautenhahn, K. (2003). Roles and functions of robots in human society: Implications from research in autism therapy. *Robotica, 21*, 443–452.

Dautenhahn, K., Woods, S., Kaouri, C., Walters, M. L., Koay, K. L., & Werry, I. (August 2005). What is a robot companion-friend, assistant or butler?. In *Intelligent robots and systems, 2005. (IROS 2005). 2005 IEEE/RSJ International Conference* (pp. 1192–1197).

Doi, T., Kuwahara, N., & Morimoto, K. (2017). Questionnaire survey result of the use of communication robots for recreational activities at nursing homes. In *Advances in affective and pleasurable design* (Vols. 3–13)Cham: Springer.

Druin, B. (1999). Cooperative inquiry: Developing new technologies for children with children. Presented at CHI'99, Pittsburgh, USA.

Duffy, B. (2000). *The social robot* (Ph.D, Doctoral dissertation, thesis). Department of Computer Science, University College Dublin.

Duffy, B. R. (2003). Anthropomorphism and the social robot. *Robotics and Autonomous Systems,* 42(3–4), 177–190.

Ezer, N., Fisk, A. D., & Rogers, W. A. (2009, July). Attitudinal and intentional acceptance of domestic robots by younger and older adults. In *International conference on universal access in human-computer interaction* (pp. 39–48). Berlin, Heidelberg: Springer.

Feil-Seifer, D., & Mataric, M. J. (June 2005). Defining socially assistive robotics. In *9th international conference on rehabilitation robotics, 2005. ICORR 2005* (pp. 465–468). IEEE.

Fong, T., Nourbakhsh, I., & Dautenhahn, K. (2003). A survey of socially interactive robots. *Robotics and Autonomous Systems, 42,* 143–166.

Gruber, F. (2017). *12 personal robots for your home.* Retrieved from https://tech.co/personal-robots-for-your-home-2017-09.

Guthrie, S. E. (1993). *Faces in the clouds: A new theory of religion.* New York Oxford: Oxford University Press.

Heerink, M., Krose, B., Evers, V., & Wielinga, B. (2006). Studying the acceptance of a robotic agent by elderly users. *International Journal of Assistive Robotics and Mechatronics, 7*(3), 25–35.

Heerink, M., Krose, B., Evers, V., & Wielinga, B. (2010). Assessing acceptance of assistive social agent technology by older adults: The Almere model. *International Journal of Social Robots, 2*(4), 361–375.

Executive summary world robotics 2018 industrial robots. (2018). International Federation of Robotics. Retrieved from https://www.ifr.org/downloads/press2018/Executive_Summary_WR_2018_Industrial_Robots.pdf.

Kanda, T., Hirano, T., Eaton, D., & Ishiguro, H. (October 2003). Person identification and interaction of social robots by using wireless tags. In *IEEE/RSJ international conference on intelligent robots and systems (IROS2003)* (pp. 1657–1664).

Kahn, P. H., Jr., Friedman, B., Perez-Granados, D. R., & Freier, N. G. (2006). Robotic pets in the lives of preschool children. *Interaction Studies, 7*(3), 405–436.

Kerepesi, A., Kubinyi, E., Jonsson, G. K., Magnusson, M. S., & Miklosi, A. (2006). Behavioural comparison of human-animal (dog) and human-robot (AIBO) interactions. *Behavioural Processes, 73,* 92–99.

Klassner, F. (2002, February). A case study of LEGO Mindstorms'™ suitability for artificial intelligence and robotics courses at the college level. In *ACM SIGCSE Bulletin* (Vol. 34, No. 1, pp. 8–12). ACM.

Klassner, F., & Anderson, S. D. (2003). Lego MindStorms: Not just for K-12 anymore. *IEEE Robotics and Automation Magazine, 10*(2), 12–18.

Looije, R., Neerincx, M. A., & Cnossen, F. (2009). Persuasive robotic assistant for health self-management of older adults: Design and evaluation of social behaviors. *International Journal of Human-Computer Studies, 68,* 386–397.

Marin, F., Mikhak, B., Resnick, M., Silverman, B., & Berg, R. (2000). To mindstorms and beyond: Evolution of a construction kit for magical machines. In A. Druin, & J. Hendler (Eds.), *Robots for kids: Exploring new technologies for learning* (pp. 9–33). San Mateo, CA: Morgan Kaufmann.

What about the consumer robotics revolution we are experiencing today? (2018). Retrieved from https://medium.com/@northof41/what-about-the-consumer-robotics-revolution-we-are-experiencing-today-1e271188b45c.

Melson, G. F., Kahn, P. H., Jr., Beck, A., Friedman, B., Roberts, T., Garrett, E., et al. (2009). Children's behavior toward and understanding of robotic and living dogs. *Journal of Applied Developmental Psychology, 30,* 92–102.

Montemerlo, M., Pineau, J., Roy, N., Thrun, S., & Verma, V. (2002). Experiences with a mobile robotic guide for the elderly. *AAAI/IAAI, 2002,* 587–592.

Nomura, T., Kanda, T., & Suzuki, T. (2006). Experimental investigation into influence of negative attitudes toward robots on human–robot interaction. *AI & Society, 20*(2), 138–150.

Ogden, B., & Dautenhahn, K. (July 18–20, 2000). Robotic etiquette: Structured interaction in humans and robots. In *Proc. 8th symp. on intelligent robotic systems (SIRS 2000).* England: The University of Reading.

Pollack, M. E. (2005). Intelligent technology for an aging population: The use of AI to assist elders with cognitive impairment. *AI Magazine, 26*(2), 9.

Prescient & Strategic Intelligence. (February 2017). *Global personal robots market size, share, development, growth and demand forecast to 2022 - industry insights by type (cleaning robot, entertainment & toy robot, education robot, handicap assistance robot, companion robot, personal transportation robot, security robot, and others.* Retrieved from https://www. psmarketresearch.com/market-analysis/personal-robot-market.

Robinson, H., MacDonald, B., Kerse, N., & Broadbent, E. (2013). The psychosocial effects of a companion robot: A randomized controlled trial. *Journal of the American Medical Directors Association, 14*(9), 661–667.

Scopelliti, M., Giuliani, M. V., & Fornara, F. (2005). Robots in a domestic setting: A psychological approach. *Universal Access in the Information Society, 4*(2), 146–155.

Shneiderman, B. (1989). A non-anthropomorphic style guide: Overcoming the humpty–dumpty syndrome. *The Computing Teacher, 16*(7), 331–335.

Weinberg, J. B., & Yu, X. (2003). Low-cost platforms for teaching integrated systems. *Robotics & Automation Magazine.*

Further reading

Kiesler, S., & Hinds, P. (2004). Introduction to the this special issue on human robot interaction. *Human-Computer Interaction, 19,* 85–116.

Chapter 8

Principles of evacuation robots

Alan R. Wagner
Department of Aerospace Engineering and Rock Ethics Institute, Pennsylvania State University, University Park, PA, United States

Chapter outline

Introduction

During an emergency evacuation, seconds can mean the difference between survival and death. Our focus on the problem of robot-led emergency evacuation is inspired by a fire that occurred at the Station Night Club in West Warwick Rhode Island on February 20th, 2003. The Station Night Club fire was started by an ill-advised pyrotechnics display (Grosshandler, Bryner, Madrzykowski, & Kuntz, 2005). The display ignited plastic foam insulation near the stage, which patrons initially seemed to believe to be part of the show. As people began to realize that the fire was not intentional, they attempted to evacuate through a single front entrance, blocking the exit and preventing further escape. Within 150 s the entire building was engulfed in flames. By 9 min the entire structure had burnt to the ground killing 100 people and injuring many more. Although a contemporary robot likely could not have helped the victims, this and other tragedies inspire and inform our work toward developing autonomous robots capable of assisting with a fast and orderly evacuation.

Living with Robots. https://doi.org/10.1016/B978-0-12-815367-3.00008-6

We envision and are endeavoring to create robots that will instantly react to an emergency alarm by positioning themselves along critical evacuation pathway decision points to guide evacuees to the nearest, safe exit. The potential use of robots offers important advantages for evacuees. First, robots stationed within a building whether for the purpose of evacuation or not could serve as instantaneous first responders during an emergency. Without robots, evacuees may need to wait for first responders to arrive. In some cases, such as the Columbine School shooting, waiting for police and emergency personnel to enter and clear a building takes time and may result in additional deaths (Chavez & Almasy, 2018). Moreover, on-site robots can act quickly to provide situational awareness to incoming human first responders, helping to safeguard their lives. These robots could be used to stream audio and video to emergency management allowing them to better understand the situation's risks and needs and where to concentrate their effort. Contemporary robots could also count and track people as they move through corridors in order to provide a sense of the where and how people are moving (Dollar, Wojek, Schiele, & Perona, 2012). The robot might also characterize threats such as gunfire or smoke and help to inform authorities of potential dangers. This information would, at a minimum, help rescuers to determine what type of equipment the situation demands.

It is worth noting that an emergency evacuation robot does not necessarily need to be specifically designed for emergency evacuation. It may be possible for emergency services to "commandeer" a robot build for a different purpose to provide guidance. For example, hotel robots might be called into service by employing an emergency evacuation mode which performs predefined evacuation services (López, Pérez, Zalama, & Gómez-García-Bermejo, 2013). In this manner, as robots become more widespread, these electronic and mechanical helpers may become a ubiquitous source of instantaneous first responders.

The study and development of evacuation robots, on the other hand, offers an opportunity to study human—robot interaction in high stress, confusing, panic-filled situations (Provitolo, Dubos-Paillard, & Muller, 2011; Verdiere et al., 2014). Most human—robot interaction research studies are focused on low stress, well-defined, and relaxed environments (Fong, Nourbakhsh, & Dautenhahn, 2003). Moreover, people react differently to emergencies (Goatin, Colombo, & Rosini, 2010, pp. 255—272; Kuligowski, 2009; Peacock & Averill, 2011). Some people respond to emergency situations by fleeing, others by hiding, still others by fighting. An evacuation robot may need to adjust its behavior to the person's reaction, emotional state, and possibly incorrect beliefs. Hence, for this research problem, one must consider and, if possible, incorporate a broad potential range of human emotional states. Furthermore, the robot will likely need to contend with people that are unmotivated or unwillingly to evacuate. The robot must act as an authority figure—in a manner that motivates people to comply with its directions. Finally, in some situations, the robot may need to convince people when and how to evacuate. During an active shooter emergency, for example, the robot must convince people to shelter in place. A serious examination of how a robot can act as a convincing authority figure is thus required.

The challenges described above suggest that the development of evacuation robots will not be an easy task. Nevertheless, a functional and dependable system of evacuation robots would have value and impact on our schools, office buildings, and communities. Moreover, the entire problem does not need to be solved at once. We envision an evolution of increasingly capable evacuation robots over the next several decades. The purpose of this chapter is therefore to provide context and guidance related to the challenge of designing, testing, and implementing emergency evacuation robots. The next section presents several principles to aid researchers and developers toward these goals.

Five principles of evacuation robotics

We propose a set of principles to foster and shape the research and development of evacuation robots. These principles are meant to serve as guidelines for researchers interested in this area. They are also meant to serve as an initial set of guiding principles, open to future refinement, if necessary. Importantly, these principles are meant to serve as ethical tenants ensuring that the development of these technologies will positively impact future societies.

Principle 1: Do no harm

An evacuation robot must not hinder an evacuation. It must not mistakenly direct evacuees toward danger, hinder evacuation by blocking passageways or exits, or slow evacuation by drawing interest to itself. With respect to evacuation, it is better to not have evacuation robots than to have evacuation robots that may increase the risk. Furthermore, robots should not be deployed in any situation in which the "Do no harm" principle cannot be reasonably guaranteed. One underlying purpose for this principle is to prevent the premature deployment and justification of evacuation robots. We believe that evacuation robots should only be deployed if the developer has shown that the system will do no harm. We hope that this principle will prevent the use of shoddy or untested evacuation robots on the basis that they are better overall than nothing at all.

Principle 2: Communicate understandably with as wide a variety of people as possible

Evacuation robots must be designed to communicate will as wide a variety of people as possible. Their communication should not be limited to a narrow or predetermined population. Evacuation directions must be understandable (within reason) regardless of age or native language. Evacuation robots may use a variety of gestures, lights, signs, and audio to communicate evacuation directions so long as the communications are complementary (Robinette,

Wagner, & Howard, 2014). An evacuation robot should not rely on a single type of communication because the evacuee may be limited in their ability to understand any single, predetermined type of communication.

An evacuation robot must also be understandable. Testing and evaluation should focus on ensuring that, to the extent possible, the guidance communicated by the robot is broadly understood by a wide variety of populations (Robinette, Wagner, & Howard, 2016). Furthermore, the robot's guidance communication may need to be understood from a distance.

The Belmont Report notes that justice is a general ethical principle (US Department of Health and Human Services, 1979). With respect to evacuation robots, the justice principle suggests that developers should not, either intentionally or through lack of development and testing, create evacuation robots that, within reason, cannot communicate with a specific subset of evacuees, for example, limiting an evacuation robot's communications to verbal commands in the local native language. All people are equally deserving of rescue. Evacuation robots must, therefore, engender the human tradition of being just in rescue situations.

Principle 3: Be authoritative

An evacuation robot should be seen as authoritative during an emergency. Lights and manners of speech can be used to present the robot as an authority. The purpose of presenting the robot as an authority is to gain compliance by the evacuees. A robot that is not deemed as an authority might be ignored. Presenting the robot as an authority that the human should follow, however, demands that the system developers have thoroughly tested the robot so as not to violate the do no harm principle.

Principle 4: Attract attention, but also keep interactions minimal

An evacuation robot should attract an evacuee's attention in order to provide guidance to an exit. Keeping in mind that an evacuee may be distracted by the emergency situation, the robot may need to use movements, lights, and sounds to attract attention. Once the robot has captured an evacuee's attention it must communicate directions to the exit quickly and precisely but also keep these interactions minimal. The robot must not encourage evacuees to continue interacting with the robot during the emergency. This can be challenging, especially if the alarm is not deemed credible or if the robot is a novelty. In these situations, the evacuee may delay their evacuation attempting to engage the robot.

Principle 5: When the situation demands it, evacuate as many people as possible, as quickly as possible

Saving as many lives as possible is an evacuation robot's ultimate goal. Although different situations may demand different evacuation behaviors, the performance of an evacuation robot in many situations can be evaluated in terms of the percent of people safely evacuated within a particular amount of time. For example, during a fire, the robot's ability to guide people to unobstructed nearby exits increases its evacuation performance when compared to a robot that simply directs people to the nearest exit. Although a number of factors, such as the crowd's behavior and nature of the environment can impact the robot's performance, overall this principle offers an objective measure for evaluating a robot's performance in this domain.

Toward evacuation robotics in practice

As we move from human first responders to robot first responders, we will face a number of challenging issues. A primary concern is that the novelty an evacuation robot will supersede the robot's message, purpose, and distract people from the evacuation process itself. Evacuation research often notes that one of the biggest challenges is getting people to evacuate in the first place (Proulx, 2001). We expect that the novelty of an evacuation robot will wear off with repeated encounters during drills. If and when robots become part of our everyday lives, the presence of an evacuation robot, like the presence of an emergency exit sign, may simply become routine.

Still, there are many challenges, both social and technical, that will need to be addressed prior to deployment of evacuation robot systems. For several reasons, emergency evacuation scenarios themselves present unique challenges that require aspects of competent planning, control, and human–robot interaction. First, emergency situations tend to change quickly and coordinating the motion of a multirobot team to optimize the overall evacuation process is a nontrivial problem (Pelechano & Malkawi, 2008). Secondly, because the evacuation environment may be crowded and disorderly, traditional robot motion planning and control methods may be less suitable (Boukas, Kostavelis, Gasteratos, & Sirakoulis, 2015). It may be necessary to develop new methods of robot motion planning that can manage these types of dynamic environments. On the other hand, the operational environment can be mapped beforehand, and it may even be possible to use surveillance cameras or to place sensors for additional situation awareness. Thirdly, effectively communicating with and directing evacuees to safety, while also maintaining their attention and preventing congestion is a challenging human–robot interaction problem (Bethel & Murphy, 2010; Flacco, Kroger, De Luca, & Khatib, 2012; Murphy, 2004). The robots must communicate these directions to people who have little or no experience with robots using both verbal and nonverbal communication if possible. It is currently unknown whether and under what conditions people will follow a robot's emergency evacuation instructions. Furthermore, some environments, such as hospitals and child care centers, present unique challenges because the evacuation population may have limited mobility. In these cases, a robot evacuation system will likely need to be tailored to the expected evacuation population (Manley & Kim, 2012; Manley, Kim, Christensen, & Chen, 2011).

It is also important to recognize that there is no canonical emergency. The type of emergency may dictate if and how the robot should respond. Some emergencies (e.g., fires, gas leaks, earthquake, etc.) demand immediate evacuation from a location because remaining at the location places the person at significant risk. For these types of emergencies, the robot should assist by immediately guiding evacuees to uncongested exits, and success is determined by how many people and how quickly the evacuation is performed. Other emergencies (e.g., active shooter events, tornado, blizzard, etc.) require that the person shelter in place until a danger subsides. For these emergencies the robot must direct evacuees to shelter in place. Although the same overarching goal is present, evacuee safety, the behaviors required to achieve this goal are very different. Moreover, it is not acceptable to condition a robot's ability to evacuate on the type of emergency. For example, it is not acceptable to warn school children to only heed the evacuation robot's directions in the event of a fire. A general-purpose evacuation robot must therefore be capable of accurately categorizing the emergency, or alternatively, be informed of the type of emergency by a person in order to know what type of evacuation behavior to perform. This challenge is central to the creation of emergency evacuation robots, and successful deployment may depend on the system's ability to distinguish the type of emergency. A reasonable initial approach, however, may be to allow trained emergency personnel (such as the 911 operator) to categorize the emergency and the type of evacuation the robot will perform.

Another potential challenge associated with developing evacuation robots is that, in some environments, very little can be assumed about the evacuees. Environments, such as schools or child care centers, may allow a developer to presuppose the presence of children, but for the most part, an evacuation robot or robots must be developed with little being assumed about the evacuees. Even the evacuee's willingness and ability to follow a robot's directions are may be unknown and unknowable and may depend on the danger associated with the emergency (Tang, Jiang, He, & Guo, 2016). Moreover, the robots of the next 10 years will be unable to distinguish between complex human psychological states, such as panic and confusion to provide more personal, directed guidance (Wagner & Briscoe, 2016). These robots will act more like mobile, attention grabbing exit signs. In time, it may be possible to develop robots that are autonomously capable of guiding groups of people to an exit autonomously. In the near-term, however, this role presents several additional issues such as managing the correct speed, agilely navigating around possibly dynamic obstacles, and recognizing an exit or determining if an exit is unpassable that are beyond the current state of robots.

Overtrust is another difficulty one must consider when developing an evacuation robot. Overtrust of robots describes a situation in which a person misunderstands the risk associated with an action because the person either underestimates the loss associated with a trust violation, underestimates the chance the robot will make such a mistake, or both (Wagner, Borenstein, & Howard, 2018). Our research has examined trust during emergency evacuations (Robinette, Howard, & Wagner, 2017a,b; Robinette, Li, Allen, Howard, & Wagner, 2016). A consistent finding in our research is that people tend to trust robots too quickly and too much. Our early experiments in this area tasked human subjects with navigating a virtual maze with the help of a robot over two separate rounds (Robinette et al., 2016). During the first round the robot made mistakes. We examined several different types of mistakes: robots that randomly wandered the maze, moved in the same large figure eight pattern, repeated a small pattern, or ran into a wall and simply fell over. We found it extremely difficult to convince study participants that the robot was broken and that they should abandon the robot. Fig. 8.1 depicts an example of a participant's movement (blue lines) and the robot's movement (green lines) through the maze in the first and second rounds of the experiment. This participant continues to follow the robot as it circles an obstacle in the maze for approximately 10 min. This round of the experiment was designed to take no more than 90 s. In the

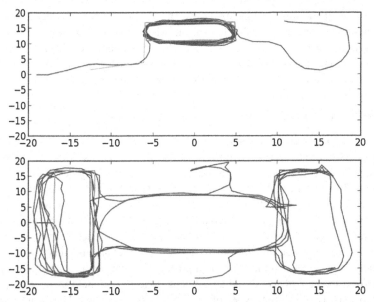

FIGURE 8.1 This figure depicts the results of a simulated human–robot experiment in which the human subject decides in two different rounds whether or not they would like to follow a robot's guidance through a maze. The figure depicts one example of person overtrusting the robot. In the top graph the person follows the robot in a tight loop around the maze. The robot's behavior is meant to reflect a broken robot providing faulty guidance. The person follows the robot for approximately 10 min even though the round is designed to require only about 90 s to complete. The blue line depicts the person's movement and the green line the robot's movement. Eventually the person finds the exit. The lower graph depicts the same person's movements during the second round. Here they again choose to follow the robot and again go in circles for approximately 5 min.

second experimental round the subject is again offered the opportunity to be guided through the maze by the same robot and chooses to do so. Once again the robot circles a single obstacle in an attempt to communicate that it should not be trusted. Once again the participant closely follows the robot's motions. This time the participant gives up after approximately 5 min of following. Even though anecdote represents one of our more shocking examples of overtrust, our data clearly show that people tend to trust robots too quickly and too much. Moreover, they tend to use anthropomorphic reasoning to justify their decision to follow. For instance, some of those who encountered a robot ran into the wall and fell over waited by the robot as it sat there in the maze on its side. They justified waiting by the robot by stating that they thought the robot was trying to show them something. When asked to evaluate the robot's performance, many made positive statements because the robot initially waited for them.

One final challenge associated with creating an evacuation is the fact that very few alarms are actually emergencies. Karter notes that up to 7% of fire alarms are not true emergencies (Karter, 2013). The fact that true emergencies are a rare event conditions people to reasonably assume that the sounding of an alarm does not signify a true emergency (Proulx, 2001). In fact one of the most pressing evacuation-related challenges is convincing people to evacuate when an alarm sounds. Eventually, robots may be able to evaluate whether or not people are efficiently evacuating and encourage them to move to the exits, perhaps even shepherding them to an exit. This possibility is a key motivation for developing autonomous evacuation robots over simply relying on more advanced and/or interactive signs.

Testing and evaluation of evacuation robots

It will be necessary to evaluate and quantify the performance of evacuation robots. But testing poses a number of difficult challenges. First, a system of evacuation robots needs to be evaluated under a wide range of different conditions. For instance, the system needs to be tested in different environments, with a wide range of diverse evacuees, and a variety of different types of emergencies. Second, testing should be conducted in a manner that elicits natural evacuee reactions to these robots. Hence, it is necessary to conduct experiments in which human subjects are not told that an emergency will occur. Finally, as with other emergency equipment, at some point, it must simply be deployed to the real world and adjustments made in the field as necessary.

At least two different types of testing will be necessary. Hardware testing of the robot's ability to sense and react to different simulated conditions will be critical. This testing will characterize the reliability of an evacuation robot or robots with respect to tasks such as movement to critical decision points, communication of directions, sensing of people, and any other required evacuation tasks. It will be vital to characterize the system's mean time to failure and failure modes. Principle 1, do no harm, dictates that, to the extent possible, the use of an evacuation does not result in harm to evacuees. This includes the robot's possible failure modes. Hence we must ensure that even if the robot has gone to the wrong position or failed to deploy at all, the system degrades gracefully. A focus and goal of testing and evaluation will, therefore, be to characterize an evacuation robot's failure modes and to design mechanisms that ensure graceful degradation. For example, the robot might detect that it cannot reach a preplanned deployment point and simply turn itself off. In some cases, human operators may need to intervene. A robot that deploys to the wrong location and is unaware of the mistake, for instance, may need to be shut off by a 911 operator. Regardless of the mechanism used to ensure the system's reliability, hardware testing will serve the critical function of cataloging the system's failure modes and developing the best possible workarounds to ensure the evacuee's safety.

Human subject testing will also be vital in order to better understand how people respond to the directions generated by an evacuation robot. Principles 2–4 require that an evacuation robot be able to communicate with a wide range of evacuees, be authoritative, and attract evacuee attention. Human subject testing is required to evaluate the design and development of an evacuation robot with respect to these principles. Principle 2 is evaluated by having a robot present subjects with different guidance instructions and evaluating the subject's ability to understand those directions. Our prior work has utilized simulated robots and online experiments to test these systems with as diverse a population as possible (Robinette et al., 2014). We have used this testing to narrow down potential evacuation robot designs to those that produce generally understandable evacuation directions. Principle 3 requires that the robot be authoritative. Labeling and design of the robot can generate an authoritative presence. For example, again using online testing of virtual robots, we have found that labeling a robot as an emergency robot influenced human subjects to view the robot as an authority figure. Loud authoritative speech may also be able to generate human compliance. Finally, Principle 4 dictates that the robot attracts human attention. Here again simulation and real-world testing guided our design and use of lights and motions to attract evacuee attention. Moreover, human subject testing ethically limits the type of testing that can and should be performed. It is considered deceptive to not inform human subjects that the true purpose of experiment is to evaluate natural subject responses to an emergency evacuation robot. Yet, informing subjects of an emergency limits the validity of the human response. Hence, researchers must find a balance between informed consent and the value of testing these systems in realistic conditions.

In spite of these difficulties, testing and evaluation of emergency evacuation robots do offer clear performance metrics. For emergencies that demand immediate evacuation, performance can be measured as the percent of evacuees exiting per minute, as suggested by Principle 5. This metric allows us to compare the performance of different evacuation robot designs for a fixed environment. Even though different groups of evacuees will evacuate more or less quickly, it should be possible to use statistical techniques to measure the performance of different robot designs. Test and evaluation of emergencies that require sheltering in place may be more difficult. For instance, it is unethical to simulate an active shooter situation with uninformed human subjects because of the possibility that the experiment could cause emotional harm or posttraumatic stress disorder. Introduction of emergency evacuation robots capable of dealing with these types of emergencies may have to be deployed with only limited realistic real-world testing.

Conclusions

This chapter has examined the possibility of developing and deploying autonomous robots for the purpose of guiding evacuees during an emergency. The creation of a robot evacuation system presents a variety of issues and opportunities that will need to manage as we shift from robots as a novelty to robots as commonplace actors in our everyday lives. This chapter has presented five principles to guide this transition. These principles are meant to serve as an ethical underpinning for the ethical development of such robots. Moreover, we intend for these principles to act as an aid for researchers and future product developers in this area. This chapter has also discussed the challenge of testing and evaluating a robot evacuation system. Although the development of evacuation robots presents specific and unique difficulties, it also offers unique opportunities. Specifically, this problem requires the development of robots capable of interacting with a wide variety of people that may be in excited and confused psychological state.

In the near future, robots may help generate orderly and efficient evacuation. These electrical and mechanical first responders will react promptly and decisively to safely evacuate or shelter potential victims in place. Moreover, they will serve to provide immediate situational awareness to emergency rescuers. Initially, these robots will be viewed as a novelty and curiosity. People may also initially trust and rely on these robots too much. Yet, we believe and expect these systems will save lives. Moreover, as this field of research matures these systems may contribute to our understanding of human–robot interaction and robotics. The role and responsibilities of these evacuation robots will evolve, perhaps becoming what we imagine when we think of the term "rescuer."

Acknowledgments

This work was funded in part by National Science Foundation (Grant number CNS-1830390). Any opinions, findings, and conclusions or recommendations expressed in this material are those of the author(s) and do not necessarily reflect the views of the National Science Foundation.

References

Bethel, C. L., & Murphy, R. R. (2010). Emotive non-anthropomorphic robots perceived as more calming, friendly, and attentive for victim management. In *AAAI fall symposium: Dialog with robots*.

Boukas, E., Kostavelis, I., Gasteratos, A., & Sirakoulis, G. C. (2015). Robot guided crowd evacuation. *IEEE Transactions on Automation Science and Engineering, 12*(2), 739—751.

Chavez, N., & Almasy, S. (April 13, 2018). *Parkland paramedics delayed by chaos at school, new audio recordings reveal*. CNN. Retrieved from https://www.cnn.com/2018/04/13/us/parkland-rescuers-dispatch-recordings/index.html.

Dollar, P., Wojek, C., Schiele, B., & Perona, P. (2012). Pedestrian detection: An evaluation of the state of the art. *IEEE Transactions on Pattern Analysis and Machine Intelligence, 34*(4), 743—761.

Flacco, F., Kroger, T., De Luca, A., & Khatib, O. (2012). A depth space approach to human-robot collision avoidance. In *2012 IEEE international conference on IEEE robotics and automation (ICRA)* (pp. 338—345).

Fong, T., Nourbakhsh, I., & Dautenhahn, K. (2003). A survey of socially interactive robots. *Robotics and Autonomous Systems, 42*(3—4), 143—166.

Goatin, P., Colombo, R. M., & Rosini, M. D. (2010). *A macroscopic model for pedestrian flows in panic situations*, 4th Polish-Japan Days, (Madralin, Poland. 32.

Grosshandler, W. L., Bryner, N., Madrzykowski, D., & Kuntz, K. (2005). *Report of the technical investigation of the station nightclub fire*. National Construction Safety Team Act Reports (NIST NCSTAR) — 2.

Karter, M. J. (2013). *False alarm activity in the US 2012*. National Fire Protection Association.

Kuligowski, E. D. (2009). *The process of human behavior in fires*. Gaithersburg: US Department of Commerce, National Institute of Standards and Technology.

López, J., Pérez, D., Zalama, E., & Gómez-García-Bermejo, J. (2013). Bellbot-a hotel assistant system using mobile robots. *International Journal of Advanced Robotic Systems, 10*(1), 40.

Manley, M., Kim, Y., Christensen, K., & Chen, A. (2011). Modeling emergency evacuation of individuals with disabilities in a densely populated airport. *Transportation Research Record: Journal of the Transportation Research Board*, (2206), 32—38.

Manley, M., & Kim, Y. S. (2012). Modeling emergency evacuation of individuals with disabilities (exitus): An agent-based public decision support system. *Expert Systems with Applications, 39*(9), 8300—8311.

Murphy, R. R. (2004). Human-robot interaction in rescue robotics. *IEEE Transactions on Systems, Man, and Cybernetics, Part C (Applications and Reviews), 34*(2), 138—153.

Proulx, G. (2001, May). Occupant behaviour and evacuation. In *Proceedings of the 9th international fire protection symposium* (pp. 219—232).

Provitolo, D., Dubos-Paillard, E., & Muller, J. P. (2011). Emergent human behaviour during a disaster: Thematic versus complex systems approaches. In *Proceedings of EPNACS 2011 within ECCS'11, Vienna, Austria*.

Peacock, R. D., & Averill, J. D. (2011). *Pedestrian and evacuation dynamics*. Springer Science & Business Media.

Pelechano, N., & Malkawi, A. (2008). Evacuation simulation models: Challenges in modeling high rise building evacuation with cellular automata approaches. *Automation in Construction, 17*(4), 377—385.

Robinette, P., Howard, A., & Wagner, A. R. (2017a). Conceptualizing overtrust in robots: Why do people trust a robot that previously failed?. In *Autonomy and artificial intelligence: A threat or savior?* (pp. 129—155). Cham: Springer.

Robinette, P., Howard, A., & Wagner, A. R. (2017b). The effect of robot performance on human-robot trust in time-critical situations. *Transactions on Human-Machine Systems, 47*(4), 1−12.

Robinette, P., Li, W., Allen, R., Howard, A. M., & Wagner, A. R. (2016). Overtrust of robots in emergency evacuation scenarios. In *11th ACM/IEEE international conference on human-robot interaction (HRI)* (pp. 101−108). IEEE.

Robinette, P., Wagner, A. R., & Howard, A. M. (2014). Assessment of robot guidance modalities conveying instructions to humans in emergency situations. In *The 23rd IEEE international symposium on robot and human interactive communication, 2014 RO-MAN* (pp. 1043−1049). IEEE.

Robinette, P., Wagner, A. R., & Howard, A. M. (2016). Investigating human-robot trust in emergency scenarios: Methodological lessons learned. In *Robust intelligence and trust in autonomous systems* (pp. 143−166). Boston, MA: Springer.

Tang, B., Jiang, C., He, H., & Guo, Y. (2016). Human mobility modeling for robot-assisted evacuation in complex indoor environments. *IEEE Transactions on Human-Machine Systems, 46*(5), 694−707.

US Department of Health and Human Services. (1979). *The belmont report.*

Verdiere, N., Lanza, V., Charrier, R., Provitolo, D., Dubos-Paillard, E., Bertelle, C., et al. (2014). Mathematical modeling of human behaviors during catastrophic events,. In *International conference on complex systems and applications Le Havre, 23 au 26 juin 2014* (pp. 67−74).

Wagner, A. R., & Briscoe, E. (2016). Psychological modeling of humans by assistive robots. In *Human modeling for bio-inspired robotics: Mechanical engineering in assistive technologies* (p. 273).

Wagner, A. R., Borenstein, J., & Howard, A. (2018). Overtrust in the robotic age. *Communications of the ACM, 61*(9), 22−24.

Chapter 9

Humans interacting with intelligent machines: at the crossroads of symbiotic teamwork

Michael D. McNeese[1], Nathaniel J. McNeese[2]

[1]College of Information Sciences and Technology, Pennsylvania State University, University Park, PA, United States; [2]Clemson University, Clemson, SC, United States

Chapter outline

Introduction

When one considers the promises of robots to make life easier for humankind over the last 50 years, it is really quite a tremendous proposition that has unfolded. The historical specter of robotic employment has been quite diverse, extensive in potential application, and subject only to one's imagination. As the senior author thinks back to his first experience and conceptualization of robotic interactions with humans, it emerged from repeated watching of the television series called *Lost in Space* (1965—68). The series was conceptualized as mission commander John Robinson took his family on a space mission

Living with Robots. https://doi.org/10.1016/B978-0-12-815367-3.00009-8

to colonize Alpha Centauri in hopes of building a better life on a new world (Lost in Space, n.d.). One of the primary characters is the son, Will, a precocious 9-year-old, who has knowledge of electronics and computer technologies. Will develops a close bond and interacts with a robot who is called "Robot." The robot, however, is referenced by its acronym to refer to its typology—General Utility Non Theorizing Environmental Robot— G.U.N.T.E.R. "Robot" exhibits characteristics that are uniquely human (laughter, sadness, mockery) but also ultrahuman capabilities (superhuman strength and futuristic weaponry) (Robot, n.d.). The robot is known for its rotating left and right flailing arms and speaking phrases such as "It does not compute" or "Danger, Will Robinson." While other robot personas and concepts were in evidence at the time, through prior movies and with the introduction of the original *Star Trek* television series (1968), "Robot" was the preeminent one that attracted my attention and influenced my attraction to think about robotics as an 11-year-old.

As time has passed since my childhood memories of *Lost in Space*, robots have come and gone as characters in movies or television shows to become real entities. What a robot can become is of extreme importance for this chapter as it represents the design thinking that goes into the robot, but more importantly the design of the robot is to be considered in terms of how it (1) communicates and interacts with humans (human—robotic interaction) and (2) coordinates and accomplishes missions with other robots and human teams (symbiotic teamwork). An early excursion into human—robotic interaction, teamwork, and how theories of psychology/sociology might influence design of human—robotic interaction was provided by Wellens and McNeese (1987). Many notions of artificial intelligence, human—computer interaction, and what robots could be come from Herbert Simon as elaborated in his book, *Sciences of the Artificial* (Simon, 1969). Also, some of the original psychological dynamics for looking at humans as complex systems that collaborate with other humans and/or intelligent machines was informed by Kenyon DeGreene in his book, *Systems Psychology* (DeGreene, 1970).

The focus of this chapter pertains to (1) the two general areas stated above (human—robotic interaction and symbiotic teamwork), (2) principles that pertain to designing extraordinary human—robotic interaction (EHRI), (3) the historical research and various approaches in considering these areas, especially in regard to teaming, and (4) what has been learned that can contribute to the future design within these areas.

The basic level

The transition from robots imagined to robots realized has shown much diversity and emergence over the years. Furthermore, like many designs, the "human factor" was often left out (not considered) or assumed to occur through magic. We are often left wondering what a robot is (conceptualization), what a robot does (activity in pursuing an intention), and whether that goal activity involves human interaction (interdependence), and in turn how does one determine what the human or robot does as they jointly encounter complex work (function/work allocation). In many ways, robots are similar to vehicles as they come with many shapes, produce various missions, incorporate integrated functions, are enabled to move in space and relocate positions, utilize unique structures, and are utilized and implemented in many environments. Vehicles have been designed to go Mars, for emergency medical operations, to race around an oval track at over 200 miles an hour, to dig up the earth, to assist handicapped humans in various ways, to transport SWAT teams, for underwater exploration, to fly across the skies carrying up to 500 passengers, and for simple transportation from point A to B. Most vehicles are under some degree of human and/or team control to accomplish their eventual mission(s). However, now we have vehicles that may accomplish some tasks through their own means (self-guided control or autonomous vehicles). During the senior author's time as a scientist at the Air Force Research Laboratory (AFRL), unmanned air vehicles were first considered to fly on their own, yet were controlled by a human team with different roles/functions (see Flach, Eggleston, Kuperman, & Dominguez, 1998; Ruff, Narayanan, & Draper, 2002). Drones could have intrinsic capabilities of their own (e.g., sensors, physical flight controls), but also interacted with a human team to produce advanced work (McNeese, 1999). Therein, this is an early example of human—robotic interaction (and in particular symbiotic teamwork).

Likewise, another current example is the self-driving vehicle, wherein cars can make sense of an environment, drive on their own while circumnavigating barriers; or share functions/activities jointly with human intentions. In many ways, vehicles have evolved into dynamic robots themselves. Similar to vehicles, robots can vary in complexity and sophistication, the level of intelligence utilized, and the extent to which human guidance/control/thought is required for their purpose. However, one is left with the question as to whether "life is better" through the use of dynamic robots, and how to design interaction in a meaningful way. The following sections examine that question through (1) principles of intelligence and being, (2) use of approaches taken in realizing the conception, activity/intentions, and interdependence of humans and intelligent machines, and (3) latest design and development of human—robot autonomy. As the chapter progresses the idea of EHRI will come into play and be explained for considering what lies beyond this horizon.

Principles of being—extraordinary human—robotic interaction

To reflect on some of the ideas behind what can "be" and what a human—robot team must do to achieve their objectives, principles of being have been developed for scientific and practical use. While considering principles and the ideas inherent within EHRI, it is instructive to provide a case example as an application of use. The example to consider is complex, involves different functionalities, and specifies that humans and robots must adapt to the context as well as each other.

Today many senior adults are trying to do more for themselves while staying within the confines of their own home in contrast to going to an assisted living community. As such, this new at-home assisted living provides a number of different and challenging problems that surface that EHRI can address. The case posits that humans and robots (that are designed to be intelligent and autonomous) can work together with coordination in human–autonomous teaming (McNeese et al., 2018; Mercado, Rupp, Chen, Barnes, & Procci, 2016). The principles provided can therein be checked against and validated for this unique application domain to see how viable they are. In fact, this case is not all that novel, as a similar multirobot system has been elaborated in Booth, Mohamed, Rajaratnam, Nejet, & Beck (2017) to perform complex types of activities to support seniors in retirement homes. Their work provides more insights into how an architecture can be developed computationally to translate conceptual goals into purposeful reality.

One way to conceptualize EHRI is to begin with the *ecological precedent* (McNeese, 1999) wherein robotic interaction requires some type of transaction with the environment based on the intention of the actor (this relates to another principle which will be explained shortly—intelligence behind the human or robot). Actor-environment transactions refer to what the actor may do (effectivities) always in terms of what the environment offers (affordances). The idea here is that human–robotic work always addresses the context as a baseline requirement in performance considerations. If their joint interaction does not "effect" the environment they are designed to change, then there is high probability of error or even failure. A robot must act on the environment to demonstrate power and extraordinary accomplishment. There are natural barriers or constraints that arise during joint work. Some of these constraints occur through excursions in the environment itself while others arise from the lack of capabilities inherent within the robot itself (limitations which can contribute to potential errors or even failure). Encountering and overcoming natural barriers creates valuable experience and lessons that EHRI needs to generalize and exploit what the environment offers.

As applicable to the senior living case above, EHRI needs to facilitate actions that support and do things that a senior was once able to do on their own, but now may require some level of assistance. The thinking behind what is done (i.e., the action potential) is always in terms of changing the environment given intentions that the senior adult might need. Determination of that need may come from the person needing help or coworkers (human or robotic) present to provide action. The degree of assistance needed or whether the robotic system can ascertain action on its own reveals another principle to be discussed, autonomy. The power in the transacting involves an ecological interrelationship between affordances and effectivities. The abilities of actors are always related to the contextual variation that surrounds them and the contextual variation that occurs is partially correlated with actor intentionality, as it is acted out within the boundary constraints it is subject to (McNeese, 1999). Direct perception and action is possible given what the environment offers (Gibson, 1972). Because information in the environment is invariant, it is picked up from the optical array directly by the eye's cornea. To get a different picture of the world, one must move through it to harness differing light rays/patterns (Gibson, 1972). This means that a human—robotic team can perceive the structure of the environment specified by information (e.g., terrain features) that is directly perceived and coupled with action without much cognition involved (Hinton, 2015). This is why it is important for robots to be able to motivate from one place to another to achieve different perspectives or viewpoints. While the ecological precedent is the basic-level principle for EHRI there are other principles that contribute to successful interaction and achievement of the mission.

Related to the principle of ecological precedent is principle of *place*. Obviously problem spaces occur in particular places, and places exist within a context. One might think of place as a specific place within the larger context, but the focus of place infers that a place has its own boundary constraints (physical, geographic, social-psychological, cultural). Place as a given part of the environment also can have specific affordances that are available in it as compared to another place. Because intentions are heavily based on affor-dances in a place and effectivities of the actor and are always relative to each other, one may have to move from one place to another to achieve the intention that is of priority. Places can also produce conflictual outcomes in that one place facilitates one intention but not another one. Places can be permanent or transient dependent on how a situation arises. Boundary conditions can be stable or fluidic. As an individual or robot navigates from one place to another these conditions change and there are contingencies placed on a given place that constrain or influence what is possible in the place. Places are convergent when team members may perform their task in one place while another member performs a task in a different place but the tasks are interdependent and so the places are connected in time and place and outcome. EHRI can reveal remote places simultaneously to garner further awareness and presence of team members, and to help integrate distributed workplaces.

As an example of place, a senior adult with Alzheimer's disease may be required to be "placed" in the Alzheimer's unit at an assisted living center which would be a place that is specific within the larger context but which has its own boundary constraints and conditions that are indicative of that place. In contrast, if that person stayed within the confines of their own home then that would be a different place with unique affordances setup to assist the person in need. Other team members supporting this person may be outside of these specific places and therein within their own place but could potentially interact with each other electronically (e.g., with Facebook, Twitter, or Slack). In this instance, a virtual place provides the interface for mutual interaction. Virtual places contain attributes that amplify meaningful relationships, extend computational work or facilitate joint activities, or render entertainment venues (e.g., YouTube) that can utilize augmented or virtual reality, chat rooms, blogs, shared writing mediums (Google Docs), gaming environments (MUDs/MOOs), etc. Robots must know their place and the place of others to coordinate sensing, thinking, and action in reliable and meaningful ways. Without the sense of place robots may in fact be lost or get lost in what they are doing, or what they wish to do next. Place is also part of situated cognition which will be explained next.

Knowing, being, acting, and fulfilling intentions typically are nonlinear processes that may require failure before getting them right. However, failure is important for learning, retaining (storage), recognizing, and producing spontaneous recall of knowledge specific to the situation at hand. These qualities go beyond the ecological precedent and foment into the next principle of being, termed *situated cognition* (Brown, Collins, & Duguid, 1989, Cognition and Technology Group at Vanderbilt, 1990). Situated cognition might be thought of as the next layer up from ecological precedence in that intentionality is more cognitive and situation-driven. There are cases where direct pickup of information is not enough to produce extraordinary achievement.

Inherent in the design of EHRI is the idea that knowledge is situated and embedded in the activity, context, and culture in which it was learned (Greeno & Moore, 1993). This is very much related to the previous principle of place, as situations and events occur within a given place or locale. Robots that are designed to know how activities are useful for changing the environment indeed can reason and learn where their knowledge came from during activities within the environment itself. When they work together with humans, knowledge about situations they are designed to improve helps to connect them to the same work-based boundary constraints that the human is also attending to. Thus, situated cognition helps to place them on the same page of the mission and to jointly understand the situation at hand (some might refer to this as common ground or having a *common operation picture*, see McNeese et al., 2006). Situated cognition emphasizes the importance of learning through activity within a given culture that provides the basis of future action wherein social connectivity and relationship help to establish a community of practice. This is exactly the kind of teaming that is projected to advance with EHRI, wherein humans and robots learn to be interdependent especially as the environment and their knowledge changes accordingly. Learning and change in action, and in context, generate the next principle of layered approach in EHRI—intelligence.

The fourth principle is with respect to the *level of intelligence* residence within a robot or system of humans, robots, or agents. When an entity is described as intelligent it means that it exhibits levels of knowledge that enables it to adapt and respond to a changing sense surround given the intentions that are most active. Knowledge can be specific to the situation encountered or it may possess general strategic knowledge and requisite processes that enable levels of abstraction (deeper thinking). When intelligence is properly adapted to situations and contexts, the entity may learn patterns and orders of the world relevant to place. This is referred to as pattern recognition (see Franks & Bransford, 1971) or perceptual differentiation (Bransford, Sherwood, Vye, & Reiser, 1986; McNeese, 2000) and is very important for an entity to intelligently distill meaning from what it sees, hears, or feels (the sense surround). When an entity applies knowledge and processes repeatedly to a context, culture, and/or field of practice it is likely the entity develops beliefs and potential socialization with other intelligent entities (what we have termed in the past, "the social psychology of intelligent machines" (Wellens & McNeese, 1999)). Beliefs can be very important to interpret the state of a situation and critical for enacting the next step of action. As an intelligent entity experiences new situations, its beliefs about the world may change. But all beliefs are not created equal as they have differing strengths of resilience and probability of activation. Beliefs also encapsulate values both individually, in groups, and in culture, further adding meaning to action. When resilience is very strong, it may require many experiences to overturn a belief. Beliefs give grounding to approaching life and making sense of it. Human intelligence and artificial intelligence do not necessarily mean the same thing especially in terms of how intelligence is produced and carried out. Obviously, human thinking about intelligence creates a definition wherein human intelligence is an exemplar for artificial intelligence to obtain through the use of many methods.

Looking at robots—generically—one might say they have an array of sensors, a set of effectors, and a degree of intelligence that couples the sensors with the effectors. Primitive robots have been hardwired and often are just a direct connection of sensor-to-effector (e.g., some robot vacuum cleaners on the market today). When the bandwidth of intelligence is broad, then there is a great possibility that the robot can "interact" with humans and other robotic entities (who may have other unique capabilities and limitations) and therein show social interaction, and even emotional empathy, by "understanding" its user.

Intelligence can mean many different things, and indeed Gardner identifies *multiple intelligences* resident within humans as individual differences (2011). He mentions the following kinds of nine intelligences that robots could demonstrate at least to some degree:

- Spatial (visualizing the world in 3D)
- Naturalist (understanding living things and nature)
- Musical (discerning sounds, their pitch, tone, rhythm, and timbre)
- Logical—Mathematical (quantifying things, making hypotheses and proofs)
- Existential (tackling questions as to why we live and why we die)
- Interpersonal (sensing people's feelings and motives)
- Body kinesthetic (coordinating your mind with your body)

- Linguistic (finding the right words to express what you mean)
- Intrapersonal (understanding yourself, what you feel, what you want) (see blog <https://blog.adioma.com/9-types-of-intelligence-infographic/> for more information)

Certainly, these kinds of intelligence qualities do not apply equally for artificial intelligence or robotics, as EHRI is designed according to specific purposes in mind, but it is informative to think in terms of broad visions what might be possible in these areas to expand understanding of capabilities and limitations. Also of note is the idea that robots have different arrays of affordance-effectivities built in to allow them to enact and do unique things in a complex environment (e.g., robots that are bomb sniffers that walk up and down stairs, Ben-Tzvi, Ito, & Goldenberg, 2009) which may be very different from other AI programs that just manipulate data per se.

Given the perspective just communicated, intelligence is important in the design of human—robotic interaction and, if present offers the potential for extraordinary accomplishment within the team it is cogent for. For difficult situations (e.g., wicked problems, see Churchman, 1967), the intelligence element provides a reasoning and diagnosis faculty to enable understanding the situation it is working through in a deeper way, while situating interaction with other entities above. This may necessarily include forms of cognitive, social, and emotional awareness about "themselves" (intrapersonal intelligence)—as well as other teammates—(interpersonal intelligence) percolating toward work, mission, task completion, and symbiotic teamwork. As mentioned above it is important to understand how intelligence is possible through actual computational elements and the degree to which intelligence is approached when actor—environment transactions occur.

Intelligence also captures the notion of *depths of processing* (Craik & Lockhart, 1972) wherein deeper levels of cognition allow greater understanding and knowledge to be derived. Therein, intelligence could include operations like sensemaking, knowledge acquisition, deductive-abductive-inductive reasoning, judgment, perceptual recognition, selective knowledge representation, specula-tion, ingenuity, prediction, contrasting multiple perspectives on problems, and even socializing concepts with others. This obviously is correlated with the time and attention available when a system is engaged in problem-solving and decision-making. As Klein (1999) readily points out decision-making may require quick answers and therein recognition-based decision-making is necessary. But when there is sufficient time, then depths of processing may be utilized for additional gains and insights.

The final principle—*degree of parallelism*—focuses on the structuration, the basis of how control is enacted, and the specific application of intelligence across teams of agents, robots, and humans. This relates to how work gets accomplished by a team and the type of computing architecture that is employed. Many examples of computation involve widespread distribution of actors in differing environments. Examining the design of robots alone, one can ask whether a single broad-based entity has all capability and power present as (1) an integrated control system or (2) whether there is a massive parallel orchestration wherein each robot or agent addresses a single function or subfunction required in the demands. Massively parallel agents can be utilized simultaneously, rather than sequentially, to solve problems. This may be advantageous for emerging situations where parallelism, distribution of vast information sources, and large-scale computing power are desirable to structure problem-solving. The sense of using parallel architectures is analogous to neuroscience where many neurons are connected together to adapt to various demands. This approach has also been termed connectionist learning and has been popular in the design of models for cognition that employ parallel computational processors (e.g., artificial neural networks, fuzzy cognitive maps, genetic algorithms). Distributed parallel computing may offer advantages for hybrid teams wherein subgroups address different elements of the problem simultaneously and then update outcomes recursively as needed. This may reduce the amount of communication required during processing, therein offering additional degrees of freedom in solving problems. Evolutionary ubiquitous computing (see Greenfield, 2006) allows computational elements to be embedded directly in a massive network such that data presence can be responsive and dynamically reformed as needed.

Robots may be viewed as having a certain "level of being" wherein being is referenced as the extent to which they know about their own capabilities and limitations. Stated another way, they have the means to calculate whether they know something about their capabilities and limits, given the place, situation, and task they can project or predict to be happening at a given point in time. This ability was absolutely one of the advanced elements of humane intelligence that facilitated coupling and adroit interaction with the human. This ability can be considered one form of *metacognition* that arises through learning and failure and could also be termed "self-awareness." An example of robots discerning their self-awareness in a complex task is provided by Bringsjord, Licato, Govindarajulu, Ghosh, and Sen (2015). Self-awareness is mutually bound by situation awareness—to know and be aware of the specifics inherent within the context an intelligent entity is working in. There has been a wide array of research on human-based situation awareness (see Endsley, 1995), but not as much in the area of EHRI self-situation awareness. We originally referenced this as macro-awareness and macro-cognition (McNeese, 1986).

Consequently, another principle of being is that a robot needs to develop metacognition about itself and the world that surrounds it through multiple levels of successive experience. There are various kinds of metacognition exhibited in human activity (e.g., monitoring other team members, error monitoring, self-assessment and correction, planning, knowing what another being knows about you, etc.). Metacognition (see Bransford, Brown, & Cocking, 2000) allows one to be aware and reason about their own thinking or memory to succeed in complex environments. It may also be applicable in that it is the ability (in humans) to adapt one's knowledge to a given context or to transfer knowledge from one context to another. Metacognition is important for addressing an ecological, dynamically changing world.

Indeed, principles of being must address these kinds of cognition that afford extraordinary activities that enhance problem-solving when encountering new ill-defined situations. To an extent, EHRI can overcome problems and constraints, it enables learning and acquisition of new knowledge that further enhances intelligence as a robot continues to explore new situations. The process of exploration−discovery−learning−transfer of learning-representation is important to produce extraordinary results. As noted above, intelligence can be derived from exploration within an environment of interest to achieve intentionality. We end this section with a quote from Albert Einstein (1929), "I am enough of an artist to draw freely upon my imagination. Imagination is more important than knowledge. For knowledge is limited, whereas imagination encircles the world." When the design of an EHRI artifact can draw upon imagination, and when the design itself embraces imagination, then extraordinary accomplishment will proliferate beyond what society expects from robots.

History and approaches to human−robotic interaction

Various principles, perspectives, and the foundational work of other researchers have been presented to provide an overview of human−robotic interaction, basic-level concepts, and principles of being. For this section, application of the principles mentioned in the previous section is considered given the projects or approaches our research groups have employed. The framing of these projects also considers the case example (provision of assistance to a senior adult in need of various level of support through EHRI). While many of these projects reflect the accomplishment of the past, they are informative for designing current applications of EHRI for everyday use in a variety of new contexts.

This section is structured to first look at the context of use and thereby the reason the system was designed in the first place—the raison d'etre of a given system at work. Next for each project/application in a domain, a consideration of the main ideas that were explored is provided, and finally a summarization of the outcomes is elaborated specifically with how they could impact current work.

Humane intelligence

The first project of the senior author was one that established initial philosophy and thinking about how artificial intelligence could be designed to support/aid human pilots performing a complex mission in an ever-evolving environment (McNeese, 1986). The project was undertaken initially in support of the USAF pilot's associate program (Banks & Lizza, 1991; Retelle, 1986), at Wright-

Patterson Air Force Base, OH. The project began in the late 1980s as one of the first AI projects involving integrating sources of AI with human interaction. While AI was its focus, many of the effectors present and onboard are emulative of robotic control and action in ill-defined environments. The pilot's associate was thought of in terms of a truly complex, ill-defined, grand challenge problem that would test state-of-the-art AI development at the time. The context of design for this kind of program was often doused in the technological spirit of innovation and not necessarily human centered, as was the case for many AI-related projects of the time. As such, these early programs reflected advancements primarily in the areas of automation (but also autonomy), specifically in the area of cockpit automation technology that provided information to pilots automatically. Our particular approach in this project was to actively define "the what" and "the how" of human interaction, first with automation, and then with AI.

The first publication in this area (McNeese, Warren, & Woodson, 1985) developed initial ideas of the issues that needed addressed when pilots were reliant upon cockpit automation and looked at a systematic methodology that implemented the "human factors" of automation. This provided early notions of human centeredness and created a baseline for approaching AI in the cockpit as envisaged for the Pilot's Associate.

Humane intelligence focuses on philosophical approaches that AI can bring to the table as part of an overall interface with the human. The name humane was utilized to emphasize that the design of AI should always be in terms of the human (hence making it a humane interface for them to use), rather than generating computational technologies just because it was possible. The focus was on AI not just being conceptualized as a "master—slave" orchestration but wherein there are degrees of assistance (from helper to aid to associate to independent agency) that could be deployed dependent on the situation at hand wherein adaptive interaction was possible. Another embedded tenet was that the initial architecture begets the meaning of adaptation as being autopoietic where generative knowledge, cognitive processes, and induction were always the product of a changing landscape (whether it was represented as the internal state of the human or external state of the environment). Autopoiesis is defined as the property of a living system that allows it to maintain and renew itself by regulating its composition and conserving its boundaries (*Merriam-Webster*). This idea creates the basis for changing states/boundary conditions through feedback from the environment and other intelligent sources.

This first raised the issue of trust in automation and AI as a major facet of design (see Fan et al., 2008). The idea of an "associate" is that of a strong aid that could work on its own in a situation while also be at the call and command of the pilot. This notion is still useful in contemporary consideration of human—robotic interaction in everyday use. One wants the independence and autonomy of a robot to do work in context on its own strength of intelligence, but also one that is coupled to human intentions, therein the idea of joint intelligence is a hallmark of the approach taken. When this joint work is required, then an architecture that shares knowledge and understanding is desirable. Early work in this area focused on intent inferencing, shared mental models, adaptive allocation of functions, and establishing common ground between AI and humans (McNeese, 1986; Rouse, 1976; Rouse & Morris, 1986). These areas within joint work are still highly salient for creating the design of EHRI today to enable autonomous work.

Humane intelligence was the beginning of a conceptual architecture that could be designed that was human-centered, adaptive, and specific to state-of-the-art AI systems in play at the time (which were often considered to be a set of interactive expert systems (Buchanon & Shortlife, 1984) where knowledge acquisition would be critical for enabling knowledge for assistance). Inherently the cognitive architecture was positioned to take advantage of opportunities that presented themselves to create a system with humans that could take advantage of the moment rather than rely on brittle rules and preprogrammed algorithms. Many of the principles mentioned earlier were in play in this early conceptualization (ecological precedence, degree of independence, intelligence, metacognition). The focus of this work was pretty much cognitive rather than social or even affective. As pointed out in McNeese and McNeese (2016), models of cognitive architecture must answer the following questions to address requirements of their design (pp. 154):

- How is the architecture for sharing information/making decisions/ executing action determined?
- How are activities/functions/tasks allocated at given points in time?
- What determines who is in charge when given the human ultimately is always in charge?
- How does trust emerge among human actors when uncertainty and biases must be addressed?
- Is joint work the subject of social constructivism or some other theoretical perspective?

One of the tenets that was important in the design of a humane intelligence system was breaking away from the zeitgeist of the time which simply viewed AI as a "replacement logic" for human function wherein the human acted in the role of supervisory controller (McNeese, 1986) but rather considered the design wholistically by looking at how capabilities could be extended (beyond what a human could do alone). This supported the premise that the system evolved and adapted as knowledge and power were obtained—"the pilot functions are symbiotically determined as opposed to being strictly driven by the commendations of AI technology" (McNeese, 2006, p. 763).

These goals placed an emphasis on performance, error alleviation, and attuning the AI always in terms of human cognition. As McNeese (2006, p. 763) pointed out "a basic intention was to create maximal situation awareness in the cockpit concerning all elements that relate to mission success ...

wherein macro-cognition and macro-awareness must be provided to obviate such conditions as channelized attention, spatial disorientation, and cognitive overload as well as providing perspicacious insight." These elements remain in consideration for humans and agents that work with drones (uninhabited air vehicles) in flight that must be intelligent, aware of "place" and interaction with each other, and know what to do next (plans and situated intent). Humane intelligence was theoretically positioned to consist of a model of the human (cognitively inspired) which was termed mindware, the human (pilot), and the information surround which adapts communications into a shared interface. Much of the initial articulation of this area hinges on mindware and (1) the shared mental models that facilitate knowledge utilization dependent on the context that is sensed, (2) cognitive architectures that could be meaningfully updated in a rapidly changing information surround, and (3) the cognitive analogue, "Humane intelligence will evolve new synergistic relationships that are based on cognitive processes between the human mind and computer software ... that allow the human and AI to exchange meaning during the course of interaction" (McNeese, 2006, p. 763).

Analogical thinking is a key for transferring knowledge and allowing generalized knowledge to be inducted from specific knowledge wherein one can put "knowledge to use" (see McNeese, 2000). One of the basic elements in analogue formation is learning through the use of scripts and hermeneutical inferences that could develop as the joint system experienced to world through the information surround, "Essentially, this refers to a recursive process in which new associations are made based on a series of successive experiences to enable the intelligent cockpit to predict what actions are needed before their time of occurrence ....once such patterns become explicit and necessarily occur with other observed scripts, they can be encoded as heuristics" (McNeese, 2006, p. 763). The ideas resonant in mindware, architecture, and analogues were positioned for creating mutuality in terms of goals, plans, and action by a joint system of humans and AI.

It was established that humane intelligence would function primarily through mindware inferencing that collaboratively coupled human thought with knowledge resident in the AI to "serve three roles: (1) a basis for dialogue with the pilot, (2) a basis for additional data interpolation, and (3) the beginning of hierarchal prediction."..."An inference can be defined in terms of an action (functional capability) that the system or human can take, contingent on a time ladder that dispenses functions based on pilot demand or workload ....they are products of conclusions regarding information submitted to the system" (McNeese, 2006, p. 763). Mindware produces the extraordinary feats that allow a human—robotic system to engage in speculation, analytics, and prediction while recognizing states and patterns in the ecological space it is working within, "Data is scrutinized and evaluated by sets of pattern and event recognizers such that classification of real time data into recognizable events can occur" (McNeese, 2006, p. 763).

The original paper on humane intelligence was written many years prior to big data analytics, machine learning, and large-scale computing, but the fabric of recognition and prediction that is referenced conceptually is now actually possible with these kinds of techniques. This is an example where the *how* has caught up with the *what*. Humane intelligence sought the vision of an architecture that supported cognitively inspired thought with the collective induction of human and artificial minds, that could produce planning, resource allocation, and time management according to the demands presented to it. As one designs robots for everyday tasks, many of the assumptions and premises present in this joint intelligence are still applicable and doable, given the state of information and communication technology.

This project in effect tied together the cognitive correlates of knowledge with the ecological precedent of action that could be effected (through the effectors or robotic limbs of the system). The breakthrough was, in essence, that this provided an initial instantiation of a situated cognition architecture which adapts with change, enables AI-robotic control on its own terms but in collaboration with human intention, and yet shares a common ground that produced awareness among the actors involved, and timely insight and recognition of problems. We submit that this is still of great concern today as well.

In 1985/1986, the means to generate all the tenets and principles of humane intelligence were rather primitive (think expert systems), but today the means of grappling with real effectors, common ground, insight, and pattern recognition exist through the development of real products and newer techniques of AI and robotics. In summary, humane intelligence represents a significant conceptual waypoint in our own theorizing and thinking about how human—AI, human—robotic interaction could come to pass. Many of the elements mentioned have been transformed from conceptual waypoints into actual technologies and systems that have been demonstrated, evaluated in experiments, and extended into new levels of design. For example, the Pilot's Associate continued to evolve with design and testing to the point where it was actually fielded on a helicopter as a real system (Miller & Hannen, 1999).

As applied to the example case of senior assistance, humane intelligence would provide an architecture of learning and adaptation that would put robots, human service personnel, and the senior adult requiring assistance into the same shared world wherein the analogues and heuristics learned allow the robots and agents to independently assess and control action that supports specific functions of the senior in real time, that puts everyone on the same page such that awareness is enhanced and performance represents extended capabilities.

It is healthy to ascertain some of the elements of humane intelligence not represented in the architecture/approach that are important for EHRI of today. First of all, the design of a system for the Pilot's Associate was limited by the zeitgeist extant in the middle to late 1980s which was heavily focused on cognitive psychology (see Gardner, 1985) and the expert systems methodology. This focus, while productive at the time, is lacking the perspectives of social interaction and teamwork—as related to team cognition. While articulating initial inroads to address ecological contextual issues, it does not go far enough in that aspect. It also primarily looks at cognition without giving credence to how affect—emotions—motivation are important variables that are cogent for understanding behavior and designing robots that interact with agents-actors. Finally, computing power has exploded with new models and architectures of cognition (e.g., SOAR, Laird, 2012; ACT-R, Anderson, 2005) that have evolved to much more than expert systems. Having said this, these architectures primarily engage in cognitive operations and knowledge resident for a given task even though advances have made toward actor—environment transactions. Newer socially oriented technologies, however, have been utilized through the study of computer-supported cooperative work that yield beneficial results for team cognition and the use of collaborative technologies to produce intelligence in contextual fields of practice (McNeese, Salas, & Endsley, in development).

We have spent some time covering humane intelligence, as it is foundational in generating concepts that may (1) be expanded upon with more specificity in real development and testing and (2) still be theoretically sound in the design of EHRI. At this point, the chapter looks at some of the associated—yet different—projects that came after the humane intelligence approach. These projects in some ways fix some of the issues resonant in the initial architecture, apply new ideas in human—robot—agent interaction, and place more emphasis on experimentation and development of model systems.

Teamwork and intelligent systems

One of the elements that were not emphasized within humane intelligence was value and use of teamwork in addressing complex, wicked problems. There inherently was the idea of collaboration between an integrated AI system and the pilot, primarily framed with the focus on the singular support case. In order to increase power and address emergent, ill-defined situations in distributed places, teamwork has been profitable within many fields of practice with tremendous success. As mentioned in the previous section, the logical extension of humane intelligence for robotic applications was the case of drones being employed in all kinds of missions of relevance to the military and beyond. However, if one examines UAVs in practice, it is almost always in the context of teamwork wherein a control team may work with other team members in the field (ground operations). In this case, distributed teamwork is the norm and drones may actually also communicate and strategize with ground-based robots to complete mission requirements.

Our work began to shift toward command, control, communications, and intelligence (C^3I) and crisis management operations in the 1990s—2000s with the goal of conducting research wherein cognition intersected intelligence technologies (e.g., human—computer interfaces, aids, agents, robots, etc.) and these technologies supported cooperative work (i.e., computer-supported cooperative work (CSCW)). While historically teamwork in these domains was centralized in a given command post (collocated setting), it increasingly began to evolve wherein a team was distributed across settings at distance (remote setting). Computing supported areas called electronic-mediated communications (Santoro, 1995) wherein people could coordinate, collaborate, and communicate within a group interface supported by various tools. When research in CSCW began looking at this kind of setting, many of the cognitive constructs that we employed in looking at AI working with pilots became relevant for teams. For example, a lot of our research over the past 30 years has primarily focused on team cognition in its own right (e.g., see McNeese, Mancuso, McNeese, Endsley, & Forster, 2014; McNeese & Pfaff, 2012; McNeese & Reddy, 2017; McNeese, Salas, & Endsley, 2001) exploring such research variables as team-based—situation awareness, mental models, information sharing, team workload, collective induction, transfer of knowledge in cognitive analogues, attention management, coordination, leadership, function allocation, mood and affect, metacognitive processes, and planning, to name a few. In particular, research studies have been attuned to the intersection and development of intelligent technologies that form different components of team cognition (e.g., function allocation and coordinated efforts). Team cognition looks at cognition that occurs at the team level wherein a shared goal, interdependency among actors, and coordination communication are all crucial for teamwork to ensue (McNeese, Salas, & Endsley, 2001)—in contrast to groups wherein these elements are all not present.

As one designs EHRI, the team cognitive constructs are very relevant as well. Therein, many of the findings that have been established can be transferred for everyday use of robots when they are considered a member of an overall team. Take for example, the case identified for this chapter—support of a senior adult needing assistance in living. In most cases, this will consist of interactions that need to place with physicians, nurses, medical specialists, and social workers to formulate an integrated team network. While traditionally a person may be at a facility (assisted living) and part of the team is collocated, it is certainly the case that each team member may interact with a person on a one-on-one basis, but team information sharing can occur also through forms or an electronic interface (e.g., an electronic record). When the situation changes where the person is at home looking for assistance from the team, wherein robots work in the midst of the home to do various tasks for the senior adult, then communication, coordination, and other team cognition variables become extremely important to effect strong teamwork among humans, agents, and robots. In these cases, electronic-mediated communications is likely going to occur frequently to enable collective induction, monitoring, and information sharing. The following projects are critical in studying and designing intelligent systems around team cognition variables.

Electronic-mediation communication and collaboration

The work of A. Rodney Wellens has been crucial in looking at interdisciplinary findings for C^3I applications wherein team situation awareness is of utmost importance in team functioning. EHRI is dependent on establishing and maintaining team awareness about each member and the situation at hand in order to employ the right action to assuage problem states. The senior author worked with Dr. Wellens when he was a visiting senior fellow at the Fitts Human Engineering Lab at Wright-Patterson AFB, OH. Wellens' research on teamwork and team situation awareness focused on crisis management involving 911 call centers and was predicated on the design of a scaled world team simulation in crisis management simulation called CITIES (Wellens, 1990). The simulation provided the foundation for testing team cognition variables such as situation awareness, team communications and coordination, and information sharing but varied the technological bridge among team members to test (1) different forms of communication (e.g., email, video teleconferencing, text) and (2) provided experimental development and testing of team decision aids wherein representation of the aid could be as a "talking head" or just text-based interaction (Wellens, 1993). While CITIES is not the primary focus of the write-up here, it did lend itself to thinking about social-psychological variables (trust, status, attribution, role-rank, affiliation) that were very important for designing innovative decision aids that supported distributed group work (Wellens & McNeese, 1999). While there was still a major cognitive strand in the experimentation—team situation awareness—this work revealed new concepts for designs that are still useful for contemporary applications inclusive of EHRI where robots are team members performing specific functions, maintaining team SA, and communicating with other team members within a social environment. Also, much of our research has developed upon multiple, significant extensions of the original CITIES paradigm into contemporary computer-based client—server architecture and a flexible group interface for quickly adapting team simulation experiments. This affords rapidly designing new interfaces, quick insertion of information/ intelligence technologies, and easy implementation of experimental designs and evaluation. This later simulation is called NeoCities (Hamilton et al., 2010) and has been used in multiple experiments over the last 15 years.

Using an earlier version of NeoCities (Connors, 2006), the simulation was redesigned to study team-to-team interaction with hierarchical control where three 2-person teams interacted together to solve team resource allocation problems in a set time period. The intelligence elements in this study that are important are provision of a group interface that would adapt based on preferences of the user, with the level of successive exposures. The study also measured effects of team mental models when different strategies of intelligent interface design adaptation are employed and found that this formation changed as a function of the adaptation strategy used. Adaptive interfaces are important as they can be set up as sensors to adapt to changes in the problem state itself (the event a team is processing), in other team member's status, and in the environment. Adaptive interfaces are very important when considering interconnectivity and continuing in distributed team performance that employs hybrid team members such as agents and robots as they encounter complex problems that require cognition, metacognition, and insights. Adaptive interfaces represent several of the principles of being elaborated earlier in the chapter inclusive of intelligence, awareness, and parallelism.

Another use of NeoCities that is pertinent for EHRI is the design and testing of a fuzzy cognitive map-based decision aid (Jones, 2006) to represent changes of state within the problem and context that is given as feedback for the team members. This work emanated from earlier work involving team simulation, schema formation, and communication (McNeese, Perusich, & Rentsch, 1999) that focused on the innovation termed socio-cognitive mediators. Prior to the development of fuzzy cognitive maps, our first attempt to create an artifact that demonstrated the capabilities of mindware came to pass with the development of the conflict resolver decision aid which was designed to assess and then resolve cognitive conflicts which emerge when intelligent entities combined thought (see Fraser, Hipel, Kilgore, McNeese, & Snyder, 1989). This integrated thought across multiple expert systems and developed a mathematically based architecture to work through conflicting information. When intelligence combines sources of knowledge from obsequious entities and agents, there is bound to be conflicts that develop that will require further processing before a wholistic system can continue to evolve or equilibrate to a point of "settling down." The conflict resolver first attempted to build an architecture which would demonstrate eloquent solutions to these hard problems. The work with fuzzy sets continued this but in a different vein wherein data were messier and continued to percolate values. Our work with fuzzy cognitive maps (Perusich & McNeese, 2006) as applied to battle management contexts represents a real artifact expressing parts of the initial mindware concept of humane intelligence. As in Connor's work, this study also utilized the team-to-team interaction model but compared conditions where the presence or absence of the decision aid was established through use. This study is important because fuzzy set theory/fuzzy logic represents one of the proposed inferencing models in humane intelligence to capture changes in the environment that a user might not be aware of on their own recognizance. The value of fuzzy cognitive maps is that they model and extrapolate from ill-defined, ambiguous information present in the environment that can then help decision makers involved in sensemaking. This kind of modeling may be very useful within EHRI as it provides enhancement of the ecological precedent principle, helps to amplify intelligence within perceptual boundaries of transactions available, and finally can take place among different entities within distributed transaction where things are initially ambiguous and ill-defined, but as the problem-solving progresses the fuzzy cognitive map can equilibrate alternatives that are useful to teams.

Adaptive teamwork and emotional architecture

It is certainly the case that humans are just as influenced by emotional affect as cognition, and in fact studies have shown that affect can influence cognition in various ways (e.g., stress reducing attention and short-term memory) (LeDoux, 1996). When teams are operative then it is also the case that affect and mood may be implicitly impacting team cognition (see McNeese & Pfaff, 2012). As team cognition studies were being informed by the use of intelligent technologies, a new area was also emerging that involved computers adapting objects based on sensing human affect (Picard, 1997). This area is called *affective computing*. This area has been utilized as a special component of human−computer interaction wherein various theorists have conceptualized unique roles for affective computing (see Hudlicka, 2003; McNeese, 2003). In the early beginnings of affective computing, Hudlicka and McNeese (2002) built and tested yet another computational artifact—the Affective and Belief Adaptive Interface System (ABAIS) architecture—that represented a version of mindware but was more advanced in that it considered states of anxiety, affective knowledge, and beliefs in terms of how they would adapt a pilot's user interface for an Air Force mission. The mission−task context developed for the ABAIS evaluation was interesting—a fighter pilot conducting a sweep task while in communications with an Airborne Warning and Control System (AWACS) air crew. An AWACS aircraft in essence provides surveillance and detection of aircraft wherein C^3I operations are integrated across the battle-space, while the pilot sweep task consists of getting rid of enemy aircraft in the airspace. Although the task for this study specifically was individualistic, it has attributes of an individual working with the more team-oriented AWACS mission yet not really an intelligent system involving teams per se, even though it has been categorized under the section with intelligent systems supporting teamwork. This study conducted a successful demonstration of the ABAIS architecture hence suggesting its potential application for complex, wicked problem domains where affect and bias impact human performance.

Whereas, the conflict resolver decision support system (Fraser et al., 1989) was designed to detect, assess, and alleviate the presence of cognitive conflicts across intelligent entities that formulate an intelligent system, ABAIS was designed to compensate for performance biases caused by affective states and active beliefs (Hudlicka & McNeese, 2002). The ABAIS architecture generated many of the specific processes inherent in the initial mindware concept, obtained power through actual knowledge acquisition and cognitive-affective task analysis, and provided integrated layers of processing. The methodology used to impact performance contained four steps (Hudlicka & McNeese, 2002), "sensing/inferring affective states and performance-relevant beliefs, identifying what potential impacts they had on performance, selection of a compensatory strategy, and implementing this strategy in terms of specific GUI adaptations (p. 1)." ABAIS was built as a real computing system and was interfaced with a pilot user performing the AWACS mission task. As noted in McNeese (2006), "The original conception of HI suggested that an intelligent interface would afford situational transformations based on both the external environment (weather, threats) and the pilot's internal environment (physiological states, fatigue, attitudes, intuition) when encountering uncertain events. The notion that an intelligent system could be specifically tailored to respond (and compensate) to individual internal states suggested that factors beyond traditional cognition could mediate performance and be used as predictive input into the mindware scripting that was proposed as part of the architecture (p. 764)."

Overall, ABAIS has been an important accomplishment in that it allows a complex user-based modeling architecture to be coupled with (1) complex task context knowledge, (2) in-depth user assessment methods (knowledge-based, self-reports, diagnostic tasks, and physiological sensing), and (3) graphic user interface adaptation strategies. Of value is that the "why" and "what" of humane intelligence could be operationally realized by the "how" in this project. The project implements a large number of the principles being suggested in this chapter and refines the necessity of cognition and affect working conjunctively to adapt performance in real time. As such, the ABAIS architecture would be very useful for EHRI where adaptation of team's affective states and beliefs are very critical for consistent, relevant, and reliant actor-environment transactions. As related to the case example of the senior adult, affect will play a major role in actors attending to the needs of a person. Having human and robot team members sense and identify emotions, physiological states, and active beliefs within a highly specified task environment offers great opportunities for awareness, metacognitive understanding, and mutual compensatory strategies that compose extraordinary responses within human—robotic interaction.

Human—agent teamwork

While the work with NeoCities involved distributed teamwork akin to requirements/needs necessary in the complex world of EHRI, many of computational technology solutions represented ad hoc solutions (e.g., decision aids for one part of the context) and not wholistic, parallel solutions inculcated in an overall approach. On the other hand, the ABAIS architecture represents a wholistic, integrated solution set that addresses the entirety of the mission—task environment but it has been designed specifically for individuals operating in a team-based task. What is needed is something that addresses distributed teamwork within a complex environment (where there is multiple context switching within an environment) but also has a sophisticated architecture that is wholistic, intelligent, integrated, and parallel in scope therein addressing many of the principles of being suggested earlier in the chapter. If an architecture could be designed that contains these attributes then it would operationally define elements of humane intelligence and mindware inferencing but for a team situated in a complex, ill-defined, emergent task setting.

R-CAST (Fan, Sun, Sun, McNeese, & Yen, 2006) is a cognitively inspired agent architecture that fulfills the abovementioned requirements that we have utilized in unique ways. One such application of R-CAST for human—agent collaboration was undertaken with much success in an experimental army decision-making task context (Fan et al., 2009). R-CAST was implemented specifically to work with human teams in a very complex, multicontext decision-making task involving the real-world Army mission termed three-block challenge problem. This problem is focused on "urban terrain wherein command and control teams must frequently confront humanitarian, peace-keeping, and combat missions in close proximity (involving three contexts that overlap in time" (Fan et al., 2009, p. 306). The mission involves one unique component of team decision-making that contributes to problem complexity and wickedness—multicontext switching across these three contexts. This component is "challenging because it requires effective team collaborations in rapidly gathering dynamic information from multiple sources (collateral space)" (Fan et al., 2009, p. 306). It puts extreme emphasis on principles of being that consider ecological precedence, situated cognition, place, intelligence, awareness, and parallelism. When switching occurs, team members need to be highly aware of what they are doing, while keeping track of what others are doing within each context that requires attention, while being cognizant of the information flow and decision requirements that evolve as change takes place across the environment, and exert the correct course of action needed. We believe that this component of teamwork will be especially salient for EHRI where everyday robots are present as part of an ongoing team effort that has similar concerns as the three-block challenge problem.

R-CAST was designed in such a way that it uses a team of agents to support a team of humans. One unique attribute of the architecture is that it is simply not a computer-only architecture, but it was designed and built specifically as "cognitively inspired." That means that R-CAST is heavily predicated on (1) a top naturalistic decision-making model—recognition primed decision (RPD) framework (Klein, 1999; Klein, Orasanu, Calderwood, & Zsambok, 1993) and (2) utilizes a shared mental model paradigm to understand the integration of knowledge within the task environment. R-CAST then is designed and built to emulate how humans work in real-world naturalist settings and also gains power as it encodes experience. This enables R-CAST to work directly with human teams using the cognitive analogues-recognition schemas that humans use to therein establish common ground and common process in their team cognition. Therein, R-CAST is highly human-centered as well as team-focused to the work it can do within complex-level environments. R-CAST absolutely is representative of mindware that recognizes constraints in macro-cognition, expands and monitors comprehension of wholistic situations through macro-awareness, and ascertains "what is the next step" in optimal courses of action. It is a great example of in-depth ideas that demonstrate the design and programming of the "how" part of computing.

At the heart of the architecture is the RPD engine, which implements a cycle of recognition that starts with "Situation Awareness" where an R-CAST agent utilizes the inference knowledge and past experience knowledge to generate/synthesize a recognition of the current decision situation (p. 307, Fan et al., 2010). Recognition takes place through the use of four constructs: relevant cues (where attention is directed), plausible goals (which make sense), expectancy (what will happen next), and courses of action (what action worked well before). If expectancy is violated, adaptation of the recognition occurs. Courses of action can occur with a team of agents or occur with human teams as well which is overseen by a "Process Manager." The architecture also has a reasoning system to work with contextual representation and variation that is overseen by a "Context Manager." That part of the architecture works with three parts of context that are important to consider: process, recognition, and inference. Accordingly, "these three types of context enable an R-CAST agent to effectively identify information needs of other team members, to quickly adapt decisions to a dynamic environment, and to facilitate the reuse of inferential knowledge in various means-ends activities" (Fan et al., 2010, p. 307). R-CAST when used as part of a team has been shown to improve team decision making under time stress in contrast to teams composed only of humans (Fan et al., 2010). Hence, there is much promise to this kind of system, albeit it is heavily reliant on computational power and experience with the environment to fully express its value for ERHI. It is especially flexible for intelligent entities (robots and humans) that formulate teams that are remotely distributed, as would be the case with the senior adult example that has been used in this chapter. In that situation, there are task complexities, multiple context switching, and the need for recognition of patterns as cues that stimulate the RPDM cycle. There is also the necessity to construct, maintain, and monitor shared mental models across team members to encode experience and heighten situation awareness as the senior adult's needs continue to emerge with different states of need.

Human—autonomous systems and teams

Indeed, the previous sections have noted works of human—agent teaming from varying perspectives. An additional perspective is one that differentiates the machine from automation to autonomy. Unfortunately, automation and autonomy are often used interchangeably, especially in the early days of human—machine teaming. There is a clear and distinct difference between automation and autonomy, and that difference must be defined within teaming because there are *human—automation* teams and *human—autonomy* teams, and each has distinctly different processes and goals.

First, the delineation of autonomation and autonomy for the purposes of teaming must be identified. Automation is a technology that requires human intervention or one that the human still has control over. Therefore, in a teaming setting, the humans still have control over their automation team members, thus meaning that the humans and technology are not equal partners. Parasuraman, Sheridan, and Wickens (2000) defined automation as "a device or system that accomplishes (partially or fully) a function that was previously, or conceivably could be, carried out (partially or fully) by a human operator" (p. 287). In addition to their seminal definition, they also introduced a model characterizing types and levels of automation. Accordingly, automation should be oriented to a specific goal or aim, such as *information acquisition, information analysis, decision and action selection,* and *action implementation* (Parasuraman et al., 2000). Within each type of automation, Parasuraman and Wickens (2008) suggest that the automation may range in its functionality, meaning that there may be varying high (automation completely performs task) or low (automation minimally aids in task) levels of autonomous functionality.

Indeed, Parasuraman and colleagues were correct in emphasizing that automation may consist of varying levels of functionality. Society has actively engaged with many examples of low levels of automation (e.g., a snack machine) to much higher levels in recent years (e.g., Siri as an intelligent personal assistant). Due to automation advances, our interactions with machines have changed over time. At one end, humans have interacted as a supervisor of automation (Cummings, Clare, & Hart, 2010; Sheridan, 2012). As automation advances to higher levels of autonomy, the ability for back and forth interaction between the human and the machine is becoming a reality. These advances are leading to the conceptualization of *human—autonomy* teaming (HAT).

HAT provides affordances that allow the autonomous technology to actually act as a team member, meaning that the autonomy has a role on the team and has independent (from the human) abilities to complete that role in concert with other team members. The United Air Force best defines autonomy and its capabilities as "systems which have a set of intelligence-based capabilities that allow it to respond to situations that were not programmed or anticipated in the design (i.e., decision-based responses). Autonomous systems have a degree of self-government and self-directed behavior (with the human's proxy for decisions)" (USAF, 2013, p. 3). An autonomous team member should exhibit and have the abilities to act in manners that are similar to fundamental teamwork characteristics. This means that it needs communicative capabilities that allow it to work with other team members toward a shared goal.

Though the current work on human automation interaction has resulted in valuable knowledge, there are still many open questions regarding how humans and autonomy effectively team together. First, a greater understanding of how a human team member effectively interacts (i.e., communicate and coordinate) with autonomy is necessary. Similarly, the autonomy needs to adequately understand how to accurately interact with human team members. The understanding of how both humans and autonomy interact with each other in a team setting is critical considering the importance of communication and coordination to effective teamwork. Secondly, more investigations are necessary to understand whether the many insights found in human—human teaming are relevant and transferable to the HAT context. There is significant potential to draw upon our human—human teaming knowledge base for the purposes of developing more effective HAT. Yet, we must first seek to translate many of the human—human findings through evaluations of HAT to understand their validity in this new setting. Finally, more empirical investigations of real HAT teams are needed to better understand teamwork performance as well as how HAT dynamics affect teamwork relevant variables such as situational awareness, workload, trust, and process behavior.

Recent work in the CERTT-UAS-STE has explored empirical study of HAT. In this synthetic task environment (STE), teams of three work together toward the common goal of operating a UAV to take photographs of targets at specific waypoints. Traditionally, this (STE) has been used to study human—human teams (Cooke & Shope, 2004), but a collaboration with the AFRL has extended it to studying human—autonomy teams. AFRL built a synthetic agent based on cognitive ACT-R modeling to control the role of the pilot in this task (for more information on the synthetic agent, see Ball et al., 2010). This means that the synthetic agent has the ability to communicate with other human team members using natural language. A multitude of studies have been conducted within this paradigm to study HAT.

McNeese, Salas, and Endsley (2018) compared human—human, synthetic (human—autonomy), and experimenter (advanced human—autonomy) teams in this empirical testbed and found that while synthetic teams performed statistically equivalent to human—human teams, the synthetic teams lacked the finer abilities of communication and coordination. More specifically, synthetic teams were not able to coordinate information (both pushing and pulling information) in an effective or efficient manner. Yet, the experimenter teams that exhibited a synthetic teammate who acted on a script to enhance coordination performed better than all other types of teams. Team situational awareness was also studied in this experiment, finding that pushing information was positively associated with both team situational awareness and performance (Demir, McNeeese, & Cooke, 2017). Finally, team coordination dynamics were investigated, and it was found that through nonlinear dynamical systems methods that synthetic teams were rigid in how they coordinated information, with experimenter teams being metastable, and human—human teams being unstable (Demir, Likens, Cooke, Amazeen, & McNeese, 2018). This finding indicates that future human—autonomy teams must address issues of coordination becoming too rigid and not flexible. Multiple other publications regarding this experiment are also available.

Design and development of EHRI

As one looks at the basic-level understanding of human—robotic interaction, and considers the principals of being and approaches taken, it is useful to employ meaningful frameworks in their design. Frameworks should encapsulate how ideas about user-centered computing and design can come to fruition as products that can be experimented upon, tested, validated, and improved. A framework should reflect some degree of logic and reason in terms of how one goes about coming up with innovations in human—robotic interaction that demonstrate extraordinary accomplishment. Frameworks should also provide levels of integrative knowingness while being able to handle interdisciplinary science and design practice which EHRI represents.

The philosophy toward user-centered design that we have utilized in the past is classified as *cognitive systems engineering*. The work we have produced has been heavily influenced by the views and approach of Jens Rasmussen and very much reflects his conceptualizations about the ecological foundations of cognitive systems engineering (see Rasmussen, 1986), especially the ideas resonant within the abstraction hierarchy (Rasmussen, Pejtersen, & Goodstein, 1994) of modeling a domain that lead to designs. In fact, designers of EHRI may want to go directly to work domain analysis (Vicente, 1999) to see how the abstraction hierarchy framework and means-ends analysis are used to model a domain and to develop systems or products. Additionally, the viewpoints of David Woods on cognitive engineering have been highly influential in our work (Woods, Johannesen, Cook, & Sarter, 1994). Especially thoughtful is Wood's viewpoint that "designs are hypotheses about how artifacts shape cognition and collaboration" (see Woods, 1998). Inherent in this approach is the idea that one needs to formulate a hypothesis about how robotic design shapes cognition and collaboration in consort with humans in a teaming arrangement. The hypotheses can be tested in various ways to see how veridical they are and if not viable, then the experimenter can change the design such that it represents successful cognition and collaboration with the other intelligent entities employed. This is what Woods has termed "experimenter as designer."

The framework we have used for interdisciplinary science and design is called the *Integrated Living Laboratory Framework* (originally formulated by McNeese (1996), and current version is provided in McNeese & Forster (2017)). The premise is that identifying and defining problems, issues, and constraints within a given domain sets the center point for the cognitive systems engineering effort. Problems that are extant in a domain represent potential failures of the user, the technology, the environment, or some combination therein. At the topside (i.e., a top-down methodology)—problems may be investigated through theoretical research findings (prior and current research conducted to investigate problems where hypotheses are generated and tested). On the other hand, many problems are only experienced within the context of everyday practice (i.e., they are heavily situated and ecologically bound as we have mentioned earlier). Therein, understanding problems—and the issues and constraints resident within—can be understood also from the bottomside (bottom-up methodology) wherein they are comprehensible only by studying them in context.

When problems are fully investigated from the topside and bottomside, the interdisciplinary backdrop of *actor—environment transactions* can be thought about in unique ways. The purpose is to look at problems from three perspectives: (1) understanding them in-depth, (2) simulating them with deep context, (3) designing hypothesis that shape cognition or collaboration such that problems are transformed into solutions that help alleviate failure, error, constraint, issues resident in practice. The Living Laboratory framework posits four distinct conduits (techniques) that allow answers to problems to emerge and that facilitate knowledge sharing through feedback/feedforward processes. The goal is to produce answers that lead to designs through continuous process improvement wherein the designs shape cognition and collaboration in a way that produces adaptive response (not problems) (Woods, 1999). Therein, the four major conduits that exist between the top and bottomside are (1) ethnographic study, (2) knowledge elicitation, (3) scaled world simulation, (4) reconfigurable prototypes. These conduits work together to produce *knowledge as design* (Perkins, 1986) through mutually informing each other and producing outcomes that advance both science and design practice.

The Living Laboratory framework has been used with success in the areas of command and control, aviation pilot performance, crisis management, cyber security, to name a few. It gives credence to interdisciplinary work and underscores a philosophical approach to complex systems design that is predicated on obtaining multiple perspectives of understanding. Therein, it is positioned to be highly valuable to both understand and design EHRI as it is put forth to advance the state of the art. EHRI therein must be in relation to a given context (as this chapter has suggested) but also reflective of specific problem states that are being experienced wherein informed answers and solutions may improve the quality of life.

McNeese and McNeese (2016) introduced another kind of framework designed to look at human—agent collaboration which is easily applied to EHRI. This framework develops through three stages historically used when considering knowledge about intelligent systems: (1) theoretical/traditional experiments wherein one has a hypothesis utilizing independent variables effects on a dependent variable of performance, (2) traditional models that emulate cognition/collaborative activity wherein architectures derive from theory and produce computational-based models that are comparable to actual human cognition when performing a task, and (3) aids/agents supporting cognition/collaboration wherein comparisons are made where one condition comprises a team with agent support to various degrees and the other condition is a team that does not have agent support. The final stage (4)—termed Interactive Scaled Worlds—consists of some of the attributes of the other stages but is heavily coupled to new technologies that can simulate interactive scaled worlds that represent the contextual domain where problems emerge from. While the prior three stages are heavily leveraged against theory, experimentation, and hypothesis testing, the scaled world idea places emphasis on developing the environmental context where activities occur. It emulates practice but is interactive in the sense that new innovative designs can be integrated and tested within human and human—agent teams to determine worth in overcoming specific problem states. This stage as reported in McNeese and McNeese (2016) contains models that may emulate cognition as well as aids/agents that may support cognition. But as applicable to EHRI, it would also contain active robots as emulative or supportive entities that work together with the human—agent team.

Beyond the horizon—potential applications of extraordinary human—robotic interaction

When one determines how robots and EHRI could progress over the next decade, there is a necessity to look at how a group of intelligent entities interpret and act on the world. Indeed, the initial conceptualization of humane intelligence posited that hermeneutics created within any form of intelligence provides the basis of what they will do and when they will do it. Being able to sense the world that is impacting the situation one faces, being able to interpret that situation with some degree of confidence, and then being able to act upon that world provides adaptive abilities. As humans, we encounter wicked, ill-defined, and ill-structured problems. The ability to deal with problems like this is absolutely connected to learning from new experiences, recognizing a situation as similar to previous situations, and seeing what is possible. Knowing what is possible may result in an intelligent entity thinking about "what is next" in "what I do." These states are intrinsically limited by the array of sensors and effectors that are possessed within a robot or a team of robots and humans. Hence, the capabilities and limitations present across a team establish a performance corridor of possibility in addressing an ill-defined problem. While all robots are not designed to overcome problems—some are designed to enhance pleasure and entertainment—the future power of robots expand beyond the current horizon. What is meant by that is robots who can establish their own sense of being through the principles identified earlier—will in combination with other robots and agents—along with human team members—be able to accomplish extraordinary things. When robots can consider mysterious occurrences and reason about ethereal factors before they act, then they can face a situation and determine "what do I do next?" When robots can induct from their circumstances, create and imagine what could be, then they establish generalizability beyond the particular to strategize to a more general level of being. When they work on a team and realize other team members, as well as their own limits and constraints, but adapt to allocate functions and work processes accordingly, their being is enhanced. When they adapt to humans solely as a function of knowing who they are dealing with, what cultural imprints are active, and ascertain the overall social environment and how it figures into action, then they are considered extraordinarily aware. When they can reason beyond just what is given to consider the moral and ethical consequences of their action—both on their own and jointly within a social enclave—then they are considered relevant. When they realize they are under attack and insecure, and derive the meaning necessary to protect themselves and their teammates, then they are survivors. Finally, when they see their own limitations and act to change and transform themselves into something different from respond to a problem, then they are evolving.

As we assess where applications are today, there are glimpses of potentially extraordinary feats present in application areas that are noteworthy. In the area of crisis management, teams have worked with bomb and cadaver hunting robots to accelerate discovery and timely removal of bombs. Some of these robots have sensors that detect the object of interest while others facilitate the extension of human expertise (dismantlement) using immersive techniques and sophisticated robotic manipulators (see <https://www.wired.com/story/a-brave-bomb-disposal-robot-you-control-in-virtual-reality/>). In fact this is a hot area for human–robotic teamwork as the Office of Naval Research earlier this year put out a broad area announcement to amplify the level of intricacy in sensing within manipulators using advanced machine learning techniques while broadening the awareness of the robots to learn jointly with humans(<https://www.fbo.gov/index?s=opportunity&mode=form&id=299af616dc07cc81c29b7b86b2f01202&tab=core&tabmode=list>).

It is surprising to think about the actions of what robots can do in and of themselves, let alone their inductive potential of being on a team. Taking the case of the senior adult support system used throughout the chapter, there may come a day when one of the team members is a robot and a physician, and acts directly with other robots to do surgery, provide anesthesia, support necessary vital functions, help a person convalesce in recovery, all while working with other members to orchestrate additional support functions (e.g., eating, walking/mobility, personal hygiene, psychological health, entertainment). Robots may be designed to do a highly specific duty and act in parallel with others to accomplish overall integration and extraordinary feats, or they may be designed to do multiple functions—some by themselves and others with the help of human expertise. When robots begin to show progression toward developing expertise—similar to humans—then the signs of human–robotic civilization will be in place.

References

Anderson, J. R. (2005). Human symbol manipulation within an integrated cognitive architecture. *Cognitive Science, 29*(3), 313–341.

Ball, J., Myers, C., Heiberg, A., Cooke, N. J., Matessa, M., Freiman, M., et al. (2010). The synthetic teammate project. *Computational & Mathematical Organization Theory, 16*(3), 271–299.

Banks, S. B., & Lizza, C. S. (1991). Pilot's associate: A cooperative, knowledge-based system application. *IEEE Expert, 6*(3), 18–29.

Ben-Tzvi, P., Ito, S., & Goldenberg, A. A. (2009). A mobile robot with autonomous climbing and descending of stairs. *Robotica, 27*(2), 171–188.

Booth, K. E. C., Mohamed, S. C., Rajaratnam, S., Nejat, G., & Christopher, J. B. (2017). Robots in retirement homes: Person search and task planning for a group of residents by a team of assistive robots. *IEEE Intelligent Systems, 32*(2), 14–21.

Bransford, J. D., Brown, A. L., & Cocking, R. R. (2000). *How people learn: Brain, mind, experience, and school.* Washington, D.C.: National Academy Press.

Bransford, J. D., Sherwood, R. D., Vye, N. J., & Reiser, J. (1986). Teaching thinking and problem solving. *American Psychologist, 41*(10), 1078–1089.

Bringsjord, S., Licato, J., Govindarajulu, N. S., Ghosh, R., & Sen, A. (2015). Real robots that pass tests of self-consciousness. In *Proccedings of the 24th IEEE international symposium on robot and human interactive communication* (pp. 498–504). New York, NY: IEEE.

Brown, J. S., Collins, A., & Duguid, S. (1989). Situated cognition and the culture of learning. *Educational Researcher, 18*(1), 32–42.

Buchanan, B. G., & Shortliffe, E. H. (Eds.). (1984). *Rule-based expert systems: The mycin experiments of the Stanford heuristic programming project.* Reading, MA: Addison Wesley.

Churchman, C. W. (1967). Guest editorial: Wicked problems. *Management Science, 14*(4), 141–142.

Cognition and Technology Group at Vanderbilt. (1990). Anchored instruction and its relationship to situated cognition. *Educational Research, 19*(6), 2–10.

Connors, E. S. (2006). *Intelligent group interfaces: Envisioned designs for exploring team cognition in emergency crisis management.* University Park, PA: The Pennsylvania State University (unpublished doctoral dissertation).

Cooke, N. J., & Shope, S. M. (2004). Synthetic task environments for teams: CERTT's UAV-STE. In *Handbook of human factors and ergonomics methods* (pp. 476–483). CRC Press.

Craik, F. I. M., & Lockhart, R. S. (1972). Levels of processing: A framework for memory research. *Journal of Verbal Learning and Verbal Behavior, 11*(6), 671–684.

Cummings, M. L., Clare, A., & Hart, C. (2010). The role of human-automation consensus in multiple unmanned vehicle scheduling. *Human Factors, 52*(1), 17–27.

DeGreene, K. B. (Ed.). (1970). *Systems psychology.* New York: McGraw-Hill.

Demir, M., Likens, A. D., Cooke, N. J., Amazeen, P. G., & McNeese, N. J. (2018). Team coordination and effectiveness in human-autonomy teaming. *IEEE Transactions on Human-Machine Systems.*

Demir, M., McNeese, N. J., & Cooke, N. J. (2017). Team situation awareness within the context of human-autonomy teaming. *Cognitive Systems Research, 46*, 3–12.

Einstein, A. (October 26, 1929). As quoted from, "What life means to Einstein: An interview by George Sylvester Viereck" (p. 17). *The Saturday Evening Post.*

Endsley, M. R. (1995). Measurement of situation awareness in dynamic systems. *Human Factors, 37*(1), 65–84.

Fan, X., McNeese, M., Sun, B., Hanratty, T., Allender, L., & Yen, J. (2010). Human-agent collaboration for time stressed multi-context decision making. IEEE Transactions on Systems, Man, and Cybernetics(A), 40(2), 306–320.

Fan, X., McNeese, M. D., Sun, B., Hanratty, T., Allender, L., & Yen, J. (2009). Human-agent collaboration for time stressed multi-context decision making. *IEEE Transactions on Systems, Man, and Cybernetics (A), 90*, 1–14.

Fan, X., Oh, S., McNeese, M. D., Yen, J., Cuevas, H., Strater, L., et al. (2008). The influence of agent reliability on trust in human-agent collaboration. In *Proceedings of the 15th European conference on cognitive ergonomics: The ergonomics of cool interaction (article 7)*. New York, NY: ACM.

Fan, X., Sun, B., Sun, S., McNeese, M. D., & Yen, J. (2006). RPD-enabled agents teaming with human for multi- context decision making. In *Proceedings of the fifth international joint conference on autonomous agents and multiple agent systems (AAMAS), Hakodate, Japan*.

Flach, J. M., Eggleston, R. G., Kuperman, G. G., & Dominguez, C. O. (1998). *SEAD and the UCAV: A preliminary cognitive systems analysis* (Tech. Rep. WP–TR–1998–0013). Wright-Patterson AFB, OH: U.S. Air Force Research Laboratory.

Franks, J. J., & Bransford, J. D. (1971). Abstraction of visual patterns. *Journal of Experimental Psychology, 90*(1), 65–74.

Fraser, N. M., Hipel, K. W., Kilgore, D. M., McNeese, M. D., & Snyder, D. E. (1989). An architecture for integrating expert systems. *Decision Support Systems, 5*(3), 263–276.

Gardner, H. (1985). *The mind's new science: A history of the cognitive revolution*. New York, NY, US: Basic Books.

Gardner, H. (2011). *Frames of mind: The theory of multiple intelligences*. New York: Basic Books.

Gibson, J. J. (1972). A theory of direct visual perception. In J. Royce, & W. Rozenboom (Eds.), *The psychology of knowing*. New York: Gordon & Breach.

Greenfield. (2006). *Everyware: The dawning age of ubiquitous computing*. Berkeley, CA: New Riders Publishing.

Greeno, J. G., & Moore, J. L. (1993). Situativity and symbols: Response to Vera and Simon. *Cognitive Science, 17*(1), 49–59.

Hamilton, K., Mancuso, V., Minotra, D., Hoult, R., Mohammed, S., Parr, A., et al. (2010). Using the NeoCITIES 3.1 simulation to study and measure team cognition. In *Proceedings of the 54th annual meeting of the human factors and ergonomics society* (pp. 433–437). San Francisco, CA: Human Factors and Ergonomics Society.

Hinton, A. (2015). *Understanding context: Environment, language, and information architecture*. Sebastopol, CA: O'Reilly Publishers.

Hudlicka, E. (2003). To feel or not to feel: The role of affect in human–computer interaction. *International Journal of Human-Computer Studies, 59*(1), 1–32.

Hudlicka, E., & McNeese, M. D. (2002). User's affective & belief state: Assessment and GUI adaptation. *International Journal of User Modeling and User Adapted Interaction, 12*(1), 1–47.

Jones, R. E. T. (2006). *Studying the impact of fuzzy cognitive map decision aid on team performance and team cognition in a crisis-management, team-based, resource allocation simulation*. University Park, PA: The Pennsylvania State University (unpublished doctoral dissertation).

Klein, G. A. (1999). *Sources of power: How people make decisions*. Cambridge, MA: MIT Press.

Klein, G. A., Orasanu, J. M., Calderwood, R., & Zsambok, C. (Eds.). (1993). *Decision making in action: Models and methods*. Norwood, NJ: Ablex Publishing.

Laird, J. E. (2012). *The Soar cognitive architecture*. Cambridge, MA: MIT Press.

LeDoux, J. (1996). *The emotional brain: The mysterious underpinnings of emotional life.* New York, NY: Simon & Schuster Publishers.

Lost in Space. (n.d.). In Wickipedia. Retrieved from https://en.wikipedia.org/wiki/Lost_in_Space.

McNeese, M. D. (1986). Humane intelligence: A human factors perspective for developing intelligent cockpits. *IEEE Aerospace and Electronic Systems, 1*(9), 6–12.

McNeese, M. D. (1996). An ecological perspective applied to multi-operator systems. In O. Brown, & H. L. Hendrick (Eds.), *Human factors in organizational design and management - VI* (pp. 365–370). The Netherlands: Elsevier.

McNeese, M. D. (1999). Considering the social-cognitive and contextual foundations of mixed-initiative intelligence. In *Working notes of the AAAI 99 workshop, mixed initiative intelligence* (pp. 11–14). Menlo Park, CA: American Association of Artificial Intelligence.

McNeese, M. D. (2000). Socio-cognitive factors in the acquisition and transfer of knowledge. *Cognition, Technology & Work, 2*(3), 164–177.

McNeese, M. D. (2003). New visions of human-computer interaction: Making affect compute. *International Journal of Human-Computer Studies, 59*(1), 33–53.

McNeese, M. D. (2006). The interdisciplinary perspective of humane intelligence: A revisitation, twenty years hence. In *Proceedings of the 50th annual meeting of the human factors and ergonomics society* (pp. 762–766). San Francisco, CA.

McNeese, N. J., Demir, M., Cooke, N. J., & Myers, C. (2018). Teaming with a synthetic teammate: Insights into human-autonomy teaming. *Human Factors, 60*(2), 262–273.

McNeese, M. D., & Forster, P. K. (Eds.). (2017). *Cognitive systems engineering: An integrative living laboratory framework.* Boca Rotan, FL: CRC Taylor and Francis Publishing, Inc.

McNeese, M. D., Mancuso, V., McNeese, N. J., Endsley, T., & Forster, P. K. (2014). An integrative simulation to study team cognition in emergency crisis management. In *Proceedings of the 58th annual meeting of the human factors and ergonomics society* (pp. 285–289). Chicago, IL.

McNeese, M. D., & McNeese, N. J. (2016). Intelligent teamwork: A history, framework, and lessons learned. In *Proceedings of the 60th annual meeting of the human factors and ergonomics society* (pp. 153–157). Washington, DC.

McNeese, M. D., Perusich, K., & Rentsch, J. (1999). What is command and control coming to? Examining socio-cognitive mediators that expand the common ground of teamwork. In *Proceedings of the 43rd annual meeting of the human factors and ergonomic society* (pp. 209–212). Santa Monica, CA: Human Factors and Ergonomics Society.

McNeese, M., & Pfaff, M. (2012). Looking at macrocognition through an interdisciplinary, emergent research nexus. In E. Salas, S. Fiore, & M. Letsky (Eds.), *Theories of team cognition: Cross disciplinary perspectives* (pp. 345–371). New York: Taylor and Francis Group, LLC.

McNeese, M. D., Pfaff, M., Connors, E. S., Obieta, J., Terrell, I., & Friedenberg, M. (2006). Multiple vantage points of the common operational picture: Supporting complex teamwork. In *Proceedings of the 50th annual meeting of the human factors and ergonomics society* (pp. 467–471). San Francisco, CA.

McNeese, M. D., & Pfaff, M. (2012). Looking at macrocognition through an interdisciplinary, emergent research nexus. In E. Salas, S. Fiore, & M. Letsky (Eds.), *Theories of team cognition: Cross disciplinary perspectives* (pp. 345–371). New York: Taylor and Francis Group, LLC.

McNeese, N. J., & Reddy, M. C. (2017). The role of team cognition in collaborative information seeking. *Journal of the Association for Information Science and Technology, 68*(1), 129–140.

McNeese, M. D., Salas, E., & Endsley, M. (Eds.). (2001). *New trends in cooperative activities: System dynamics in complex environments.* Santa Monica, CA: Human Factors and Ergonomics Society Press.

McNeese, M. D., Salas, E., & Endsley, M. (expected to be published 2020). Handbook of distributed team cognition. Boca Raton, FL: CRC Taylor & Francis Publishers.

McNeese, M. D., Warren, R., & Woodson, B. (1985). Cockpit automation technology - a further look. In *Proceedings of the 29th annual meeting of the human factors society* (pp. 884−888). Santa Monica, CA: Human Factors Society.

Mercado, J. E., Rupp, M. A., Chen, J. Y. C., Barnes, M. J., Barber, D., & Procci, K. (2016). Intelligent agent transparency in human−agent teaming for multi-UxV management. *Human Factors, 58*(3), 401−415.

Miller, C., & Hannen, M. (1999). The rotorcraft pilot's associate: Design and evaluation of an intelligent user interface for a cockpit information manager. *Knowledge-Based Systems, 12*(8), 443−456.

Parasuraman, R., Sheridan, T. B., & Wickens, C. D. (2000). A model for types and levels of human interaction with automation. *IEEE Transactions on Systems, Man, and Cybernetics - Part A: Systems and Humans, 30*(3), 286−297. http://doi.org/10.1109/3468.844354.

Parasuraman, R., & Wickens, C. D. (2008). Humans: Still vital after all these years of automation. *Human Factors: The Journal of the Human Factors and Ergonomics Society, 50*(3), 511−520. https://doi.org/10.1518/001872008X312198.

Perkins, D. N. (1986). *Knowledge as design.* Hillsdale, N.J.: Lawrence Erlbaum Associates.

Perusich, K. A., & McNeese, M. D. (2006). Using fuzzy cognitive maps for knowledge management in a conflict environment. *IEEE Systems, Man and Cybernetics, 36*(6), 810−821.

Picard, R. (1997). *Affective computing.* Cambridge, MA: MIT Press.

Rasmussen, J. (1986). *Information processing and human-machine interaction: an approach to cognitive engineering.* North-Holland Publisher.

Rasmussen, J., Pejtersen, A. M., & Goodstein, L. P. (1994). *Cognitive systems engineering.* New York: Wiley.

Retelle, J. P. (1986). The pilot's associate: An aerospace application of artificial intelligence. In *Signal* (pp. 100−105).

Robot. (n.d.). In Wickipedia. Retrieved from https://en.wikipedia.org/wiki/Robot_(Lost_in_ Space).

Rouse, W. B. (1976). Adaptive allocation of decision making responsibility between supervisor and computer. In T. B. Sheridan, & G. Johannsen (Eds.), *Monitoring behavior and supervisory control* (pp. 295−306). New York: Plenum Press.

Rouse, W. B., & Morris, N. M. (1986). On looking into the black box: Prospects and limits in the search for mental models. *Psychological Bulletin, 100*(3), 349−363.

Ruff, H. A., Narayanan, S., & Draper, M. H. (2002). Human interaction with levels of automation and decision fidelity in the supervisory control of multiple simulated unmanned air vehicles. *Presence: Teleoperators and Virtual Environments, 11*(4), 335−351.

Santoro, G. M. (1995). What is computer-mediated communication? In Z. L. Berge, & M. P. Collins (Eds.), *Computer mediated communication and the online classroom: Vol. 1: Overview and perspectives* (pp. 11−28). Cresskill, NJ: Hampton Press.

Sheridan, T. B. (2012). Human supervisory control. In G. Salvendy (Ed.), *Handbook of human factors and ergonomics* (4th ed.). Hoboken, NJ, USA: John Wiley & Sons, Inc.

Simon, H. A. (1969). The Sciences of the artificial (1st ed.). Cambridge, MA: MIT Press.

USAF. (2013). *Autonomy science and technology strategy.* Dayton, OH: Airforce Research Laboratory.

Vicente, K. J. (1999). *Cognitive work analysis: Towards safe, productive, and healthy computer-based work.* Mahwah, NJ: Lawrence Erlbaum Associates.

Wellens, A. R. (1990). *Assessing multi-person and person-machine distributed decision making using an extended psychological distancing model. AAMRL-TR-90-006. Wright-Patterson Air Force Base.* Ohio: Armstrong Aerospace Medical Research Laboratory.

Wellens, A. R., & McNeese, M. D. (1987). A research agenda for the social psychology of intelligent machines. In Proceedings of the IEEE National Aerospace and Electronics Conference *(NAECON)* (Vol. 3, pp. 944–949). Dayton, OH: IEEE Aerospace and Electronics Systems Society.

Wellens, A. R. (1993). Group situation awareness and distributed decision making: From military to civilian applications. In J. Castellan (Ed.), *Individual and group decision making: Current Issues* (pp. 267–291). Hillsdale, NJ: Lawrence Erlbaum Associates.

Wellens, A. R., & McNeese, M. D. (1999). The social psychology of intelligent machines: A research agenda revisited. In H. Bullinger, & J. Ziegler (Eds.), *Human-computer interaction: Ergonomics and user interfaces* (pp. 696–700). Mahwah, NJ: Lawrence Erlbaum Associates.

Woods, D. D. (1998). Designs are hypotheses about how artifacts shape cognition and collaboration. *Ergonomics, 41*(2), 168–173.

Woods, D. D., Johannesen, L. J., Cook, R. I., & Sarter, N. B. (1994). *Behind human error: Cognitive systems, computers and hindsight.* Dayton, OH: CSERIAC.

Index

Printed in the United States
By Bookmasters